IOWA

OFF THE BEATEN PATH®

OFF THE BEATEN PATH® SERIES

ELEVENTH EDITION

IOWA

OFF THE BEATEN PATH®

LORI ERICKSON

Globe
Pequot

Essex, Connecticut

All the information in this guidebook is subject to change. We recommend that you call ahead to obtain current information before traveling.

**Globe
Pequot**

An imprint of Globe Pequot, the trade division of
The Rowman & Littlefield Publishing Group, Inc.
4501 Forbes Blvd., Ste. 200
Lanham, MD 20706
www.rowman.com

Distributed by NATIONAL BOOK NETWORK

British Library Cataloguing in Publication Information available

ISSN 1540-1340
ISBN 978-1-4930-7816-5 (paperback)
ISBN 978-1-4930-7817-2 (e-book)

♾️™ The paper used in this publication meets the minimum requirements of American National Standard for Information Sciences—Permanence of Paper for Printed Library Materials, ANSI/NISO Z39.48-1992.

Contents

About the Author

Lori Erickson grew up on a farm near Decorah and earned a BA from Luther College and MA from the University of Iowa. She has written about her home state for a wide variety of publications and is the author of books that include *Sweet Corn and Sushi*, *Holy Rover*, *Near the Exit*, *The Soul of the Family Tree*, and *Every Step Is Home*. She lives in Iowa City with her husband, Bob Sessions.

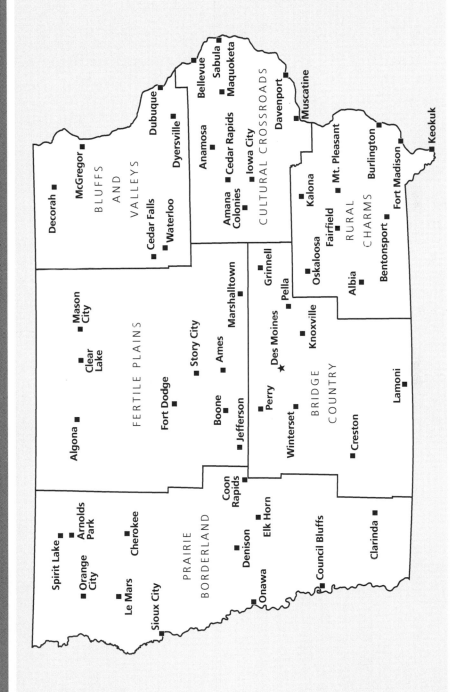

IOWA

Introduction

One of my favorite Iowa stories happened several years ago on a trip to another region of the United States. I was at a conference and found myself seated next to a woman from Germany. She was elegant and sophisticated, and I learned she had a position as an executive in her home country.

"And where do you live?" she asked.

When I said I was from Iowa, her face lit up.

"Iowa is my second home!" she said. "I love Iowa."

She went on to say that decades before she'd been a high school exchange student in a small town in eastern Iowa. She had been a spoiled and difficult teenager, she recalled, but when she arrived on the farm owned by her host family, her life changed dramatically. The family had four children, and everyone pitched in to help. She was immediately treated as a member of the family and warmly welcomed into the community at the small local high school. She was even voted homecoming queen during her year in Iowa.

"I try to come back to visit my Iowa family every year," she said. "Iowa changed my life. I wouldn't be who I am today if it wasn't for my time there."

I can't promise all Iowa visitors such a life-changing experience, but I love what that story says about my home state. There are rich treasures here—in the landscape, in the culture, and in the people. And if you allow yourself to stay awhile, to visit, explore, and immerse yourself, you, too, may find that some of Iowa rubs off on you.

Iowa isn't nearly as much of a well-kept secret as it was when the first edition of this book came out in 1991. While you can still find the occasional misguided person who mistakes Iowa for Idaho, you can also find many Americans who have come to view Iowa as a place that produces poets and writers as well as corn, a place of unexpected beauties, surprising strengths, and even (thanks to the movies *Field of Dreams* and *The Bridges of Madison County*) a touch of romance.

While Iowa's tourism industry has grown, what hasn't changed, thankfully, are the traits and values that have long defined the state. Here you'll still find generous and friendly people, wonderful small towns, dynamic cities, fascinating museums and historic sites, and beautiful nature areas. If this is your first visit, you're in for a treat. And if you've been here before, venture farther afield this time to discover even more of the state.

As with previous editions, this eleventh edition has been substantially revised and updated. I'm grateful to Tracy Stuhr, who assisted with previous editions of this book, and to my husband, Bob Sessions, who helped with the research and updating of this one. Jessica O'Riley of the Iowa Tourism Office has been a great help with this project, as well as with many others relating to Iowa.

On my travels through Iowa, I have found many things to cherish and admire. Everywhere the land, its people, and its landmarks are finding new ways to survive and prosper. Prairie is being replanted, historic buildings have been restored and rededicated to new uses, and bike trails are being created. I've been particularly impressed by the large number of heritage museums and historic restorations. No county and hardly a single town are without some remnant of the past that has been saved, in one form or another, for the wandering traveler to explore.

Another major development in Iowa has been the growth of farmers markets and the sustainable agriculture movement. A quiet revolution is occurring in this agricultural state, mirroring the growing national interest in organic and locally grown foods. Iowa has some of the best soil in the world, and an increasing number of farmers, gardeners, cooks, and restaurateurs are using it to work culinary magic. You really haven't lived until you've tasted a freshly picked Iowa heirloom tomato, sampled a bit of Templeton Rye whiskey, or

Fun Facts about Iowa

- Iowa leads the country in pork, beef, corn, soybean, and grain production.
- Iowa averages thirty-four tornadoes annually.
- More than 25 percent of the nation's best crop soil is found in Iowa.
- Iowa is the only state name that starts with two vowels.
- One Iowa farm grows enough food to feed 279 people.
- Iowa boasts the highest literacy rate in the nation (99 percent).
- After the Civil War, Iowa was the first state to give the vote to African Americans.
- Iowa has more golf courses per capita than any other state.
- Iowa is home to the World Food Prize, an international award recognizing the achievements of those who advance human development by improving the quantity, quality, or availability of food in the world.
- Iowa is the only state whose east and west borders are formed by water (the Missouri and Mississippi Rivers).
- Iowa's weather ranges in temperature from below zero in winter (with wind chills dipping into negative double digits) to more than one hundred degrees in summer. Temperatures can fluctuate by as much as fifty degrees in one day.

Famous Iowans

President Herbert Hoover: thirty-first president of the United States

First Lady Mamie Doud Eisenhower: wife of President Dwight D. Eisenhower

Bix Beiderbecke: jazz musician

Johnny Carson: comedian and television talk-show host

Carrie Chapman Catt: suffragist leader

Buffalo Bill Cody: frontier scout and Wild West showman

Norman Borlaug: Nobel Peace Prize winner and father of the Green Revolution in agriculture

Grant Wood: regionalist painter

John Wayne: movie star

Ashton Kutcher: film and television actor

Elijah Wood: star of the *Lord of the Rings* film trilogy

Glenn Miller: big band musician

Simon Estes: opera singer

Donna Reed: star of the film *It's A Wonderful Life*

James Van Allen: space physicist

Famous Fictional Iowans

Radar O'Reilly: *M*A*S*H;* born in Ottumwa

Captain James T. Kirk: *Star Trek;* born in Riverside

---

nibbled on a piece of Maytag Blue Cheese. If you're traveling through Iowa during the months between June and October, stop by a farmers market on a Saturday morning. And at any time of year, you can patronize the growing number of restaurants that make use of seasonal, locally grown produce.

Although many new entries have been added to this edition, this book does not, by any means, provide a complete list of attractions in the state of Iowa. But it does provide a diverse sampling of the interesting sites and activities Iowa has to offer travelers. While much of the text has remained the same, some of it has been updated to reflect current hours and prices. I've also added new sidebars to include some personal perspectives and reminiscences, as well as to highlight a selection of each area's attractions, events, and stories.

As you use this book, you'll note that each section features a list of *New Deal murals* in the area. Grant Wood and his Stone City Art Colony received federal funds through President Franklin Roosevelt's New Deal program. The money was given to artists to paint murals depicting life "in their own backyard."

The work was commissioned to grace the public building projects that were being built as part of the effort to get Americans working again during the Great Depression of the 1930s. More than fifty murals were painted in Iowa between 1934 and 1942, and many of these wonderful paintings can still be found across the state. While they vary in style and subject matter, most favor the Regionalist style of painting that Grant Wood had helped to popularize.

A few pointers on this guidebook: Keep a state map in your glove compartment as you travel because many of these attractions are off the interstates, and you may find yourself lost without a good map. I also recommend that you call ahead to verify hours and prices. Though all were correct at press time, they change frequently. Restaurants are described as inexpensive (entrees less than $20), moderate ($20 to $35), and expensive (more than $35). Lodgings have a similar rating system: inexpensive (less than $125 per night), moderate ($125 to $175), and expensive (more than $175).

FOR MORE INFORMATION

For more information on the state of Iowa, contact the following:

Iowa Tourism Office
(800) 345-IOWA
traveliowa.com

Eastern Iowa Tourism Association
(563) 875-7269
easterniowatourism.org

Central Iowa Tourism Region
(515) 832-4808
iowatourism.com

Western Iowa Tourism Region
(712) 662-7383
visitwesterniowa.com

Iowa Department of Natural Resources
(515) 725-8200
iowadnr.gov

Iowa Department of Transportation
(800) 288-1047 or 511
iowadot.gov or 511ia.org

State Historical Society of Iowa
(515) 281-5111
iowahistory.org

Iowa Bed & Breakfast Guild
(800) 743-IOWA

Iowa Bicycle Coalition
(515) 309-2867
iowabicyclecoalition.org

From the limestone bluffs bordering the Mississippi River to the Loess Hills flanking the Missouri, from the picturesque lakes in the north and across the rolling central plains to the southern border, Iowa is, above all, a place to savor, to enjoy, to visit, and to revisit. Welcome—and happy exploring!

—Lori Erickson

Bluffs and Valleys

Northeast Iowa is a land of thickly wooded hills, steep bluffs, secluded valleys, and scenic vistas—countryside that in many places seems more like that of New England than the Midwest. From river towns rich in history to immigrant enclaves where old-world traditions remain strong, northeast Iowa offers a host of unique treasures.

River Region

Begin your tour of northeast Iowa in *Dubuque*, one of my favorite destinations in the state. Much of what makes the city so appealing relates to its long and colorful history as a Mississippi River town. The city is named after Julien Dubuque, a French-Canadian fur trader who received permission in 1788 from the Fox Indians to work the lead mines in the area. The territory was opened to white settlement in 1833, and soon hundreds of new residents—many of them immigrants—were pouring into the new town. The next century saw a decline in mining and the growth of the lumbering, boatbuilding, shipping, and meatpacking industries. As the city grew rich, its

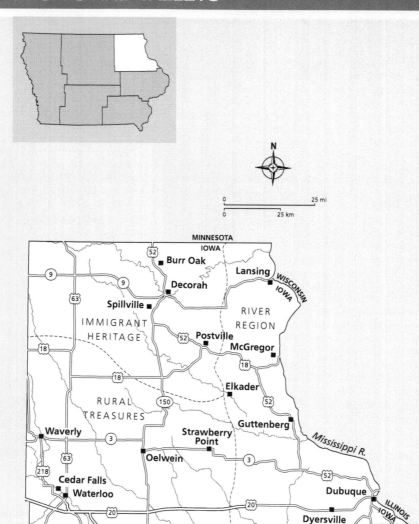

citizens filled its streets with magnificent homes and buildings, structures that stand today as eloquent reminders of the city's past.

The crown jewel of Dubuque is its waterfront, which has a complex of sites celebrating the historical, environmental, educational, and recreational majesty of the mighty Mississippi. Begin your explorations at the ***National Mississippi River Museum & Aquarium***. An affiliate of the Smithsonian Institution, the museum is the best place in the nation to explore the cultural and natural history of the Mississippi River. Its ***William Woodward Discovery Center*** contains large freshwater aquariums, live animals (including alligators, otters, turtles, fish, and snakes), touch pools, stream tables, living-history demonstrations, and the National Rivers Hall of Fame. Here you can "pilot" a steamboat, touch stingrays from the Gulf of Mexico, see a simulated flood, and marvel at massive catfish and peculiar longnose gar (fish with long, rod-like noses).

The adjacent ***Fred W. Woodward Riverboat Museum*** is the city's original museum, located on the site of a boat works that once manufactured some of the largest boats and paddle wheelers in the nation. Inside are displays that bring to life the history of the river, including exhibits on Native Americans, river explorers, the lumber industry, and recreation on the river.

Outside you'll find more attractions, including the **William M. Black**. The *Black* is a large dredge boat (almost the size of a football field) that once roamed the waters of the Missouri River digging up tons of mud and muck in order to make the channel safe for navigation. Today visitors can tour the boat and even (for an additional fee) stay overnight in the crew's quarters.

The harbor area outside the museum also features a wetlands walk with a Native American wickiup home and a boatyard area featuring steamboat artifacts, boatbuilding demonstrations, and a children's play area. ***The Depot Café***, located in the restored Chicago Burlington Northern Railway Depot, sells inexpensive snacks, sandwiches, and refreshments.

AUTHOR'S FAVORITES

Effigy Mounds National Monument	World's Smallest Church
Seed Savers Heritage Farm	Fenelon Place Elevator
Hayden Prairie	Waverly Midwest Horse Sale
WW Homestead Dairy	Backbone State Park

thegreat mississippi

The **Mississippi River** is the second-longest river in North America, passing through ten states as it winds 2,350 miles from its headwaters in northern Minnesota to the Gulf of Mexico in Louisiana. The river serves as a water source for more than four million people and drains 40 percent of the continental United States. It is also a major flyway for migratory birds.

The National Mississippi River Museum & Aquarium is located in the port area of downtown Dubuque. It's open daily from 9 a.m. to 5 p.m. (during the winter months 10 a.m. to 4 p.m.). Admission is $21 for adults; $15 for youth. Call (563) 557-9545 or visit river museum.com for more information.

The **Grand Harbor Resort and Waterpark**, located adjacent to the museum, is a great family destination. The resort overlooks the river and features 193 guest rooms, and its 25,000-square-foot indoor water park has enough slides, tubes, waterspouts, rope ladders, water cannons, and wading pools to keep children entertained for hours. You can visit the water park even if you're not staying at the hotel. For more information, visit grandharbor resort.com or call (563) 690-4000.

Other parts of the waterfront complex include the **Alliant Energy Amphitheater**, which features special events and live entertainment, the **Mississippi Riverwalk**, and the **River's Edge Plaza**. The Riverwalk is part of a 44-mile trail connecting the Mississippi River to the Field of Dreams in Dyersville, another popular Iowa attraction that is described later in this section. The River's Edge Plaza serves as a docking site for the Delta Queen Company riverboats and other large excursion vessels.

Al Capone's Hideout

During the Prohibition Era, Al Capone was a frequent guest at the **Hotel Julien**, and there's evidence that at one time he was actually part owner of the hotel. Local lore says that Capone and his entourage would come to Dubuque when things got too hot for him in Chicago. He used a nearby underground garage to hide his cars and would take over the hotel's entire top floor for weeks at a time. Conveniently, the location provided an excellent view of the bridge that led to Illinois, so Capone would have warning if federal authorities or rival gangs came looking for him.

Today the hotel's Capone Suite recalls the hotel's most notorious guest. Located on the second floor, it includes two bedrooms, a living room, and a kitchen, all decorated in a luxurious style that likely would have pleased the gangster.

TOP ANNUAL EVENTS

JUNE

My Waterloo Days
Waterloo, June
(319) 291-2038
experiencewaterloo.com

Strawberry Days
Strawberry Point, second weekend
in June
(563) 933-4482
strawberrypt.com

Sturgis Falls Celebration
Cedar Falls, last full weekend in June
(319) 268-4266
sturgisfalls.org

JULY

Nordic Fest
Decorah, last full weekend in July
(563) 382-3990
nordicfest.com

SEPTEMBER

German Fest
Guttenberg, fourth Sat in Sept
(563) 581-6149
guttenbergiowa.net

OCTOBER

Fall Arts & Crafts Festival
McGregor, first and second weekends
in Oct
(563) 873-3795
cityofmcgregoriowa.com

NOVEMBER

National Farm Toy Show
Dyersville, first weekend in Nov
(800) 533-2727
toyfarmer.com

Two more riverfront attractions are the ***Diamond Jo Casino*** (which offers gaming year-round) and the **Celebration Belle**, an 800-passenger, four-deck non-gaming riverboat that cruises between Dubuque and the Quad Cities. The boat is the largest luxury excursion boat on the Upper Mississippi. For information on its cruises, call (309) 764-1952 or visit celebrationbelle.com.

Thanks in part to the rebirth of the riverfront, downtown Dubuque has also undergone a renaissance. The area known as ***Lower Main*** includes fine restaurants, galleries, coffee shops, and stores, attracting locals and visitors alike.

Built in 1913, the ***Hotel Julien*** at the corner of Main and Second Streets is a historic gem as well as a luxurious lodging place. After declining into shabbiness by the early 2000s, a multimillion-dollar renovation made it into the city's showplace.

Thankfully, a treasure trove of artifacts had been saved from prior restorations, from Victorian-era mirrors and vintage art prints to original wrought-iron tiles. A design team scoured drawings, blueprints, and photographs to re-create the interior furnishings, using original materials when possible and installing artisan-crafted reproductions when necessary.

"Going Up?"

Dubuque's most unusual attraction is the **Fenelon Place Elevator**. Described as the "world's steepest, shortest railway," the elevator connects downtown Dubuque with the residential neighborhoods on top of a steep bluff. It was built in 1882 by J. K. Graves, a businessman who worked downtown but liked to return home each day for lunch and a nap. The problem was that it took him a good hour to drive his horse and buggy there and back again. To solve the problem, he commissioned a small cable car modeled after those he had seen on trips to Europe and had it installed on the bluff near his home. Now he could easily fit in both lunch and a nap, and he returned to work each day a happy man.

Then Graves's neighbors started asking permission to use the elevator, and soon it had become a fixture of the city. In the intervening years, the cars and support structure have been rebuilt several times, so even if it seems like you're going to tumble to the ground as you're riding it, rest assured, the cars are safe. The elevator is even listed on the National Register of Historic Places—quite an honor for a machine designed to give a businessman time enough for a nap.

The Fenelon Place Elevator is located at 512 Fenelon Place. It is open Apr 1 through Nov 30, from 8 a.m. to 10 p.m. Round-trip rates are $4 for adults and $2 for children. (And while you're in the area, browse through the Cable Car Square shopping district at the foot of the elevator, an area of renovated homes and buildings that now houses gift shops, antiques stores, and boutiques.)

While the Hotel Julien remains true to its historic roots, it also offers the latest in comfort and amenities to its guests. The **Riverboat Lounge** offers a retreat just off the lobby for drinks and conversation, while **Caroline's Restaurant**, located in the hotel's lower level, serves American cuisine with a gourmet twist and is open daily for breakfast, lunch, and dinner. The hotel's **Potosa Spa** offers pampering in a dimly lit, soothing oasis. For information visit hoteljuliendubuque.com or call (563) 556-4200. Prices are moderate to expensive.

For a delicious meal head to **Pepper Sprout**, which specializes in seasonal, locally raised ingredients prepared in creative ways. It's one of eastern Iowa's finest restaurants and well worth every penny. You'll find it at 378 Main St. For information call (563) 556-2167 or see peppersprout.com.

A lovely place to stay in Dubuque is the **Hancock House**, a magnificent Queen Anne mansion with a spectacular view of Dubuque and the Mississippi River valley. The house, which is listed on the National Register of Historic Places, features 9 guest rooms, some with whirlpools and fireplaces. A full breakfast is served each weekend morning. The Hancock House (563-235-0000; thehancockhouse.com) is at 1105 Grove Ter. Rates are moderate to expensive.

During the growing season, visit the **Dubuque Arboretum and Botanical Gardens**. The gardens showcase many different plant and tree collections, including a Japanese garden, woodland wildflowers, lily ponds, and one of the largest public hosta gardens in the United States. You will be accompanied by the sound of trickling waterfalls and on Sunday by musical concerts. All of this was developed by volunteers from the community, and admission is free. The arboretum is located at 3800 Arboretum Dr. Call (563) 556-2100 or see dubuquearboretum.net for more information.

For evening entertainment in Dubuque, two performance centers in the downtown area offer a variety of shows in elegant settings. The **Five Flags Theater** was built in 1910 and was modeled after the great music halls of Paris. Today it has undergone a plush restoration that will make you think you've gone back a century in time. A few blocks away is the **Grand Opera House**, a hundred-year-old stage where Ethel Barrymore, George M. Cohan, and Sarah Bernhardt once performed. After years of service as a movie house, it is once again home to live community theater. And according to its resident acting company, the venerable old building is haunted—literally—by the spirits of actors who once performed here. "Where else would old actors go once they died?" asks one performer who's heard the ghostly voices. "It seems logical they'd go back to the place they'd loved best."

Regardless of whether ghosts make an appearance during a performance, you're likely to enjoy a show at either one of the stately old theaters. Five Flags Theater is located at Fourth and Main Streets; (563) 589-4254; fiveflagscenter .com. The Grand Opera House is at 135 Eighth St.; call (563) 588-1305 or see thegrandoperahouse.com for more information.

St. Luke's United Methodist Church has a splendid collection of stained-glass windows designed by Louis Comfort Tiffany. Its Good Shepherd window was created for the Columbian Exposition of 1893, and Tiffany is said to have considered it his finest creation in glass. The Good Samaritan window, installed in 1916, is another masterpiece, created with deep purple and lavender shades. It shows the Samaritan tenderly cradling the injured man, wrapping his cloak around him for protection.

St. Luke's was founded in 1833, making it Iowa's oldest congregation. The present Romanesque building was finished in 1897 and included 5 large and 90 small Tiffany windows. Two more windows were added in 1916 and another two in the 1930s. Between 1999 and 2002, the church spent nearly $1 million to restore the sanctuary's eight largest windows—money well spent. St. Luke's is at 1199 Main St.; call (563) 582-4543 or visit stlukesdbq.org to arrange to see the windows.

For more information on what to see and do in the city, call Travel Dubuque at (800) 798-8844 or see traveldubuque.com.

Five miles south of Dubuque on US 52 is the **Crystal Lake Cave**. This incredible natural cave was discovered accidentally in 1868 when some miners were drilling for lead and happened upon it. In 1932 one of these miners christened it and opened it to the public. Tours through the cave wind along a 3/4-mile track, and the temperature hovers around fifty degrees, so you will want to dress accordingly. You will see anthodites—otherwise known as cave flowers—a rare form of aragonite crystals, as well as large formations of brown onyx, which only take about a million years or so to form. There are delicate hollow "soda straw" stalactites through which water flows and a crystal "chandelier" formed of still-growing, active stalactites. The cave is open from 9 a.m. to 6 p.m. daily from May through Aug; the rest of the year the hours vary. Call (563) 556-6451 or see crystallakecave.com for more information.

Ten miles northwest of Dubuque on CR C9Y is an Iowa dining landmark that you shouldn't miss: **Breitbach's Country Dining** in the small town of **Balltown** (563 Balltown Rd.). Breitbach's likes to boast that it's the only restaurant in the world to be visited by both the outlaw Jesse James and the actress Brooke Shields, but that's not the restaurant's only claim to fame. Breitbach's has been refreshing the palates of weary travelers since 1852, making this the oldest bar and restaurant in continuous operation in Iowa history.

Breitbach's has endured through adversity. On Christmas Eve 2007, its historic building was totally destroyed in a fire, after which the local community rallied to help sixth-generation owner Mike Breitbach and his family rebuild. Just ten months later another fire destroyed the new building. Mike wasn't certain he had the strength to rebuild yet again, but once more loyal patrons and friends came to his aid. The restaurant was rebuilt, and today it draws patrons from a wide region. The key to Breitbach's longevity is simple: homemade, delicious food, reasonable prices, and a welcoming and cozy atmosphere. The restaurant has won an America's Classics Award from the James Beard Foundation, which is given to only a handful of restaurants each year—a well-deserved accolade for an Iowa treasure. Breitbach's is open for breakfast, lunch, and dinner (closed Mon from Nov through Apr). For information call (563) 552-2220 or see breitbachscountrydining.com.

didyouknow?

One dairy cow produces seventy-two glasses of milk a day.

One cow hide provides enough leather for twelve basketballs.

Before heading north along the Mississippi, you may want to take a short detour east to the small town of **Dyersville**. One of its attractions is the **National Farm Toy Museum**, a facility housing more than 30,000 rare and antique farm toys as well as miniature farm replicas that reflect the agricultural heritage of the nation.

The National Farm Toy Museum is located at 1110 Sixteenth Ave. Court SE; (563) 875-2727. Hours are 9 a.m. to 6 p.m. Mon to Sat and 10 a.m. to 4 p.m. Sun. Admission is $7 for adults and $5 for children (under six free). For more information see nationalfarmtoymuseum.com.

Dyersville has become known as the Farm Toy Capital of the World, not only because of the museum, but also because of the fact that three major farm toy manufacturers are located here: TOMY, Scale Models, and SpecCast. Each November the town hosts the ***National Farm Toy Show***, an event that attracts thousands of toy collectors and exhibitors.

Another attraction in Dyersville is the ***Basilica of St. Francis Xavier***, one of the finest examples of Gothic architecture in the Midwest. The church has a main altar of Italian marble and Mexican onyx, a pulpit of butternut, and twin towers that rise to a height of 212 feet. It was given the title of basilica in 1956 in recognition of its outstanding architecture and spiritual significance and is one of only fifty-three basilicas in the United States.

Visitors are welcome to visit the church at 104 Third St. SW. Information packets are available at the main entrance for self-guided tours. The basilica is open daily from 7 a.m. to 8 p.m. For more information call (563) 875-7325 or see xavierbasilica.com.

Doll lovers won't want to miss the ***Dyer-Botsford Doll Museum***, home to a collection of more than 2,000 dolls plus rare Christmas ornaments. The Victorian-era structure was once the home of Dyersville's founder and is open daily from May through Nov. The museum (563-875-2414; dyersvillehistory .com) is at 331 First Ave. E in Dyersville.

Three miles northeast of Dyersville is the **Field of Dreams** *Movie Site*. *Field of Dreams*, filmed here in 1988, tells the story of an Iowa farmer who plows up his field to build a baseball diamond so that "Shoeless" Joe Jackson and his fellow players can return to play (the men were banned from baseball for allegedly throwing the 1919 World Series). Since then, thousands of fans from as far away as Japan have visited the diamond, which still remains among the cornfields. Visitors can sit and dream on the bleachers, walk the bases, and toss a few baseballs. The baseball diamond is open free of charge 9 a.m. to 5 p.m. From Dyersville take IA 136 to the north edge of town and follow the signs to the farm. The address is 28995 Lansing Rd. For information see fieldofdreamsmoviesite.com or call (563) 875-8404.

From Dyersville head north for 25 miles on IA 136 and US 52 to the Mississippi River port of ***Guttenberg***. Lovely scenic overlooks are on both the north and south ends of town on US 52. While you're here, you can enjoy

Toys 'R' Dyersville

Dyersville's first toy factory was founded after World War II by Fred Ertl Sr. During the war all metal toy production had stopped, and after the conflict ended there was a tremendous demand for toys (think of all those newly hatched baby boomers). Ertl started making toy tractors in his basement to earn some extra money, and soon it became his full-time business.

Over the next four decades, the *Ertl Company* grew to become the world's lead-ing farm toy manufacturer. In 1999 it merged with Racing Champions, a maker of die-cast collectibles, to become *RC2* (now *TOMY*). While the company now makes its toys overseas, its Dyersville plant continues to serve as a sales and distribution center.

Fred's son, Joe Ertl, meanwhile, carries on the family toy-making tradition at *Scale Models*, a Dyersville company he founded in 1971. The company's employees make farm toys in a wide variety of designs, tiny models of the huge machines made by companies like John Deere, Massey Ferguson, and Allis-Chalmers.

Guttenberg's 1-mile river walk or visit its charming historic district. For more information about the mighty Mississippi that flows by the town, tour the **Guttenberg Fish Aquarium and Hatchery**, which is operated by the Iowa Department of Natural Resources. Inside its tanks are many of the species that inhabit the river and local streams, from northern pike and catfish to turtles. You'll find the aquarium (which is open daily May through Oct) at 331 S. River Park Dr., south of Lock and Dam 10. Call (563) 252-1156 for information.

West of Guttenberg, visit the charming town of **Elkader**, the only town in Iowa named for a Muslim leader. Abd el-Kader led the fight for Algerian independence in the nineteenth century. His revolutionary spirit so impressed the town's founders that they named the new settlement after him.

Schera's Algerian-American Restaurant at 107 S. Main St. is owned and operated by two men inspired by that story. Brian Bruening, a native of New Hampton, and Frederique Boudouani, who is of French-Algerian descent, opened the eatery in 2006, naming it after Scheherazade of *1001 Arabian Nights*. The restaurant serves delicious and moderately priced Algerian, North African, and Mediterranean dishes. Call (563) 245-1992 or see scheras.com for information.

The **Elkader Whitewater Park** was created in 2013 on the Turkey River that flows through the town. Its main feature is the Gobbler, a 22-foot-wide wave of varying difficulty, depending upon water levels. In the middle of the river, Boulder Island provides a great place to rest—or, if the river is high enough, it creates a high-flow wave that challenges even advanced whitewater paddlers. For information see elkaderwhitewater.com or call (563) 245-2098.

Spend a delightful (and informative) hour or two at the **Osborne Nature Center**, 5 miles south of Elkader at 29862 Osborne Rd. Set on 300 acres of diverse and well-maintained grounds along the Volga River, the Osborne is an educational treasure, with live animals, nature exhibits, a pioneer village, and hiking trails. Call (563) 245-1516 for more information or see claytoncounty conservation.org.

North of Clayton is **McGregor**, a river town that's one of the loveliest in the state. The explorers Marquette and Joliet passed through here in 1673, followed by Zebulon Pike in 1805. Pike lent his name to the 500-foot bluff that towers above the town (though the peak he later climbed in Colorado would gain greater fame). The scenic spot—one of the most beautiful along the entire Mississippi River—is part of **Pike's Peak State Park**, located 2 miles southeast of McGregor on IA 340. Nearby are hiking trails and picnic and camping facilities.

In 1837 an enterprising fellow named Alexander MacGregor came to settle here. The son of Scottish immigrants, MacGregor established a ferry business that transported furs and other goods between the new settlement of MacGregor's Landing on the west bank of the river and Prairie du Chien on the east bank. The town bustled with steamboat traffic and commerce, and by 1865 the town's population had grown to more than 5,500.

The nineteenth century saw a number of memorable characters pass through the town. The best known of early residents was the Ringling family of circus fame. The five Ringling brothers spent part of their childhood in

Iowa Whitewater Parks

You don't have to go to the mountains to experience whitewater rafting, thanks to some creative engineers who are making Iowa's rivers more attractive to paddlers. Whitewater parks in Elkader, Charles City, and Manchester are great places for beginners to learn how to whitewater raft. Side chutes allow for a quick exit from the rapids and make them easy to run over and over again. But these rivers also appeal to more advanced rafters, who come for special competitions and events as well as practice. The artificially constructed courses are free and are suitable for kayaks, rafts, canoes, tubes, and paddleboards.

The whitewater parks have other benefits as well. They replace low-head dams that are dangerous for swimmers and boaters and improve fish habitat by aerating the water downstream and creating "ladders" that allow the fish to move more easily upstream.

A Haven for Wildlife

The Mississippi River and surrounding shoreline near McGregor are part of one of the nation's ecological treasures: the *Upper Mississippi River National Wildlife and Fish Refuge*. Established in 1924, the refuge stretches from Wabasha, Minnesota, to the Quad Cities and is the longest wildlife refuge in the lower forty-eight states. It encompasses more than 240,000 acres of water, wetlands, wooded islands, forest, and prairie along 261 river miles.

Hundreds of species of birds, mammals, reptiles, amphibians, and fish make their home here. The refuge is critically important because of the reduction of habitat elsewhere throughout the Midwest. Natural lakes are increasingly scarce, bottomland forests are vanishing, and more than half of the wetlands have been lost.

More than one hundred bald eagle nests are present in the refuge, which also provides a vital migratory bird corridor for thousands of waterfowl, songbirds, and raptors each year. You can also see muskrat, mink, beaver, otter, weasel, fox, raccoon, and jackrabbits.

The best way to see the refuge is by paddling its secluded backwaters. For more information on this national treasure, see fws.gov or stop by the visitor center on US 18 North just outside of McGregor.

McGregor (the "a" having been dropped from its original name) and staged their earliest shows here before leaving for larger venues. Diamond Jo Reynolds was another larger-than-life resident. He operated a thriving riverboat business from a building that still stands at 123 A St.

The decline of the steamboat era brought a decline in the town's fortunes as well, with the population eventually dwindling down to a few hundred people. But through the next century McGregor attracted a faithful cadre of residents who treasured the slow pace of life along the river. Visitors came to the area as well, people drawn to the beauty of the Mississippi and also to the town's many antiques stores.

The most recent chapter in the town's history began about three decades ago, when a new generation of residents began to revitalize McGregor's fortunes. The area's beautiful scenery is still the primary draw, especially in the fall when the surrounding hills are full of color. McGregor holds a popular arts and crafts festival on two weekends in October, but increasingly it's a year-round destination as well, with a number of fine stores and restaurants.

The *Old Man River Restaurant and Brewery* is a microbrewery and restaurant located in the 1880s building once owned by Diamond Jo Reynolds at 123 A St. Quench your thirst with a dunkel lager; then try the Sleepy Old Man burger with the ale-battered onion rings. Call (563) 873-2002 for information.

Another bright spot in the downtown is **Paper Moon**, a bookstore and gift shop owned by the mother-and-daughter team of Jennifer and Louise White. The store's resident cats draw nearly as much attention as its whimsical range of merchandise, which includes household accessories, jewelry, and books. Paper Moon (563-500-1994; papermoonbooks.com) is at 206 A St.

A few miles north in Marquette, visit the **Driftless Area Wetlands Centre** (563-873-3537; driftlessareawetlandcentre.com) at 509 Highway 18. This environmental education facility has a visitor center, wetlands, prairie, wildlife displays, and animals native to the Driftless Area (the term refers to the hilly, scenic region in northeast Iowa and southwest Wisconsin that was spared the leveling effects of the last ice age). The facility's wetlands are home to ducks, turtles, frogs and other species, while inside the center you can learn about topics that include geology, birding, and prairie restoration. Young children will especially enjoy the interactive stations along the outdoor nature play trail here, which has balance beam logs, stepping-stones, and willow huts that double as

Sandhill Cranes

Sandhill cranes migrate to and from their winter campground in Florida over a large portion of the upper Midwest in the spring and fall. Spring is a more popular time to watch for them because their fall migration is much more relaxed and leisurely than the businesslike one they make in the spring. This is because they have to make accommodations for their young that cannot fly either as fast or as far. They may fly as much as 300 miles a day at an altitude below 5,000 feet. You can recognize them by their appearance during flight—long necks stretched out in front, longer legs trailing behind—and their bugling calls can be heard for miles. During migration the birds "paint" themselves, preening mud into their gray feathers for camouflage. When you see them in the Midwest, they will appear to be brown.

Younger birds form "bachelor flocks," feeding and nesting together until they settle down. Males and females mate for life at about four years of age. Their nests are adequate yet plain (just a bunch of marsh plants piled on the ground), but they seem content. Sandhill cranes are most active just before sunrise and just after sunset.

Listen for their unison calls during these times, the one-noted male and the two-noted female singing together. The female usually lays two eggs in April or early May, and incubation takes about a month. When one bird leaves the nest to forage, the other takes over incubation duties. Unison calls, I am told, are particularly loud at this time. Cranes, like people, have difficulty deciding what to have for dinner.

The International Crane Foundation sponsors the **Midwest Sandhill Crane Count** every year. Volunteers take to the fields on a designated morning in April to count cranes. If you are interested in participating, contact the foundation at savingcranes .org. What a great way to learn about some fly-by-night neighbors!

wildlife blinds. The visitor center is open Tues through Sat, 11 a.m. to 4 p.m., April through Oct, and Tues through Fri the rest of the year. Admission is free.

Next head to *Spook Cave*, 9 miles west of Marquette near the junction of US 52 and US 18. Here you can take what's billed as "America's longest underground boat tour." Bring your sweater (the temperature is usually forty-seven degrees) and take a half-hour guided cruise. The tour is the perfect activity for a hot, Iowa summer afternoon.

Spook Cave tours are $16 for adults and $11 for children. The cave is open from 9 a.m. to 5:00 p.m. daily May through Oct. Call (563) 539-4114 for more information or see spookcave.com. The site also has a campground and cabins.

Five miles north of McGregor, you'll find one of northeast Iowa's premier attractions, *Effigy Mounds National Monument*. This 1,500-acre area preserves outstanding examples of more than 2,000 years of prehistoric Indian mound building. Within its borders are nearly 200 known burial mounds, 29 of which are in the shape of bears or birds (most of the rest are conical or linear in form). The Great Bear Effigy is one of the most impressive mounds, stretching 70 feet across the shoulders and forelegs, 137 feet long, and more than 3

The Mysteries of the Mounds

High on the bluffs above the Mississippi River in northeast Iowa, a chain of mysterious mounds stand as mute reminders of a civilization that flourished here more than a thousand years ago.

The first animal-shaped mounds were built around AD 650. Each was constructed by digging up soil from the forest floor and clay from the riverbank and then depositing it inside an outline drawn on the ground, a laborious process that likely took hundreds of trips.

While conical-shaped mounds were usually used as burial places, most of the effigy mounds appear to have been used solely for ceremonial purposes. Perhaps they acted as territorial markers or totems for the people who built them, visible symbols of a spiritual tie to the land. Burnt residue indicates that fires were set on the head, flank, or heart regions of the animal effigies.

Effigy mound building ended here around 1300, for reasons unknown. As white settlers began moving into this region in the early 1800s, many of the mounds were destroyed by farming, road building, and logging. Others were plundered for grave offerings such as stone tools and pottery. Out of an estimated 10,000 mounds that likely once existed in the region, fewer than 1,000 remain today.

Fortunately, local groups recognized the priceless value of these northeastern Iowa mounds and worked to protect the site. Their efforts resulted in the establishment of *Effigy Mounds National Monument* in 1949.

feet high. The mounds are all the more impressive when you realize that their builders didn't have the ability to see the giant shapes from the air but instead worked out all the shapes from ground level.

The visitor center at the monument has exhibits explaining the mounds and the artifacts found within them, plus a film on the culture of the Indians who lived here. The center is open daily and admission is free. Call (563) 873-3491 or see nps.gov/efmo for information.

From Effigy Mounds continue north on the river road (IA 76 and IA 364) through the towns of **Waukon Junction** and **Harpers Ferry**. A few miles north of Harpers Ferry, the scenic river road takes you to one of the loveliest spots in the state, the tiny **Wexford Immaculate Conception Church**. Inside the exquisite stone building covered with ivy are simple wooden pews, a floor of colored mosaic tile, and an altar of lovely murals and statues. The church was built in the 1860s by a group of immigrants who journeyed here from County Wexford, Ireland. On the back wall of the church is a framed photocopy of the passenger list from the boat that brought the Wexford immigrants over the ocean, their names written in a beautiful flowing script. A peaceful cemetery surrounds the building, and just north of the church there's a shrine with a statue of Mary surrounded by blooming flowers.

Continue north on CR X52 to the town of **Lansing**, where you can enjoy a lovely view of the Mississippi from Mount Hosmer, a city park perched atop a high bluff.

Six miles north of Lansing off IA 26 are the **Fish Farm Mounds**, a smaller cousin of Effigy Mounds to the south. The site includes at least twenty-eight mounds overlooking the Mississippi River. The mound group is one of the few sites that remains of the many that once dotted bluffs and terraces along the Mississippi River.

Immigrant Heritage

From Lansing take IA 9 west for 35 miles to **Decorah**, a picturesque community that is likely the most Norwegian-American town in the United States. Settled by Norwegian immigrants in the 1850s, it has long taken great pride in its Norse roots. Throughout the town you'll see evidence of Decorah's ethnic past, from the Norwegian *nisse* (gnomes) peeking out of windows to shops decorated with rosemaling, a type of Norwegian flower painting. Each year on the last full weekend in July, the town celebrates its heritage with **Nordic Fest**, a three-day festival featuring parades, ethnic foods and music, historical displays, and arts and crafts demonstrations.

To learn more about Decorah's past, visit ***Vesterheim National Norwegian-American Museum***, which tells the story of Norwegian immigrants from their lives in Norway to their assimilation as Americans. The name means "home in the west," and throughout the facility you'll see the clothes, tools, household objects, and everyday items used by the immigrants, as well as replicas of homes and displays on the arduous sea crossing the settlers endured. There are also many examples of Norwegian folk crafts on display, a gallery of paintings by Norwegian-American artists, and an extensive outdoor exhibit area. This is regarded as the largest and most comprehensive museum in the United States devoted to a single immigrant group, so plan to spend several hours touring the entire complex.

To immerse yourself more fully in Scandinavian traditions, sign up for a class through the ***Vesterheim Folk Art School***. Classes are offered in a wide range of crafts and are taught by master teachers from throughout the United States and Scandinavia. Learn how to carve wooden spoons, dye and weave

Foodie Heaven

When it comes to food, the northeast Iowa town of Decorah used to be best known for its Norwegian specialties, including lefse, a soft flatbread made from potatoes, and lutefisk, a fish dish that can best be described as an acquired taste.

But today, Decorah and the surrounding region draw foodies from a wide radius. The Decorah area has a long tradition of small-scale, sustainable agriculture, and the produce from those farms is helping fuel growth in the quality and size of the restaurant scene.

When you dine out in Decorah, there's a good chance that much of what you're eating and drinking was grown, raised, or crafted within a few miles of the restaurant. Local farms here raise a cornucopia of products that include shiitake mushrooms, microgreens, rare vegetable varieties, artisan cheeses, and humanely raised meats. In the hands of skilled chefs at restaurants that include La Rana and Rubaiyat, the ingredients become a feast for the palate and the eye.

The **Oneota Food Co-op** (312 W. Water St.; 563-382-4666; oneotacoop.com) is another good place to take the pulse of the town's food scene. Its shelves stock a wide variety of locally raised and artisan foods, and visitors can enjoy a casual meal in its light-filled atrium.

A block away, the **Decorah Farmers Market** hosts vendors from May through Oct. Held on Saturday mornings and Wednesday afternoons, the market has freshly picked vegetables and fruits, homemade jams, local honey, eggs from free-range chickens, and an array of baked goods.

cloth, cook Norwegian specialties, and much more. Both online and in-person classes are offered.

Vesterheim is located at 520 W. Water St., Decorah, and is open daily. Admission is $12 for adults, with reduced rates for children and senior citizens. For more information visit vesterheim.org or call (563) 382-9681.

Another Decorah attraction is the **Porter House Museum** (401 W. Broadway St.; porterhousemuseum.org), an 1867 Tuscan-style villa that was home to Adelbert Field Porter and his wife Grace Young Porter. Bert, as he was commonly called, was a gentleman naturalist and photographer who traveled the world. The museum showcases his impressive collections of rare butterflies, rocks, and other artifacts. The Porter House is open daily from June through Aug, weekends in May and Sept, and a small admission is charged. After touring the museum, take a stroll through the nearby Broadway-Phelps Park Historic District, an area of lovely homes and stately trees.

While you're in Decorah, walk the lovely campus of **Luther College**, which is one of the most scenic in the Midwest. The Decorah area also has many fine parks, including Dunning's Spring, which has a beautiful waterfall, and Phelps Park, which offers hiking along a network of trails. The Upper Iowa River, which runs through the center of town, is popular with canoeing enthusiasts. *National Geographic Explorer* magazine named it one of the "world's top one hundred adventures." The area also has many well-stocked trout streams.

The **Hotel Winneshiek** is a boutique hotel with historic roots. Built in 1904–5, the brick structure was extensively renovated three decades ago. A three-story octagonal lobby with a stained-glass skylight serves as the hub for thirty-four luxurious rooms and suites. The downtown hotel is at 104 E. Water St. (563-382-4164; hotelwinn.com). Rates are in the expensive category.

Decorah's **Trout Run Trail** is an 11-mile, paved recreational trail that encircles the town. Along the way you'll pass limestone bluffs, blooming prairie, and bucolic farms. You can get a trail map by calling (563) 382-3990 or at visitdecorah.com.

One of the stops on the trail is the **Decorah Fish Hatchery**, site of the **Decorah Bald Eagle Cam**. Since its launching in 2011, the eagle's nest video cam has racked up millions of views, making it one of the most-watched live wildlife streams on the Internet. During nesting season, viewers can watch in real time as the birds nurture their young. Visitors to the fish hatchery can peer upwards at the nests in cottonwood trees (the bald eagle pair has two nests, both of which are observed by cameras). The Decorah Fish Hatchery is at 2325 Siewers Spring Rd.

After a day of touring, two Decorah breweries offer places to relax and sample craft beers. **Toppling Goliath** has received international recognition for its craft beers, including being rated the world's second-best brewery by the Rate Beer website. You'll find its tasting room at 1600 Prosperity Rd. (563-387-6700; tgbrews.com). The brewery also has a restaurant serving upscale pub food.

Pulpit Rock Brewing is fast making a name for itself as well. It has a cozy tasting room and patio at 207 College Dr. (563-380-3610; pulpitrockbrewing.com).

From Decorah take US 52 north for 6 miles to *Seed Savers Heritage Farm* at 3074 N. Winn Rd. The farm is the headquarters of the Seed Savers Exchange. This unique 890-acre farm is a living museum of historic varieties of endangered fruits and vegetables and is the largest nongovernmental seed bank in the United States. The farm is set beside limestone bluffs and century-old stands of white pine woods. Seeds are multiplied and gathered from the organic gardens and offered for sale in the visitor center, which was built by Amish carpenters. Seed Savers preserves more than 20,000 rare vegetable varieties. About 10 percent of the varieties are grown each summer, on a ten-year rotation, to ensure fresh seeds for the collection.

The Seed Savers Exchange has also developed the most diverse public orchard in the United States—900 varieties of apples are grown there. And don't miss the Ancient White Park cattle! They're from the British Isles and are distinguished by their white coats, black-tipped lyre-shaped horns, and black noses, ears, and hooves. The visitor center is open daily from Mar through Oct. For more information call (563) 382-5990 or visit seedsavers.org.

North of Decorah you'll also find *Winneshiek Wildberry Winery*. Owners Ken and Yvonne Barnes worked for decades as dairy farmers until their two

Uff da!

One expression you're likely to hear in Decorah is the all-purpose, ever-useful "Uff da!" Brought to America by immigrants, Uff da is the Norwegian-American equivalent of "Oy vey"; just the thing to say when you put too much butter on your *lefse* or lost your chewing gum on the chicken coop floor.

Norwegian jokes are also popular in Decorah. It's a testimony to the good nature of Decorah residents that they love to tell these jokes on themselves. Have you heard the one about the Norwegians and Germans who went ice fishing together? They're all casting away like mad, but while the Germans are catching lots of fish, the Norwegians aren't catching anything at all. Finally one of the Norwegians tells his friend to go over to the other group to see why they're catching all those fish. Off the man goes and comes back a few minutes later to report, "Well, it looks like the first thing they do is cut a hole in the ice."

daughters helped them launch a wine-making business in 2005. In addition to 22 acres of grapes, they grow 2 acres of rhubarb plants, a tart plant that makes a surprisingly good wine.

The farm's former dairy barn houses the winery, its interior refurbished into an airy tasting room and gift shop with a cathedral ceiling and oak floor. In the basement, fermentation tanks, pressing machines, and other wine-making paraphernalia stand where once the Barnes milked cows. You can find the winery at 1966 337th St. For information call (563) 735-5809 or see wwwinery.com.

For more information on the Decorah area, call (563) 382-3990 or visit decoraharea.com.

Continue north on US 52 to the site of the ***Laura Ingalls Wilder Museum***, located at 3603 236th Ave. in Burr Oak. This National Historic Landmark was once home to the author of the famous Little House series of children's books. In the fall of 1876, the Ingalls family moved to ***Burr Oak*** following disastrous grasshopper plagues in Minnesota. Laura's father managed the hotel that is now the museum, while Laura, her mother, and her sister waited tables, cooked, and cleaned. The Ingalls family lived here for one year before moving back to Walnut Grove, Minnesota.

Local Ingalls fans borrowed $1,500 to purchase the hotel in 1973 and launched a campaign to raise money for its restoration. With public dances, benefit auctions, book sales, donations, and a "Pennies for Laura" campaign, enough funds were raised to open the old hotel as a museum. This building is the only childhood home of Laura Ingalls Wilder that remains on its original site. It's open daily May through Labor Day and limited days the rest of the year; call for hours. Admission is $10 for adults and $6 for children. Call (563) 735-5916 for information or see lauraingallswilder.us.

Prairie lovers will want to take a detour east of Burr Oak to see one of the state's largest remaining sections of native grasslands, ***Hayden Prairie State Preserve***. The 242-acre tract is located 3 miles south of Chester on CR V26 and shows what much of Iowa looked like before it was broken by the plow. Owned and managed by the state of Iowa, Hayden Prairie contains more than 200 plant species and attracts a diverse range of birds and wildlife.

Next head southeast for 35 miles to the ethnic enclave of ***Spillville***. While Decorah is known for its Norwegian heritage, Spillville was settled by Czech immigrants. The little town takes great pride in one of its former residents, the famed Czech composer Antonin Dvořák, who spent a summer here in 1893. Homesick for the companionship of his countrymen after a year's work as director of the New York Conservatory of Music, Dvořák came to Spillville and spent the summer composing his "American Quartette" and found inspiration for "Humoresque," which was written after he left.

The Secrets of Midwestern Prairies

When it comes to loving prairies, I was a late bloomer. Raised on an Iowa farm, I had a farmer's disdain for wasted land that didn't produce crops or feed livestock. A wild meadow or stand of woods could be pretty, but in the end it wasn't worth as much as a well-plowed field.

And then I discovered **Hayden Prairie**. A stretch of grassland marked only by a modest sign, it is easy to miss as you drive north to the Minnesota border. A botanist friend took me there and spent an hour introducing me to the life within its boundaries. I was interested, but it took something more to begin the love affair.

I came back on my own one day, looking for a place to stretch my legs on a trip north. I parked the car and began to wander through the grasses, and I eventually found a spot away from the road, where I lay down on a soft mat of last year's vegetation. I breathed in the freshness of the air, felt the prickle of plants against my skin, listened to the restless whisper of the wind, and slowly, ever so slowly, the prairie began to weave me into its web.

Since then I've returned often to Hayden Prairie, and any other prairie I can find. If you're looking hard, you can discover them scattered throughout the Midwest, hidden treasures tucked away in parks, along gravel roads, and scattered in patches on the occasional farm—a small section the farmer "just can't bear to plow because it's so pretty in the summer." These are the paltry remnants of an expanse of grassland that once extended from Pennsylvania and Ohio to the Rocky Mountains and from southern Canada to the Gulf of Mexico.

At a distance these may seem to be just another stand of pasture, but come closer and they have a wild, ragged appearance. Come closer still, spend an afternoon, a season, or a lifetime, and the prairie will begin to reveal its secrets to you.

The building where Dvořák lived that summer is now the home of **Bily Clocks**, a museum filled with the hand-carved clocks of brothers Frank and Joseph Bily. The two were local farmers who whiled away long winter days and evenings by carving. In thirty-five years they created twenty-five intricately carved clocks ranging in height from a few inches to 10 feet, using woods from various foreign countries as well as butternut, maple, walnut, and oak from America. Among the outstanding clocks on display are an apostle clock from which the twelve apostles parade every hour, an American pioneer clock showing important historical events, and a clock built to commemorate Lindbergh's crossing of the Atlantic in 1928.

Bily Clocks is located at 323 S. Main St. It is open daily May through Oct, with shortened hours the rest of the year. Call (563) 562-3569 or see bilyclocks .org for more information or to arrange a visit during the winter months. A small admission is charged.

Before you leave Spillville, pay a visit to the lovely St. Wenceslaus Church, where Antonin Dvořák played the organ for daily Mass during his stay in the village. St. Wenceslaus is the oldest Czech Catholic church in the United States.

South of Spillville on IA 24 is the town of **Fort Atkinson**, site of the **Fort Atkinson State Preserve**. A fort was built here in 1840–42 as part of the campaign to remove the Ho-Chunk (Winnebago) people from their ancestral lands. The state of Iowa acquired the property in 1921, and reconstruction of the old fort began in 1958. Part of the original barracks is now a museum housing documents relating to the history of the fort.

A good time to visit Fort Atkinson is during its annual **Rendezvous**, held on the last full weekend in Sept. The event draws buckskinners from several states who re-create the days of the frontier. Events include cannon drills, skillet- and tomahawk-throwing contests, anvil shooting, and melodrama performances—and when you get hungry you can sample frontier treats such as venison stew and Indian fry bread.

Fort Atkinson (563-425-4161; iowadnr.gov) is open daily, with museum admission by appointment only.

On a country road near the town of **Festina**, east of Fort Atkinson, is the **St. Anthony of Padua Chapel**, better known as the **World's Smallest Church**. The stone chapel is only 14 by 20 feet and holds four tiny pews. It was constructed to fulfill a vow made by Johann Gaertner's mother, who promised God she would build him a chapel if her soldier son survived Napoleon's Russian campaign. The son did indeed return home unharmed, and the chapel was built of locally quarried stone in 1885. A small, peaceful graveyard filled with old cedar trees is located in back of the little church and includes the grave of Johann Gaertner (who died a natural death, one hopes).

To reach the chapel, follow the signs from Festina. The building is open during daylight hours and has no admission charge.

Twenty miles east of Festina you'll find **Greens' Sugar Bush** at 1437 111th Ave., **Castalia**. This maple syrup operation is one of the oldest continually operating businesses in Iowa, now in its sixth generation in a single family. Each spring they hold a pancake day, its date depending upon how the sap is flowing, and you can buy maple syrup at their farm throughout the year while quantities last. Call (563) 605-1168 for more information.

Northeast of Castalia is Waukon, where you'll find an Iowa artistic treasure: **Steel Cow** (steelcow.com). Located at 15 Allamakee St. NW, the gallery showcases the work of Valerie Miller, who takes her inspiration from the state's bovine citizens. You'll find her huge murals of cows on buildings throughout northeast Iowa. You can stop by her studio to purchase smaller versions of her work, from canvas prints and Christmas ornaments to refrigerator magnets.

To continue the cow theme, visit **WW Homestead Dairy** at 850 Rossville Rd. (563-568-4950; wwhomesteaddairy.com). The dairy uses milk from local farms to create tasty cheeses and dozens of flavors of ice cream, all made with 14 percent butterfat. The dairy is especially known for its cheese curds, which visitors can see being made through the windows that overlook its production facility.

Peake Orchards (563-419-0449; peakeorchards.com) at 323 North Line Dr. in Waukon offers hayrides to its grove of apple trees on Sunday during harvest season. Guests can pick their own varieties off the trees (the orchard is noted for its Honeycrisp apples) and browse a gift shop with apple-related items. Come on a Saturday to enjoy their delicious apple cider donuts.

A mile away at 1352 Apple Rd. is **Empty Nest Winery** (563-568-2758; emptynestwinery.com). Owners Dave and Pam Kruger gave up their dairy business five years ago to become vintners. They make a variety of grape and other wines, made with whole berries rather than juice for bolder flavors. A tasting room and banquet area overlook the rolling fields of northeast Iowa.

Take US 18 south of Frankville to **Clermont**, where you'll find **Montauk**, a lovely mansion that was home to Iowa's twelfth governor, William Larrabee. Larrabee built the Italianate house in 1874 high on a hill overlooking the Turkey River valley, and his wife, Anna, named it after the lighthouse on Long Island that guided her sea-captain father home from his whaling voyages.

didyouknow?

It takes forty gallons of sap to make one gallon of maple syrup.

The fourteen-room home is built of native limestone and local brick kilned in Clermont, and it is surrounded by 46 acres of flower gardens and trees. Inside are the home's original furnishings, including Tiffany lamps, Wedgwood china, statues from Italy, onyx tables from Mexico, a large collection of paintings, and thousands of books. The elegant and cultured mansion reflects the character of its owner, a man of boundless energy and ambition as well as great intelligence and charisma. He ran for governor on a platform that called for tighter control of the railroads, women's suffrage, and strict enforcement of Prohibition (his campaign slogan was "a schoolhouse on every hill and no saloons in the valley").

Montauk is located 1 mile north of Clermont on US 18. Hours are noon to 4 p.m. daily from Memorial Day through early Sept. A small admission is charged. Call (563) 423-7173 or see montaukiowa.com for more information.

From Clermont head 3 miles south to **Elgin**, where you'll find the **Gilbertson Conservation Education Area** (563-426-5740). Run by the Fayette County Conservation Board, the 1,000-acre site on the banks of the Turkey

River has a variety of attractions, including a nature center, summer petting zoo, campground, displays on local wildlife, and ten miles of trails.

Rural Treasures

Southeast of Montauk at the junction of IA 3 and IA 13 lies the town of **Strawberry Point**. Though the town has only 1,300 residents, it's difficult to miss, for a huge strawberry has been erected at its city hall. The name was given to the town by soldiers, traders, and railroad workers who enjoyed the bountiful wild strawberries once found along the area's trails and hillsides. Each year in June the town holds **Strawberry Days**, a community celebration that culminates with the serving of free strawberries and ice cream on the last day of the festival.

Strawberry Point is also home to the **Wilder Memorial Museum**, 123 W. Mission St. The museum is best known for its collections of dolls and of Victorian glass, porcelain, lamps, and furniture. Much of its collection was donated by Marcey Alderson, a local music teacher and avid antiques collector who spent his lifetime acquiring exquisite pieces. Dresden, Limoges, and Haviland porcelains, beautiful glassware and lamps, and ornately carved furniture are all on display here. (A favorite with many visitors is a lamp once used on the set of *Gone With the Wind*.) The Wilder Museum is located on IA 3 and is open Tues through Sat, Memorial Day through Labor Day, and on weekends in Sept and Oct. Admission is $7 for adults and $5 for students. For more information call (563) 933-4615 or see wildermuseum.org.

Just south of Strawberry Point on IA 410 is one of Iowa's loveliest nature preserves, **Backbone State Park** (563-924-2527; iowadnr.gov). The park's most prominent feature is an unusual spinelike rock formation that is known in local lore as the "devil's backbone." Legend has it that the devil lost his nerve one day and left his backbone behind as he slithered east to the Mississippi River. The park has campsites, cabins, hiking trails, and wonderful views of the Maquoketa River and surrounding countryside.

didyouknow?

Backbone State Park was dedicated in 1920, making it Iowa's first state park.

From Strawberry Point travel south to the small town of **Quasqueton**, where you can visit one of the state's most significant architectural landmarks at **Cedar Rock State Park** (2611 Quasqueton Diagonal Blvd.). The park preserves a house that was designed by famed architect Frank Lloyd Wright and built between 1948 and 1950. It was commissioned by wealthy businessman

Lowell Walter and his wife, Agnes, who later bequeathed their home to the Iowa Conservation Commission and the people of Iowa.

Nearly every item in the Walter house bears the imprint of the famous architect. The overall design is strongly horizontal, lines that Wright felt reflected prairie landforms. The long, low structure is skillfully integrated into the landscape and sits on a limestone bluff overlooking the Wapsipinicon River. Wright designed the furniture, selected the carpets and draperies, and even helped pick out the china, silverware, and cooking utensils. In addition to the house, the wooded 11-acre site has a river pavilion, a fire circle, and an entrance gate that were all designed by Wright. The Walter house is one of the most complete designs Wright had the opportunity to create in his long and productive career. The house is open May through Oct, Wed through Sun from 10 a.m. to 5 p.m. Admission is free. Call (319) 934-3572 for more information.

From Quasqueton go west on US 20 to the adjoining cities of **Waterloo** and **Cedar Falls**.

Cedar Falls is best known as the home of the **University of Northern Iowa**, a school founded in 1876 to train public school teachers. Today it enrolls about 9,500 students in a wide variety of undergraduate and graduate degree programs. One of the most prominent landmarks on campus is the UNI Campanile, a 100-foot-tall structure built to commemorate the school's fiftieth anniversary. The UNI-Dome is the other most recognizable landmark on campus. The bubble-topped building houses various sports facilities and also hosts many nonathletic events. The university is also home to the Gallagher-Bluedorn Performing Arts Center. See gbpac.com or call (319) 273-7469 for an events schedule.

Also in Cedar Falls is the **Ice House Museum**, a structure containing artifacts of the ice-cutting industry as well as other historic items. In the days before mechanical refrigeration, natural ice was cut from the Cedar River and stored year-round in this unusual circular building constructed in 1921. Each year some 6,000 to 8,000 tons of ice were stacked within its 100-foot diameter (the circular shape allowed only one wall to touch the stacked blocks rather than two, thus slowing the melting process). In 1934 the icehouse owner lost his business, and the structure was used for a variety of purposes in the following years. In 1975 it escaped demolition when a group of local citizens raised money to restore it and open it as a museum. Today you can see the array of equipment once used in ice cutting plus photographs of the entire process, from harvesting to selling. A visit here is certain to make you appreciate your refrigerator and freezer at home.

The Ice House Museum is located at 121 Center St. It's open on weekends from May through mid-Oct. Call (319) 266-5149 for more information.

Two other museums operated by the Cedar Falls Historical Society are the **Victorian House Museum**, a historic Civil War–era home at 308 W. Third St. and the **Little Red Schoolhouse**, an early twentieth-century country school moved in 1988 to a location near the Ice House Museum. For more information call (319) 266-5149 or see cfhistory.org.

The **Hartman Reserve Nature Center** (319-277-2187; hartmanreserve .org) has lakes and prairie as well as century-old oaks and a rare grove of huge native cottonwood and hawthorn trees. Tour the center and then explore the 6 miles of trails that wind through the grounds. You'll find the 340-acre property at 657 Reserve Dr.

In the neighboring city of **Waterloo**, visit the **Grout Museum District**, a complex of attractions off US 218 at 503 South St. Begin your tour at the **Sullivan Brothers Iowa Veterans Museum**, which honors Iowans who have served in the US military. Everyone who tours this museum in a sense becomes a veteran, because each visitor is given a dog tag at the entrance that invites them to take on the persona of an Iowan who served in the military. As visitors wander through the exhibits detailing each combat period, they can scan the dog tag in a kiosk that gives information on how their veteran experienced the events of that war. There are eighteen different profiles that are composites based on the experiences of actual veterans.

An emphasis on storytelling is a hallmark of the entire museum. Interactive exhibits with weapons, uniforms, battle maps, vintage photos, and period memorabilia give the broad outlines of each conflict, but the displays also interweave the individual stories of Iowans in war. A video in the World War II exhibit, for example, features an elderly man fighting back tears as he recalls what it was like to watch his comrades being killed during the bombing at Pearl Harbor. In the Vietnam exhibit, a woman who had served as an Army nurse talks about her experiences during the war and after, including the emotions she felt the first time she walked in a Veterans Day parade.

Next visit the **Grout Museum of History and Science**. Here you can wander through an impressive variety of exhibits describing area history and the natural environment. On the lower level are five full-scale dioramas depicting a log cabin, toolshed, blacksmith shop, carpenter shop, and general store. On the upper level are displays that will inform you about the geology of Iowa, its first inhabitants, and the plant and animal life of the state. There's also a gallery for changing exhibitions and an impressive exhibit, "Engine of the Heartland," that traces the evolution of Waterloo from a small town into an industrial center.

Science buffs will enjoy the **Norris Corson Family Planetarium**, which features a 17-foot dome and a star projector that dramatically displays the stars,

The Fighting Sullivans

Iowa's most famous veterans were the five Sullivan brothers, who were killed in 1942 when their ship sank during World War II's Battle of Guadalcanal in the Pacific.

When the brothers enlisted in the Navy, they asked to be stationed on the same vessel, a request that the Navy initially rejected, but then granted. Their deaths were the largest single combat loss for any family in American military history. The tragedy generated a huge amount of media attention and made the Sullivan Brothers a national symbol of the nation's sacrifice as well as its determination to win World War II.

The *Sullivan Brothers Iowa Veterans Museum* in Waterloo honors their memory. One of its exhibits is a reproduction of their family's living room in Waterloo, where hundreds came to extend condolences after the brothers' deaths. The exhibit also includes the Gold Star flag that was once displayed at their home, a flag that bears five stars to show how many family members they had lost in combat.

The Navy named two destroyers after the brothers, and they were the subject of the 1944 movie *The Fighting Sullivans*. Steven Spielberg also referenced their deaths in *Saving Private Ryan*, where their loss becomes part of the reason why the Ryan brothers do not serve in the same place.

moon, and planets in the night skies, and the *Bluedorn Science Imaginarium*, a three-floor, interactive science center filled with exhibits on how science affects everyday life.

Finally, fans of historic architecture will want to visit the *Rensselaer Russell House Museum*, which is one of the best examples of Italianate architecture in Iowa. It was built by Rensselaer Russell, a Waterloo businessman who completed the house in 1861 at the then-princely cost of $6,000. Today it has been restored to its original Victorian splendor and is open to the public by appointment.

For information on hours and admission prices in the Grout Museum District, see groutmuseumdistrict.org or call (319) 234-6357.

Waterloo's *Lost Island Theme Park* is a family-friendly magnet. The site expands upon Lost Island Water Park, a popular Midwestern destination since 2001. In addition to all the attractions of the water park, the amusement park has five themed areas with three roller coasters, go-karts, adventure golf, and rides appropriate for a wide variety of ages. Lost Island is at 2600 E. Shaulis Rd. For more information call (319) 455-6700 or visit thelostisland.com.

For wrestling fans, the *National Wrestling Hall of Fame Dan Gable Museum* is a pilgrimage destination. But even if you're not well-versed in the sport, this site is still worth visiting. The museum is named after wrestling legend Dan Gable, a 1972 Olympic gold medalist who is regarded as one of the greatest amateur wrestlers in the history of the sport. The Waterloo native went on to coach at the University of Iowa, where his teams won fifteen NCAA national wrestling titles. The museum has exhibits on Gable's life and the history of wrestling going back to the ancient Greeks. It's located at 303 Jefferson St. in Waterloo and is open 10 a.m. to 4 p.m., Mon through Fri. Call (319) 233-0745 or see nwhof.org/waterloo for information.

For more information on area attractions, contact Experience Waterloo at (319) 233-8350 or see experiencewaterloo.com.

newdealmurals

During the Depression, the Works Progress Administration commissioned artists to paint murals across the state. You can see these WPA murals in towns that include:

Cresco: Post Office

New Hampton: Post Office

Waverly: Post Office

Waterloo: Public Library

Independence: Post Office

Manchester: Post Office

Dubuque: Post Office

Southwest of Waterloo, visit **Hansen Dairy** (319-242-1074; hansendairy.com) at 8461 Lincoln Rd. in Hudson. Book a tour to learn how milk gets from the cow to your table. Admission includes a trolley ride to the farm, then a walking tour to see its animals and facilities. Participants can feed a calf, milk a cow by hand, make butter, and sample products made on the Hansen farm. An added treat is getting the chance to meet the farm's resident kangaroos (they're not native to Iowa but they're certainly cute). Tours are $20.

From **Waterloo** and Cedar Falls head north on US 218 for 15 miles to **Waverly**, the site of the **Waverly Midwest Horse Sale**. Twice a year this event draws buyers and sellers from around the country and the world. With a sale bill that includes more than a thousand horses and mules, plus hundreds of harnesses, saddles, wagons, carriages, cutters, and sleighs, the sale is the largest event of its kind in the country. The majority of the horses sold here are draft horses—the massive Percherons, Shires, Belgians, and Clydesdales, breeds that once farmed the country. Today they're bought and sold by a varied clientele who include Amish farmers, lumber companies that use them in areas inaccessible to machines, ranchers who buy them to haul hay, and places like Disney World that use horses in parades and to pull trolleys. Even if you're not in the market for a Belgian or a Clydesdale, the sale is a fascinating slice of rural life. The sales are held each year in Mar and Oct on the grounds of the Waverly Sales Company, on US 218 on the northwest side of Waverly. For more information call (319) 352-2804 or visit waverlysales.com.

The Church in the Wildwood

The story behind Iowa's *Little Brown Church in the Vale* begins in 1857 when William Pitts, a young music teacher, was traveling west from Wisconsin to visit his fiancée, who lived in Iowa. On the way he stopped to take a stroll along the Little Cedar River and came across a place that he thought would make a lovely location for a church. On his return home he sat down to write a hymn describing what he had imagined, a song with a refrain of *"Oh, come to the church in the wildwood, Oh, come to the church in the vale."*

The years passed, and eventually Pitts returned to the area to teach music at a local academy. He was stunned by what he found, for a small church was being built at the very spot he had visualized in his hymn. On dedication day in 1864, Pitts's vocal class sang the song in public for the first time, and the church and the hymn became inseparable. The song later gained wider fame when it became the theme of a popular gospel group that toured the country in the early twentieth century.

From Waverly head north on US 218 for 17 miles to *Nashua*, home to perhaps the most famous church in Iowa, the *Little Brown Church in the Vale*. The church was immortalized in the hymn "The Church in the Wildwood" and has become a popular spot for weddings. More than 76,000 couples have been married in this simple Congregational church. The Little Brown Church is located 2 miles east of Nashua on IA 346, at 2730 Cheyenne Ave. The church is open for weekday tours, and worship services are held on Sun at 10:15 a.m. For more information (or to arrange a wedding) call (641) 435-2027. Visit its website at littlebrownchurch.org.

Adjacent to the Little Brown Church is the *Old Bradford Pioneer Village*, a reconstruction of what was once a thriving village in the area. The fourteen-building complex includes log cabins, a railroad depot, a country school, and the building where William Pitts had his office. The village (641-435-2567; oldbradfordvillage.org) is open May through Oct and is located at 2729 Cheyenne Ave. in Nashua.

East of Nashua, visit the *Hawkeye Buffalo & Cattle Ranch* (641-229-6701; hawkeyebuffalo.com) at 3034 Pembroke Ave. in Fredericksburg. On a wagon ride, you can meet the farm's bison herd and learn about the farm, which has been in the same family since 1854. Its owners take pride in raising ethically grazed bison and cattle.

Places to Stay in Bluffs and Valleys

CEDAR FALLS

The Black Hawk Hotel
115 Main St.
(319) 277-1161
theblackhawk.com
expensive

Three Pines Farm
9611 Wagner Rd.
(319) 404-2942
threepinesfarm.org
moderate

DECORAH

B & B on Broadway
305 W. Broadway St.
(563) 382-1420
bandbonbroadway.com
moderate to expensive

DUBUQUE

The Richards House
1492 Locust St.
(563) 557-1492
therichardshouse.com
inexpensive to expensive

GUTTENBERG

Court House Inn
618 S. River Park Dr.
(888) 224-2188
thecourthouseinn.biz
moderate

LANSING

McGarrity's Inn on Main
203 Main St.
(563) 538-2080
mcgarritysinn.com
moderate

MCGREGOR

Hickory Ridge Bed, Breakfast & Bridle
17156 Great River Rd.
(563) 873-1758
hickoryridgebbandb.com
inexpensive

Places to Eat in Bluffs and Valleys

CEDAR FALLS

Montage
222 Main St.
(319) 268-7222
montage-cf.com
moderate

DECORAH

Mabe's Pizza
110 E. Water St.
(563) 382-4297
mabespizza.com
inexpensive

La Rana
120 Washington St.
(563) 382-3067
laranadecorah.com
moderate

Rubaiyat
117 W. Water St.
(563) 382-9463
rubaiyatrestaurant.com
moderate to expensive

DUBUQUE

Copper Kettle
2987 Jackson St
(563) 845-0567
inexpensive

L. May Eatery
1072 Main St.
(563) 556-0505
lmayeatery.com
moderate

DYERSVILLE

Textile Brewing Company
146 Second St. NE
(563) 207-0357
textilebrews.com
inexpensive

WATERLOO

Mersim's
126 E. Ridgeway Ave.,
Suite A
(319) 883-3055
mersims.com
inexpensive

WAVERLY

East Bremer Diner
117 E. Bremer Ave.
(319) 352-2455
eastbremerdiner.com
inexpensive

Cultural Crossroads

East central Iowa is truly a cultural crossroads. Here you'll find two of Iowa's largest metropolitan areas, the Quad Cities and Cedar Rapids, as well as the cosmopolitan charms of Iowa City, home of the University of Iowa. This region also includes one of the state's most popular tourism attractions, the Amana Colonies, which were founded as a religious communal society and where German traditions still remain strong. Here in east central Iowa you can also explore the legacies of two of Iowa's most famous native sons, President Herbert Hoover and artist Grant Wood.

Village Charm and City Sophistication

If I had to name my favorite destinations in Iowa, the *Amana Colonies* would certainly be near the top of my list. Part of the reason is sheer gluttony: The restaurants in these seven picturesque villages are among the best in the state, each serving bounteous portions of hearty German food. If I ever get to heaven, I hope the cafeteria there is staffed by Amana natives.

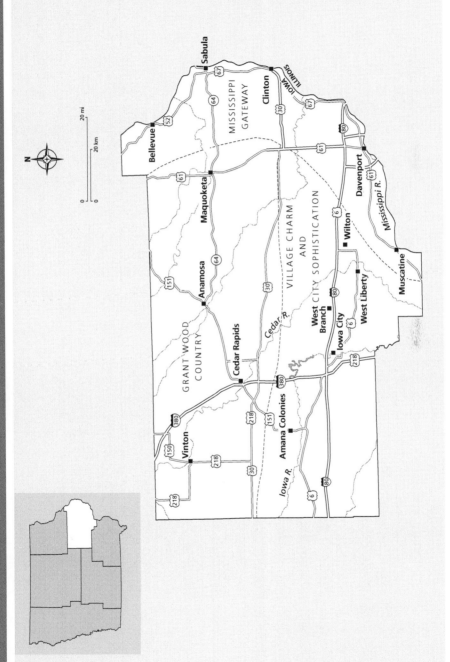

But the food is not the only reason to visit this community, located 20 miles southwest of Cedar Rapids on US 151. Its rich history alone makes it a fascinating stop. The villages were settled by a group of German immigrants, bound together by a common religious belief that has its roots in the Pietist and Mystic movements that flourished in Germany during the early 1700s. The group fled religious persecution in Germany in 1842 and settled in New York State, but eventually they sought a larger and more isolated location for their community.

They came to Iowa in 1855 and built their new home on 26,000 acres of timber and farmland in the rolling countryside of eastern Iowa. Soon they had established a nearly self-sufficient communal society, sharing work, meals, and all worldly goods. This system continued until 1932, when the pressures of the modern world and the Depression combined to convince the villagers that changes were needed. A profit-sharing corporation was formed to manage the farmland and businesses, and the community kitchens served their last meal. So ended one of America's longest-lived and most successful experiments in utopian living.

Visit the Amanas today, however, and all around you'll see reminders of the past. These tidy brick villages look more European than midwestern, with their houses clustered in the center and weathered barns on the periphery. For a better understanding of their history, visit the ***Amana Heritage Museum*** (4310 220th Trail), housed in three nineteenth-century buildings set on spacious grounds. There you can view exhibits about the history of the Amana Colonies, their culture and religious life, and the various crafts and industries of the society. The museum also operates several other historic sites in the Amana Colonies, including the Communal Kitchen in Middle Amana, the High Amana General Store, and the Homestead Church. Each gives additional insights into the world of the Amanas before the Great Change of 1932.

The Amana Heritage Museum is open daily Apr through Oct, with reduced hours during the rest of the year. A ticket that is good for admission to all the

AUTHOR'S FAVORITES

The Amana Colonies	Prairie Lights Books
NewBo Market	Rochester Cemetery
The Black Angel	Grant Wood Scenic Byway
Maquoketa Caves State Park	Twilight Riverboat

sites is $10 for adults. For more information call (319) 622-3567 or see amana-heritage.org.

While you're in the village of Amana, take the time to stroll its streets and browse in the many shops filled with the handcrafted items that have made the Amanas famous. The Amana Furniture and Clock Shop sells beautiful walnut, cherry, and oak furniture and has a room devoted entirely to grandfather clocks, which create a delightful cacophony of ticks and chimes. Another popular spot is Warped & Woven Mill Mercantile, which is Iowa's only remaining working woolen mill. It's been in continuous operation since 1857, making it the oldest business in the Amanas. It's a great place to shop for blankets, sweaters, jackets, mittens, and other items. Across the road is the ***Millstream Brewing Company***, where premium local beers are brewed. Elsewhere in the village are wineries, gift shops, bakeries, and enough specialty shops to keep you occupied for several hours.

Though Amana has the most shops and visitor attractions, don't confine yourself to just one village. A leisurely drive through the countryside will take you on a tour of the other villages, most of which have their own shops, restaurants, wineries, and historical sites. In ***Middle Amana*** you'll drive past the villages' best-known industry, Amana Refrigeration Products. The business was founded by Amana native George Foerstner and is the largest employer in Iowa County. (It is currently owned by the Whirlpool Corporation.)

From any of the seven Amana villages—Amana, East, Middle, High, West, South, and Homestead—it is easy to get on the Amana Colonies Trail, the roads that link the seven villages. Each village has its own unique flavor, and a pleasant day or two can be spent exploring them. Take your time admiring the houses and buildings of brick, stone, or wood. If you are planning a picnic during the summer months, make sure you stop at the ***Lily Lake***, located on IA 220 on the outskirts of Middle Amana. This small lake is covered with water lilies during mid- to late summer and offers a luxuriant display of green, gold, and creamy white foliage and flowers.

And before you leave the Amanas, enjoy a meal in one of the village restaurants, known for such German specialties as sauerbraten, Wiener schnitzel, smoked pork chops, and pickled ham. Most serve their meals family style, with overflowing bowls of salads, potatoes, and vegetables, plus delicious homemade pies and desserts. In the words of one Amana native, "If you leave here hungry, it's your own fault."

Several other attractions in the villages may also strike your fancy. One is the ***Amana Colonies Nature Trail***, located at the junction of US 151 and US 6 near Homestead. The trail winds for more than 3 miles through hardwoods

TOP ANNUAL EVENTS

MAY

Maifest
Amana, first weekend in May
(319) 622-7622
amanacolonies.com

Houby Days
Cedar Rapids Czech Village
second weekend in May
(319) 731-4560
tourismcedarrapids.com

JUNE

Snake Alley Art Fair
Father's Day
(319) 754-8069
btownart.com

JULY

Iowa City Jazz Festival
weekend nearest July 4
(319) 337-7944
summerofthearts.org

AUGUST

Bix Beiderbecke Memorial Jazz Festival
Davenport, early Aug
(563) 324-7170
bixsociety.org

Hoover's Hometown Days
West Branch, first weekend in Aug
(319) 643-5888
hooverdays.org

OCTOBER

Iowa City Book Festival
Mid-October
(319) 356-5245
iowacityofliterature.org

and along the Iowa River, reaching its turnaround point on a scenic bluff overlooking an Indian dam built some 250 years ago.

Another fine trail is the *Amana Kolonieweg*, a 3.1-mile route that connects the villages of Amana and Middle Amana. The trail circles Lily Lake, and it is especially lovely when the water is abloom with lilies in mid-July and early Aug. You can also watch for geese, pelicans, herons, and bald eagles.

Overnight guests to the Amanas can choose from a variety of accommodations, from motels and campsites to intimate bed-and-breakfasts. In Amana, the *Hotel Millwright* (hotelmillwright.com; 319-838-5015) occupies part of the Amana Woolen Mill complex of buildings. The boutique hotel has sixty-five guest rooms and suites done in a modern, industrial-chic style. Its *Indigo Room* serves upscale versions of classic American dishes.

Die Heimat Country Inn (4434 V St., Homestead; 319-622-3937; dieheimat.com) offers fifteen rooms with private baths and is furnished with Amana antiques. In the late 1850s, Die Heimat (which is German for "The Home Place") was an inn for travelers, and later the building became a communal kitchen. Today it is a gracious small hotel offering a mixture of old-fashioned style and modern amenities. See dheimat.com for more information.

The Amana Colonies Visitors Center, 622 Forty-Sixth Ave. in Amana, will give you a complete listing of attractions as well as hotel accommodations in the area. The center, which is open daily, also has an informational video presentation on the Amanas and a gift shop. Call (319) 622-7622 for information about the Amana Colonies or visit amanacolonies.com.

If you like to shop, one more destination should be on your itinerary before you leave this part of the state: ***Outlets & Marketplace Williamsburg*** near the town of ***Williamsburg*** off I-80 (exit 220). Here you'll find nearly forty shops selling merchandise from nationally known manufacturers at savings up to 70 percent off retail prices. From Liz Claiborne dresses to Mikasa dinnerware, this is the place to find bargains. Call (319) 668-2885 or visit shopomw.com for information.

UNESCO City of Literature

Walk the downtown streets of Iowa City and you don't have to look far for evidence of the town's love for literature: The sidewalks on Iowa Avenue and in the Northside Neighborhood feature bronze panels bearing quotations from writers ranging from Flannery O'Connor and Tennessee Williams to W. P. Kinsella and Gail Godwin. The ***Literary Walk*** honors more than fifty authors who have a connection to Iowa City and is a testimony to how much the people of Iowa City treasure the writers in their midst.

Iowa City is a literary mecca because of the ***Iowa Writers' Workshop***, the nation's oldest and most respected program for creative writing. Based in an 1857 Victorian-style house overlooking the Iowa River, the workshop is a two-year graduate program at the University of Iowa that nurtures the next generation of fiction writers and poets.

The workshop was founded in 1936 as the first creative writing degree program in the United States, pioneering a model that other universities would later follow. Its graduates include US Poet Laureates, more than a dozen Pulitzer Prize winners, and a host of writers who have won National Book Awards and other major literary prizes. The contributions that the workshop has made to the nation's cultural life were honored in 2003 when it was awarded a National Humanities Medal from the National Endowment for the Humanities, the first medal ever given to a university.

Iowa City received another major honor in 2008, when it was named one of the world's first three Literary Cities by the United Nations' UNESCO organization (along with Edinburgh, Scotland, and Melbourne, Australia).

The Writers' Workshop is just one of several highly regarded writing programs at the University of Iowa. The campus is also home to the ***International Writing Program*** (a residency program that attracts authors from around the world), the Iowa Playwrights Workshop, and a writing program in literary nonfiction.

Next head east on I-80 for 20 miles to *Iowa City*, which is home to the *University of Iowa*, a Big 10 school with more than 30,000 students. Aside from the Saturdays when the football team has a home game, the pace here is as relaxed as the leisurely current of the Iowa River, which flows through the center of town. The university sits in the heart of Iowa City and is the focus of much of its life, but stroll just a few blocks from downtown and you'll find yourself on tree-lined, peaceful residential streets. (One neighborhood you shouldn't miss is Summit Street, a stately expanse of Victorian homes and beautifully kept lawns about 0.25 mile east of the downtown area.)

Iowa City's nickname is the Athens of the Midwest, and though the title may seem a bit exalted, there are an extraordinary number of cultural attractions here for a town of its size.

The best way to see the University of Iowa is to take a stroll along the river walk that runs through its center. If you're an animal lover, be sure to bring along some bread crumbs, for you're likely to encounter the determined ducks that waddle down the sidewalks here with all the swagger of frontier cowboys. Frequent feedings have made them bold and sassy, and their raucous conversations are a steady accompaniment to the bustle of university life.

Just up the hill from the river is the *Old Capitol*, a lovingly restored Greek Revival structure that served as the state's first capitol from 1842 until 1857. Its golden dome can be seen throughout Iowa City; thus, if you're given directions by local residents they're likely to begin, "From the Old Capitol it's about . . ."

Designed by John Francis Rague, the building served as the first permanent seat of Iowa's territorial and state governments until 1857, when the capital was moved to Des Moines. For the next 113 years, the building was used for various university purposes until a restoration effort was begun in 1970. Today the centerpiece of the Old Capitol is a magnificent self-supporting spiral staircase that leads to the restored legislative chambers upstairs. This National Historic Landmark (319-335-3491; oldcap.uiowa.edu) is open Wed through Sat. Admission and guided tours are free.

Next door to the Old Capitol is the venerable Macbride Hall, home for many years to the *University of Iowa Museum of Natural History*. Its *Iowa Hall* offers a comprehensive look at Iowa's geology, archaeology, and ecology. As you move through the gallery's exhibits, you'll witness the passage of five billion years. One of the most impressive exhibits is a diorama depicting the arrival of Europeans in the state in 1673, seen from the perspective of two Ioway Indians looking out over the Mississippi River from tall bluffs on the Iowa shore. Another highlight is a life-size re-creation of a giant ground sloth, a sight that never fails to draw a gasp from young children. Two other galleries at the museum will intrigue those with a scientific bent. Hageboeck Hall features more than 1,000 birds, including nearly every species recorded as residents or seasonal visitors of Iowa. Mammal Hall displays animals ranging from aardvarks to zebras. Its specimens represent nearly every order and family of mammals, including a giant panda from China and an orangutan from the Borneo jungle. The museum's lobby features a small gift shop, plus displays on the pioneering work of Iowa's early naturalists. The Museum of Natural History is open Wed through Sat. Admission is free. Call (319) 335-0480 or see mnh .uiowa.edu for more details.

The new **University of Iowa Stanley Museum of Art** (stanleymuseum .uiowa.edu; 319-335-1727) has one of the nation's foremost university art collections. Works from around the world can be seen here in a beautifully designed, three-story building in the heart of campus. Highlights of the collection include works by Jackson Pollock, Grant Wood, Joan Miró, and Max Beckmann, as well as stellar examples of African, Oceanic, and Asian art. Don't miss its fiber arts gallery, especially the stunning pieces of cloth from West Africa. Admission to the museum is free. You'll find it at 160 W. Burlington St.

Though the University of Iowa tends to overshadow the rest of Iowa City, there are many other attractions to explore here. The pedestrian mall downtown is the perfect place to people-watch, and during the summer months food vendors peddle their wares. Stop by any of the food carts on the pedestrian mall or at any of the downtown area's numerous restaurants.

Theater buffs should book tickets at **Riverside Theatre**, Iowa City's very own professional company at 119 E. College St. It's been entertaining audiences since 1981 with provocative, thought-provoking performances of classics and contemporary works. During the summer months, Riverside presents a free outdoor production of a Shakespeare play at the Festival Stage in Lower City Park. For more information, call (319) 259-7099 or see riversidetheatre.org.

Don't leave Iowa City without spending an hour (or two or three) at **Prairie Lights Books**, one of the Midwest's best independent bookstores. The downtown landmark offers readings by nationally touring authors throughout the year, but it's also a great place to visit if you just want to have a cup of coffee or glass of wine as you browse through a book or newspaper. Prairie Lights is open daily and is located at 15 S. Dubuque St. in Iowa City. Call (319) 337-2681 or see prairielights.com for information.

There are many fine restaurants in Iowa City, including the downtown eateries **Basta** (bastaiowacity.com; 319-337-2010) for Italian cuisine, the **Bluebird Diner** (thebluebirddiner.com; 319-351-1470) for hearty American fare, and **Crepes de Luxe Café** (crepes-de-luxe.com; 319-887-2233) for sweet and savory crepes.

Another local landmark is **The Sanctuary** at 405 S. Gilbert St. The Sanctuary serves some of the best pizza in town (as well as a good variety of other choices) and has a huge selection of international beers, in addition to offering entertainment on the weekends—usually a folk singer or a small band. The ambience is delightfully bohemian and the Pizza Fontina (a pizza covered with broccoli, tomatoes, mushrooms, and fontina cheese) is a personal favorite. The Sanctuary (sanctuarypub.com; 319-351-5692) is open daily.

Don't pass up a visit to **Plum Grove** at 1030 Carroll St. in Iowa City. The Greek Revival structure was once the home of Robert Lucas, Iowa's first territorial governor from 1838 until 1841. Called Plum Grove after a thicket of plum trees on the property, the home was a showplace in frontier Iowa. In the late 1930s the state of Iowa agreed to purchase it, thanks to a local preservation effort led by a grandson of Lucas. Today it's fully restored and furnished with period antiques.

Interesting to those who garden, and even to those who don't, are the heritage garden plots on the grounds of Plum Grove. Planted with only the flowers, vegetables, and herbs that would have been used before the 1850s, these plots re-create a different, growing kind of history. Plum Grove is open weekends from Memorial Day weekend through Oct, from 1 to 5 p.m. Admission is free. Call (319) 351-5738 for more details.

didyouknow?

The fur of the giant sloth located in the Iowa Hall on the University of Iowa campus was made out of 500 cow tails.

Another attraction in the Iowa City area owes its existence to a natural disaster. During the Flood of 1993, massive amounts of water surged over the emergency spillway at Coralville Lake and eroded a 15-foot-deep channel. When the waters receded, a geologic treasure emerged: an ancient seabed filled with thousands of fossils. The **Devonian Fossil Gorge** has become a popular spot for anyone interested in geology—and a good spot to see first-hand the awesome power of a flood. The gorge is located 3.4 miles north of I-80 on Dubuque Street (turn right at West Overlook Road).

On Dubuque Street about 1 mile north of I-80 at exit 244, you can see the **World's Largest Wooden Nickel**. This giant wooden coin is 16 feet wide and weighs nearly 4,000 pounds. It was erected in 2006 by Jim Glasgow as a protest against widening the highway and raising speed limits in the area. Go ahead and snap a picture with your hands outstretched like you're holding it—it's an Iowa City tradition.

Iowa City's neighboring city is **Coralville**, a town named after the coral formations left behind by the same sea that created the Devonian Fossil Gorge.

Iowa City's Black Angel

No sojourn to Iowa City is complete without a visit to the enigmatic *Black Angel*, a grave marker that is a source of local tradition and speculation. Dozens of legends cling to the marker: One of the most popular says that a grieving husband spent his savings to place a white angel over the grave of his wife, only to have it turn black overnight because of her unrevealed infidelity to him.

Another cheery story says that anyone who touches the angel will die within the year. There's a happier bit of folklore associated with it as well—college students say that you're not a true University of Iowa coed until you've been kissed in the shadow of its wings.

The real story behind the angel is a bit more prosaic, though it has its share of intrigue as well. The statue was commissioned in 1911 by a Bohemian immigrant named Teresa Feldevert for the graves of her son and her second husband. When the statue arrived in Iowa City, however, Teresa refused to pay for it, saying that it wasn't what she had ordered. The dispute ended up in court, and the woman was ordered to pay the Chicago sculptor $5,000. The disgruntled Teresa decided to have the statue erected in spite of her dislike of it—and ever since it's been a source of fascination for Iowa City residents.

This hauntingly beautiful grave marker, located in the Oakland Cemetery (1000 Brown St.), stands 9 feet tall and really has to be seen to be appreciated—I can promise you she is not what you will expect. Does her posture admonish or beckon, forbid or entreat? I leave it for you to decide.

Coralville's **Johnson County Historical Society Museum** has exhibits that bring to life the history of the area, from descriptions of the Mormon migration through the area during the 1840s to information on Meskwaki Indian history. The Heritage Museum (johnsoncountyhistory.org; 319-569-4502) is open Tues through Sun afternoons. It is located at 200 E. Ninth St., Suite 101.

The **Iowa Children's Museum**, located in the Coral Ridge Mall at exit 240 off I-80, offers fun for the wee ones as well as their parents. A kid-sized grocery, hospital, farm, and art studio are among its attractions. The museum (319-625-6255; theicm.org) is open Tues through Sun. Admission is $10.

Another attraction in Coralville is the **Iowa Firefighters Memorial**. The monument recognizes the sacrifices of those who have lost their lives while fighting fires. The larger-than-life bronze statue depicts a firefighter rescuing a child, and the memorial wall at the end of the plaza lists the names of Iowa firefighters killed while rescuing others. The memorial is located at exit 242 off I-80.

For more information about attractions in the Iowa City and Coralville area, call (319) 337-6592 or see thinkiowacity.com.

Eight miles east of Iowa City lies the historic small town of **West Branch**, birthplace of President Herbert Hoover and the location of the **Herbert Hoover National Historic Site** (210 Parkside Dr.). Here you'll find his official presidential library, a museum detailing his life, the cottage where he was born, a blacksmith shop, an 1853 schoolhouse, and the Quaker meetinghouse where the devout Hoover family attended services. All are set on expansive, beautifully kept grounds, making this a favorite picnic spot for many visitors.

If you're like me, the thought of visiting the Hoover site might not fill you with excitement. My only memory of Hoover before I visited was a vague knowledge of "Hooverville" shantytowns and the grim man who plunged the country into the Great Depression. After I spent a fascinating afternoon in West Branch, however, I came away surprised and impressed. The much-maligned Hoover, I learned, was a complex man of extraordinary abilities.

Tour the library and museum and you'll learn the history of his life. The son of an Iowa blacksmith, Hoover was orphaned at the age of ten and went on to become a noted mining engineer and businessman. He made his entry into public life during World War I as the director of food relief programs that fed an estimated 318 million victims of war and drought in Europe and the Soviet Union (take special note of the display of embroidered flour sacks sent to Hoover by grateful children). Later he became secretary of commerce and in 1928 was elected the thirty-first president of the United States—a position for which he refused to accept a salary. Defeated for reelection during the depths of the Depression, the indomitable Hoover continued his work as an active public servant until his death at age ninety. By the end of his life, he had once again regained the respect of his fellow citizens, and his passing was marked by tributes from around the country and the world.

Be sure to visit the various buildings on the Hoover site, and don't miss the large statue near the library that was given to Hoover as a gift from the people of Belgium. The figure is a larger-than-life woman wearing a veil, a depiction of the Egyptian goddess Isis. Her air of mystery is irresistible.

The Hoover Library-Museum complex is open from 9 a.m. to 5 p.m. daily, and admission is $10 for adults. A fun time to visit is during **Hoover's Hometown Days**, held the first weekend in Aug. Call (319) 643-5301 for more information or visit hoover.archives.gov.

Before you leave West Branch, take the time to tour its charming downtown, an area that has been named a National Historic District. Don't miss **Main Street Antiques and Art**, located at 110 W. Main St. Not only will you find an eclectic and unique assortment of antiques, but also, in the back of the shop, is a gallery of paintings by proprietor Lou Picek. Noted for their colorful and "primitive" style, they offer a unique depiction of the artist's experiences or, as Lou says, his "everyday life with a touch of humor and fantasy." Main Street Antiques (319-643-2065) is open Mon through Sat from 10 a.m. to 5 p.m. and from noon to 5 p.m. on Sun.

From West Branch head southeast to the small town of **West Liberty**, where a vibrant Hispanic community flourishes in rural Iowa. Walk its streets and you'll find several Mexican restaurants, a Mexican bakery, and a *tortilleria* where homemade tortillas by the hundreds roll off the grill each day. If you're looking for a piñata for your birthday or an order of chiles rellenos washed down with a margarita, West Liberty is the place to visit.

About 50 percent of the town's residents are Hispanic, hailing from Mexico, Guatemala, Colombia, Honduras, and other Latin American nations. The best way to sample the flavor of West Liberty is to pull up a chair in one of its Mexican restaurants. All are informal, inexpensive, and unpretentious, with menus that feature such traditional favorites as enchiladas as well as meat-for-the-more-adventurous (brain or tripe tacos, anyone?). Many consider **El Patio** (214 N. Columbus St.; 319-627-7334) to be the best, but you won't go wrong at any of these eateries.

West Liberty is also home to the **Eulenspiegel Puppet Theatre**, a nonprofit company that has entertained both children and adults for more than forty years. The theater has experimented with almost every type of puppet, often collaborating with other artists in witty productions featuring handmade

Wildflowers and Gravestones

If you're in the West Branch area, make sure you plan a stop at the **Rochester Cemetery**, located just southeast of the Cedar River bridge in Rochester. Particularly during the spring and summer months, this remarkable cemetery, set amid 13 acres of prairie, comes alive with wildflowers and prairie grasses. Around Mother's Day the cemetery is filled with swirling galaxies of shooting stars and mayapples. Later, false dandelion predominates, punctuated by prairie phlox and golden alexanders. In late June and July, there are beautiful patches of black-eyed Susans sprinkled among the other flowers, and in August the prairie grasses glow with their subtle inflorescence. All told, more than fifty species of wildflowers have been counted here.

Don't miss the grave of Mary King in the southwest portion of the cemetery. This grave is the source of a Cedar County legend that claims that Mary King was the mother of the great actress Sarah Bernhardt. Once, immediately before Miss Bernhardt took the stage in Iowa City in 1904, a gigantic bouquet of red roses was placed on the grave. The rumor has it that the Divine Miss Sarah was in reality little Sarah King, who had run away earlier with an acting troupe and was never heard of—at least under her own name—again.

puppets and live music. Most performances are held at the New Strand Theatre in downtown, which was built in 1910 as an opera house. For information call (319) 627-2487 or see owlglass.org.

Mississippi Gateway

Begin your tour along east central Iowa's portion of the Mississippi River in **Muscatine**. Life in this river port has always been dominated by the Mississippi River. In 1835 an influx of white settlers came to the area, and two years later James Casey started a trading post here to service the flourishing riverboat industry. Soon people began calling the area "Casey's wood pile"—though by 1850 the growing town had adopted the more elegant name of Muscatine. The word was taken (depending on whom you believe) either from the Mascoutin Indians who lived here or from an Indian word meaning "burning island." (It's interesting, however, to speculate on what the town's sports teams would have been called had the original name been kept. Casey's Wood Pile Termites, perhaps?)

You can find out more about Muscatine's history at the **National Pearl Button Museum** at 117 W. Second St. In the early twentieth century, Muscatine was the Pearl Button Capital of the World. Visit the museum to see the complete button-making procedure, from collecting shells from the bottom of the Mississippi River through processing, cutting, and dyeing. The museum is open Tues through Sat, 10 a.m. to 4 p.m., and a small admission fee is charged. Call (563) 263-1052 or see muscatinehistory.org for information.

The **Muscatine Art Center**, a combination museum and art gallery, is located at 1314 Mulberry Ave. The museum is housed in a 1908 mansion donated to the city by the Laura Musser family. The first floor is furnished in the fashion of the Edwardian era, and upstairs is gallery space for various exhibits and an art library. Connected to the elegant mansion is a modern three-level facility with gallery space for the art center's collections, which include works by Grant Wood, Georgia O'Keeffe, and Mauricio Lasansky, as well as a Great River collection of works featuring the Mississippi River. Outside is a landscaped area featuring a Japanese garden and native Iowa wildflowers.

The Muscatine Art Center is open Tues through Sun. Call (563) 263-8282 or visit muscatineartcenter.org for details. Admission is free.

While you're in the Muscatine area, plan a stay at the **Merrill Hotel** (563-263-2600; themerrill.com) at 119 W. Mississippi Dr. This luxury boutique hotel overlooks the Mississippi River and has 122 rooms named after local notables. Works by Muscatine artists adorn its interior and its **Maxwell's On The River**

The Pearl of the Mississippi

Muscatine's nickname, the Pearl of the Mississippi, recalls its former status as the world's center for pearl-button production. Though the first major industry in Muscatine was lumber, by the late 1890s button-making had become the city's main source of revenue.

John Boepple is credited with launching the industry. Not satisfied with the quality of buttons he could make out of animal horns in his native Germany, Boepple experimented with freshwater clams he had obtained from the Illinois River. He was pleased to find that their iridescent interior produced a sturdier and more attractive button. Eventually he immigrated to Muscatine, where, he had heard, there was a rich supply of clams that collected naturally along the Mississippi River.

Boepple opened Muscatine's first pearl-button factory in 1897, and by 1905 the area was producing nearly 40 percent of the world's annual production of buttons. Button-making was a labor-intensive operation requiring a great deal of handwork. More than forty factories employed 3,500 people—more than 50 percent of the local work force—and Muscatine became known as the Pearl Button Capital of the World.

The invention of the zipper and the development of plastic buttons, alas, stifled this thriving industry. By the 1960s the last factory had closed. Thankfully, pearl button history is preserved in Muscatine.

Restaurant serves dishes made with fresh, local, and sustainably raised produce and meats.

If you visit Muscatine during the summer months, don't leave without buying one of the region's renowned melons. The sandy soil here is ideal for growing sweet-tasting muskmelons. Among the best places to buy them are *Mairet's Garden Center* (563-263-2338) at 4707 US 61 and *Taylor's Market* (563-264-1393) at 2637 Stewart Rd.

One of my favorite parks is located near Muscatine: *Wildcat Den State Park*, a beautiful area with winding trails and some lovely river views. Here you will also find the *Pine Creek Grist Mill*. The mill, originally built in 1848 at a cost of $10,000, was bought by the state of Iowa in 1927 for $87.50 after it had gone out of business. It is open May through Oct. For hours call (563) 263-4337 or see iowadnr.gov.

Next head to the largest metropolitan area in Iowa, the Quad Cities. The name is misleading, for there are five cities that come together here on the Mississippi: *Davenport* and *Bettendorf* line the Iowa side, while Rock Island, Moline, and East Moline hug the Illinois bank.

The first thing to realize is that these are river towns, each with a rich history that stretches back some 200 years. The area was a trading center for the

American Fur Company and a battleground during the War of 1812. Davenport was the first city in Iowa to have railroad service, and it was here that the first train crossed the Mississippi in 1856. (The railroad bridge was later the cause of a historic lawsuit between the river trade and the railroad. Successfully defending the railroad interests was a young Illinois lawyer who would later make quite a name for himself—Abraham Lincoln.) During the Civil War, a prison camp for Confederate soldiers was located in the area, and nearly 2,000 Southern soldiers are buried here, far from their homes. In the years following the war, the area became a major port for river travel between New Orleans and St. Paul.

Arsenal Island, the largest island in the upper Mississippi, is an excellent place to learn more about the history and military importance of the Quad Cities. The arsenal was established by the US Army in 1862 and continues to manufacture weapons parts and military equipment. With 7,500 civilian and military workers, the Rock Island Arsenal is one of the area's largest employers. (Visitors to the island must pass a security check; see visitquadcities.com for details.) Arsenal Island lies in the Mississippi River channel between Davenport and Rock Island and can be reached through two entrances, one on the Illinois side in Moline and one via the Rock Island Bridge.

Begin your tour of the island at the *Colonel Davenport House*. A native of England, George Davenport came to the island in 1816 under contract to provide food to the soldiers building Fort Armstrong. He later resigned his Army position to establish a lucrative trading post, becoming wealthy enough to build this stately Federal-style home overlooking the Mississippi in 1833–34. When a new town was founded across the river in 1836, it was named in his honor.

Today the house is furnished in period style, with living accommodations on the ground floor and an upstairs room that replicates an early trading post. Guides explain how furs were highly prized in frontier America, particularly the beaver pelts that were used to make fashionable hats. In 1820 a single beaver pelt was worth the equivalent of $200 in today's money, giving an indication of the large sums that passed through Davenport's trading post. Unfortunately, that wealth also led to the businessman's death, for in 1845 he was murdered by bandits looking for gold. The Colonel Davenport House (309-786-7336; davenporthouse.org) is open noon to 4 p.m., Thurs through Sun, May through Oct.

To learn more about the military history of the island, visit the *Rock Island Arsenal Museum*, which is the second-oldest US Army museum after West Point. Opened in 1905, it's known for its large firearms collection, including several guns used in the Battle of the Little Big Horn. Its historical exhibits describe how the arsenal has played an important role in the nation's defense

for more than 150 years, with generations of military and civilian workers labor-
ing in its manufacturing areas. The building is open daily except for Mon, and
admission is free (309-782-5021).

After touring the museum, walk the peaceful grounds of the **Rock Island
National Cemetery**, where white headstones are arranged in orderly rows.
The nearby **Confederate Cemetery** holds the remains of those who once
fought against some of those veterans. The main difference between the two
graveyards is that the Confederate grave markers are pointed at the top (it's
said that they're shaped in this way because the Confederates didn't want any
Yankees sitting on their graves).

The **Mississippi River Visitor Center** is a fitting place to end a tour
of the island, for the river has shaped the island's history and character in
countless ways. Operated by the US Army Corps of Engineers, the center
describes the workings of the lock and dam system that maintains a nine-
foot channel on the river. Without this system, barge traffic would not be
possible and the many tons of freight carried by the boats would have to be
hauled in some other fashion. An observation deck allows close viewing of

A Small Island with a Big History

Just 3 miles long and less than a mile wide, Arsenal Island has more history per
square foot than almost anywhere in the Midwest. This smidgen of land in the middle
of the Mississippi River played a vital role in two wars and has more than twenty-six
buildings on the National Historic Register. The lush lawns of its National Cemetery
hold the graves of 29,000 veterans, while nearby rest 1,960 Confederate soldiers
who died on the island during the Civil War.

Congress recognized Arsenal Island's strategic importance in 1809, when it set aside
its 946 acres as a federal military reservation. During the Blackhawk War of 1832,
the island's Fort Armstrong served as headquarters for the US Army. The Civil War
brought even greater prominence to the island when the Rock Island Arsenal was
established by Abraham Lincoln and the island became the site of an Army prison.
More than 12,000 Confederate POWs were held here between 1863 and 1865 (fans
of the novel Gone With the Wind will recall that this is where Ashley Wilkes was
imprisoned). Soldiers who died of illness—a common fate during the period—are
buried nearby.

After the Civil War the arsenal continued to play a vital military role. One indication of
its national significance was the building of Quarters One to house its commanding
officer. With 21,000 square feet and fifty-four rooms, the Italianate villa was for many
years the second-largest residence maintained by the US government, second only
to the White House. The Army also constructed rows of imposing buildings made of
Joliet limestone, stately structures that are still in use today.

Lock and Dam 15, giving visitors the chance to admire the skill of pilots as they maneuver their huge loads into the narrow confines of the lock. The visitor center is open Wed through Sat, 9 a.m. to 4 p.m. Call (309) 794-5338 for more information.

Downtown Davenport is enjoying a renaissance thanks to a multifaceted redevelopment project along its riverfront. The **Figge Art Museum** houses the former Davenport Museum of Art, which was founded in 1925 as the first regional art museum in Iowa. The $47 million structure more than triples the size of the former facility and is the first civic project in the United States designed by the British architect David Chipperfield. Rising dramatically from the riverbank, the Figge is a work of art in itself, a simple block form enveloped by glass surfaces that reflect the movements of sun and clouds. Its interior includes exhibit and educational spaces, a library and resource center, a lecture hall, and a two-story Winter Garden that offers spectacular views of the Mississippi.

The Figge is particularly known for its Regionalist collection, an art movement that, beginning in the 1930s, explored the landscape and themes of small-town and rural America. The museum also boasts one of the most significant collections of Haitian art in the world. Its Mexican Colonial collection, which is one of the largest outside of Mexico, is also highly regarded. Other prominent works include pieces by artists Salvador Dalí, Andy Warhol, and Winslow Homer, as well as landscapes from the nineteenth-century Hudson River School and European works presenting every major artistic period from the Renaissance to Fauvism.

The Figge Art Museum is at 225 W. Second St. and is open Tues through Sun. For more information call (563) 326-7804 or see figgeartmuseum.org.

The **Putnam Museum** is another major attraction in the Quad Cities. Inside you'll find exhibits on the region's heritage and the wildlife of the Mississippi River valley, as well as Asian and Egyptian galleries and a hands-on science lab. The Putnam also boasts an IMAX 3-D Theater. The Putnam Museum (563-324-1933; putnam.org) is open daily. It is located at 1717 W. Twelfth St. in Davenport.

The **Family Museum** in Bettendorf is a fun stop whether or not you have young children in tow. I recommend borrowing a child for the day if you don't have one of your own; watching kids explore the exhibits within is as much fun as looking at them yourself. The museum features exhibits designed with curious young children in mind. While most museums say, "Don't Touch," this one says, "Please Do!" During your visit you can go down a rabbit hole, visit an old-fashioned farm kitchen from 1940, and turn into a bird in the Kinder Garten. The Family Museum is open daily except for Sunday. It is located at

2900 Learning Campus Dr. For more information call (563) 344-4106 or see familymuseum.org.

Vander Veer Botanical Park (214 W. Central Park Ave., Davenport) is a peaceful place to recover from all your sightseeing. The Rose Garden is considered one of the finest in the Midwest, with 1,800 roses representing nearly 145 varieties. The peak blooming period normally begins in early June and continues through the summer. The conservatory presents five special floral displays throughout the year, and at any time it's a lush and quiet place to wander through and enjoy.

The *Hotel Blackbawk* is located in downtown Davenport, 2 blocks from the Mississippi riverfront. Originally opened in 1915, it underwent a multimillion-dollar renovation in 2010 and is now a luxury boutique hotel. *Bix Bistro*, its elegant restaurant, is named after Davenport native son and famed jazz musician Bix Beiderbecke. The hotel also has a spa and the retro-chic Blackhawk Bowl, a place that makes bowling-for-two romantic. The Hotel Blackhawk (855-958-0973; hotelblackhawk.com) is at 200 E. Third St. Prices are moderate to expensive.

One stop you shouldn't miss during your visit here is the *Machine Shed*, one of the state's best restaurants. The walls are covered with old farm implements and antiques (including a large collection of seed corn hats), and the food is home-style Midwestern cooking at its best: dinners of crispy fried chicken, thick pork chops, and tasty stuffed pork loin; savory soups; and mouthwatering desserts, all served family style with big bowls of vegetables and freshly baked bread.

The Machine Shed is open for breakfast (don't miss their huge cinnamon rolls), lunch, and dinner and is located off I-80 at exit 292, at 7250 Northwest Blvd. in Davenport. Prices are moderate; call (563) 391-2427 for information or see machineshed.com.

> ## didyouknow?
>
> D. D. Palmer performed the first chiropractic adjustment on September 18, 1895, in Davenport. He later opened the Palmer Institute and Chiropractic Infirmary, which became the Palmer College of Chiropractic in 1905 under his son, B. J. Palmer.

Another attraction in the Quad Cities is the *Village of East Davenport*, an area of historic buildings that date back to 1851. Here you'll find unique shops, galleries, pubs, and restaurants.

You can experience the power and mystique of the Mississippi River by stepping on board the *Celebration Belle* (see page 5), which offers a variety of cruises, including lunch and dinner, sightseeing, and specialty cruises. Call (309) 764-1952 or see celebrationbelle.com for more information.

Another way to see the river is on board the Quad Cities' **Channel Cat Water Taxi** ride. This wonderful transport functions as a "water bus," departing from and returning to various spots along the river. Each landing is visited approximately every half hour. It serves as a watery link between Quad Cities' bicycle trails (each taxi has space for bicycles), but non-bikers are welcomed as well. Tickets are for all-day unlimited use. The *Channel Cats* run from Memorial Day to Labor Day, then weekends only through Oct. Call (309) 788-3360 or see gogreenmetro.com for schedule information and ticket prices.

Walnut Grove Pioneer Village, located 9 miles north of the Quad Cities near the town of **Long Grove** on US 61, is a pleasant place to unwind after visiting the Quad Cities. Walnut Grove was a crossroads settlement in the pioneer days of Scott County in the 1860s. Today, the three-acre site contains eighteen historic buildings, including a blacksmith shop, a schoolhouse, a church, and pioneer family homes. The surrounding **Scott County Park** offers nature trails, camping facilities, playground equipment, and a nature center.

Walnut Grove Pioneer Village (scottcountyiowa.gov) is open daily from 9 a.m. to 6 p.m. Apr through Oct. Admission is free.

While you're in the Quad City area, plan a stay at the **Beiderbecke Inn**, 532 W. Seventh St. in Davenport. This magnificent Victorian "painted lady" was built by local jazz legend Bix Beiderbecke's grandparents. In this grandly spacious bed-and-breakfast, you can truly sample the life of the well-to-do of yesteryear. Not only that, it is close to the river and even has a tower room. Rates are moderate. Call (563) 323-0047 or see beiderbeckeinn.com for more information.

didyouknow?

The World's Largest Truck Stop is at the Walcott exit off I-80, just east of Davenport.

A few miles north of the Quad Cities lies the charming river town of **LeClaire**. Founded in 1833, LeClaire was once a boatbuilding center and home to many steamboat captains, who used to hire on with riverboats traveling past the treacherous rapids near the Quad Cities. The lucrative trade helped make the town a bustling commercial center, but after the Mississippi was tamed by the lock and dam system, LeClaire faded into somnolence.

About a decade ago, LeClaire began to wake up—and it now has nearly as much activity as during the days when women in hoop skirts strolled its streets and steamboats lined its dock. The renaissance is due to the town's scenic location on the Mississippi River, its convenient access to I-80, and a host of creative entrepreneurs. Its attractive downtown has a growing number of unique shops and restaurants.

On the bank of the Mississippi, the **Buffalo Bill Museum** tells the story of the town's connection to the colorful Wild West showman, who was born in LeClaire in 1846. Other exhibits cover the town's Native American and Steamboat Era history. The museum complex also features the Lone Star, a wooden-hulled steamer that plied the waters of the Mississippi for nearly a century. Visitors can scramble up and down its decks to learn more about shipping on the nation's greatest river. The museum (563-289-5580; buffalobillmuseumle claire.com) is at 199 N. Front St. and is open Tues through Sat. Admission is $5 for adults.

LeClaire is also home to the **Twilight**, a paddle-wheel riverboat that offers a two-day cruise along one of the prettiest sections of the entire Mississippi. Modeled after the classic steamboats of the 1880s, the *Twilight* is trimmed with wrought iron filigree, encircled by promenades and fitted with lounges perfect for watching the river flow by, and topped by a wood-and-glass pilot house. Anyone who's read *The Adventures of Huckleberry Finn* is likely to look at the *Twilight* and imagine a certain white-suited gentleman with bushy white hair smoking a cigar in one of its rocking chairs.

I've taken a number of cruises on the Mississippi, and I consider the trips offered by the *Twilight* to be among the very best. The food is delicious, the scenery magnificent, and the live entertainment enjoyable. Three types of river cruises are offered, including one that departs from LeClaire in the morning, travels upriver all day, and docks at Dubuque, where guests spend the night. The next day you can tour Dubuque and then board the boat again for a leisurely trip back to LeClaire. Cruises run late-May through Oct, and reservations are required. Tickets for the two-day cruise start at $429 (double occupancy)

Treasure Hunters

LeClaire has gotten national attention thanks to "American Pickers," a History Channel show that chronicles the adventures of Mike Wolfe as he travels the country foraging for treasures in junkyards, cluttered barns, and other out-of-the-way spots. Wolfe launched the show from LeClaire in 2010 and the show continues to prominently feature the town, bringing a steady stream of visitors from around the world to Wolfe's **Antique Archaeology** store just off the main thoroughfare.

Antique Archaeology includes Wolfe's original shop as well as a newer building. Each is stocked with off-beat treasures, from a stuffed albino raccoon named Paul to rusting Indian motorcycles and a bumper car from a 1950s county fair. During the summer, the store can get up to 1,000 visitors a day. Its offerings are always changing, depending upon what Mike and his crew find in their travels. You'll find Antique Archaeology (563-265-3939; antiquearchaeology.com) at 115½ Davenport St.

and include all meals, entertainment, and lodging. For more information call (800) 331-1467 or visit riverboattwilight.com.

A popular stop in LeClaire is the ***Mississippi River Distilling Company***, where visitors can sample whiskeys, vodkas, and other spirits. The company prides itself on sourcing all of its corn, wheat, barley, and rye from within a 25-mile radius. "We go out to the farms and pick up the grain ourselves," says Scot Schaar, distiller. "I remember a farmer telling us it was the first time he's ever known what's happened to his corn after it left his farm." The distilling company (563-484-4342; mrdistilling.com) is at 303 N. Cody Rd.

From LeClaire head north to the river port of ***Clinton***. Like the Quad Cities, Clinton is a town dominated by the Mississippi River. During the late nineteenth

Amaizing Mazes

As a full moon rises over a cornfield in central Iowa, a rustling noise can be heard amid the stalks. Something big is racing through the plants, a creature whose pounding feet make a rhythmic sound as it runs at full speed. Its gasping breath grows louder as it nears the edge of the field, until suddenly it bursts into a clearing.

"I won!" shouts the young man in triumph as a group of his friends emerge from the corn a few seconds later, their laughter filling the evening air.

Similar scenes are repeated across Iowa each fall, as a growing number of farmers are finding a new use for corn, that most quintessential of Iowa crops.

The first corn maze in Iowa opened in the late 1990s. Because corn grows to a height of 12 feet, the intricate, looping paths of a maze create a genuine challenge, especially because of the many dead ends that are incorporated into most designs. Once the growing season is over, the corn that forms the maze is simply harvested along with other crops.

Most corn mazes are open only in the fall, with October being the busiest month. Many farmers combine them with additional attractions like pumpkin patches, hayrides, and petting zoos. For many visitors, corn mazes have become a fall tradition as beloved as trick-or-treating.

Major mazes in Iowa include:

Bloomsbury Farm, near Cedar Rapids, (319) 446-7667, bloomsburyfarm.com.

Center Grove Orchard, near Des Moines, (515) 383-4354, centergroveorchard.com

Ditmars Orchard, near Council Bluffs, (712) 256-7053, ditmarsorchard.com

Harvestville Farm, near Fort Madison, (319) 470-1558, harvestvillefarm.com.

Pinter's Gardens & Pumpkins, near Decorah, (563) 382-0010, pintersgardensandpumpkins.com.

century, Clinton became an important transportation and lumbering center. Today it continues to be an active industrial area.

Clinton takes great pride in its history as a river town, and you can enjoy an echo of that past at the **Clinton Area Showboat Theatre**. This is a theater group that performs each summer aboard the *City of Clinton* showboat—an authentic paddle wheeler permanently dry-docked on the riverbank in Clinton's Riverview Park. Recalling the days when lavish showboats plied their way up and down the river, the theater is the perfect place to complete a day's touring along the Mississippi.

These aren't amateur productions, either. Each spring the theater recruits nationally to produce its June-through-August summer stock season. Performances are given in a 225-seat air-conditioned theater and include contemporary works as well as old standards. Musicals, comedies, and dramas are offered each season.

The *City of Clinton* showboat is docked along the Mississippi at 303 Riverview Dr. Call (563) 242-6760 or see clintonshowboat.org for more information.

Travel to the north end of Clinton, and you'll find **Eagle Point Park**, a recreation area perched high on a bluff overlooking the river. The park itself contains 200 acres of numerous hiking trails and picnic areas. Be sure to see the 35-foot observation tower built of locally quarried stone that stands on a promontory above the river.

Another lovely nature area is the **Bickelhaupt Arboretum** at 340 S. Fourteenth St., Clinton. This fourteen-acre horticultural showplace features more than 2,000 plants and 600 trees and shrubs. It is open from sunrise until sunset, year-round, and no admission is charged.

From Clinton travel north on US 67 and US 52 to **Bellevue**, one of the Mississippi River's most charming towns. Begin your tour at Lock and Dam No. 12 in the middle of town and then wander through Bellevue's shopping district, an area lined with century-old stone and brick buildings. Many now house stores selling antiques, collectibles, and arts and crafts.

For a treat of a different sort, visit the **Butterfly Garden** at **Bellevue State Park**. This one-acre garden is carefully planned to provide for the care and feeding of nature's most beautiful and delicate creatures. In it is a mixture of plants that range from radishes and carrots to milkweeds and stinging nettles— plants that play host to some sixty species of butterflies that hover here each spring, summer, and fall. Interspersed among the plants are large rocks that make ideal basking spots for butterflies, plus a small pond where they can get water. The Butterfly Garden is located in Bellevue State Park, 0.5 mile south of town off US 52.

Iowa's Island City

The mighty Mississippi rolls past hundreds of towns and cities on its long journey from northern Minnesota to the sea, but none is as intimately tied to the river as the small town of *Sabula*. Located on a narrow island reached only by bridge, causeway, or boat, the town of 500 residents is a haven for people who have Mississippi River water flowing through their veins.

Sabula's many links to the surrounding river are visible throughout the town. Many of the modest houses that line its quiet streets have a fishing boat or a speedboat parked on their lawns, and on warm summer days the town empties as nearly everyone heads for the water.

Thanks to Sabula's location, they don't have to travel far. The town, which is just 4 blocks wide and 9 blocks long, covers the entire island. To the east lies the main channel of the Mississippi, its powerful current carrying massive barges loaded with grain bound for New Orleans, jet skiers out for an afternoon spin, and fishing boats trolling at a leisurely pace. The rest of the island is surrounded by a maze of backwaters, perfect habitat for the hundreds of great blue herons and other birds that nest in the area. A portion of these backwaters just north of town forms the 4,000-acre *Green Island Wildlife Area*, home to recently reintroduced trumpeter swans.

Native Americans were the first inhabitants on the island, which wasn't discovered by white settlers until 1835. In 1864 the town was incorporated, its name taken from the Latin word *sabulum*, meaning "sandy soil." Its location made it a desirable steamboat landing, and the little settlement later grew into a major meat-packing center. Another early industry was the making of buttons, combs, and jewelry fashioned from mussel shells harvested from the river bottom.

One of Bellevue's magnificent old mansions is **Mont Rest**, a bed-and-breakfast inn built in 1893. Nestled into a wooded hillside overlooking the town and river, Mont Rest is especially known for its murder mystery packages. Held nearly every weekend, they include a mystery script, costumes, gourmet dinner, and removal of dead bodies. You can come just for the evening or stay overnight.

Mont Rest is located at 300 Spring St.; (563) 872-4220; montrest.com. Rates are moderate to expensive.

Before you leave Bellevue, pay a visit to **Potter's Mill**, a six-story former mill built in 1843. During the nineteenth century the mill sold its flour to wholesalers as far away as New York and Boston. Over the years it had fallen into nearly total disrepair, but it was refurbished in the 1980s and is now listed on the National Register of Historic Places. Potter's Mill houses **Flatted Fifth Blues & BBQ**, which serves a menu of moderately priced Southern-style favorites and hosts frequent live jazz performances. You'll find the mill at 300 Potter's Dr. Call (563) 872-3838 or see pottersmill.net for information.

Travel north on US 52 for 10 miles and you'll reach *St. **Donatus***, a small village known for its old-world architecture and traditions. Its settlers were immigrants from Luxembourg, who tried to duplicate the architecture, dress, and customs of their native land in their new home.

One of the village's main attractions is the ***Outdoor Way of the Cross***, the first of its kind in America. Completed in 1862, it consists of fourteen brick alcoves scattered along a winding path behind the St. Donatus Catholic Church. Each alcove contains an original lithograph depicting Christ's journey on Good Friday. At the top of the hill is the Pieta Chapel, a replica of a church in Luxembourg.

Grant Wood Country

Iowa's most famous native artist, Grant Wood, drew rich inspiration from this part of eastern Iowa, depicting its rolling countryside in many of his paintings. You'll find this region easy to explore on the ***Grant Wood Scenic Byway***, a series of county roads and highways that take you past many attractions relating both to Wood's life and to Iowa history. The 75-mile route stretches between Stone City and Bellevue and is marked by signs.

On your tour of this part of the state, follow the winding roads of the byway to ***Maquoketa***. North of town on US 61 is ***Banowetz Antiques*** (563-580-9391), one of the Midwest's largest antiques shops, with more than 2 acres of merchandise.

The ***Hurstville Interpretive Center*** celebrates the natural resources and history of the area. Located next to an 18-acre wetland, the center features ecological exhibits that include a beehive display, with insects busily flying in and out of a small escape hatch that leads outdoors. You can also tour displays and watch a video to learn about the Hurstville Lime Kilns, which in the nineteenth century supplied lime (an important ingredient for construction) around the Midwest. Then head outside to see rare trumpeter swans that live in a protected enclosure in the wetland area. The center is at 18670 Sixty-third St. (563-652-3783).

A nice place to stay in Maquoketa is the ***Squiers Manor Bed and Breakfast***, located at 418 W. Pleasant St. This lovely, Queen Anne–style mansion was built in 1882. Guests enjoy desserts by candlelight each evening and a full gourmet breakfast every morning. Rates range from moderate to expensive. For more information call (563) 652-6961 or visit squiersmanor.com.

Nearby you'll find **Maquoketa Caves State Park**, one of Iowa's most unusual geologic formations. This 272-acre state park contains a labyrinth of underground caverns and woodland trails. You can reach the thirteen caves scattered throughout the park by well-marked and sometimes rugged trails. Although two of the main caves are lighted, flashlights are needed in the others. Don't miss the 1,100-foot Dancehall Cave, so named because dances were once held here on warm summer nights.

Native American pottery, arrowheads, spears, and other artifacts found in the caves provide proof that they were used by indigenous tribes for hundreds of years. When the caves were first discovered before the Civil War, lovely stalactites and stalagmites were found, but unfortunately, souvenir hunters have robbed the caves of most of these. Two monuments that remain are a balanced rock and a natural bridge.

Camping and picnic sites are available in the park. Call (563) 652-5833 or visit iowadnr.gov for more information.

For some local color and hearty food, visit **Bluff Lake Catfish Farm**, at 9343 Ninety-fifth Ave. It is 1 mile from Maquoketa Caves at the end of a long

Iowa Wine Country

Thanks to a creative and hardworking group of vintners and farmers, the Iowa wine industry is blossoming. And as wineries prosper, Midwestern travelers are discovering the sensual pleasures of wine country: the chance to sample diverse vintages, chat with vintners about their complex art, observe the steps that go into the harvesting of grapes and bottling of wine, and enjoy the inviting ambience of a well-tended vineyard.

The growth of Iowa wineries is actually a rebirth, for during the early years of the twentieth century Iowa was the sixth-largest grape producer in the nation. The industry declined as a result of Prohibition, the growing market for corn and soybeans, and damage to grapevines caused by the drift of corn herbicides. For decades the industry was kept alive mainly in the small wineries of the Amana Colonies, establishments that buy most of their juice from outside the state to create primarily sweet dessert wines.

The past decades, however, have seen a remarkable renaissance in the Iowa wine industry. Today there are more than 100 wineries and more than 300 commercial vineyards scattered across Iowa, numbers that are growing each year.

One of the best ways to sample Iowa vintages is to follow the **Iowa Wine Trail**, a consortium of eleven wineries in eastern Iowa. The Wine Trail sponsors a variety of special events.

For more information see iowawinetrail.com.

and winding gravel road (follow the signs once you leave the park). This bustling establishment specializes in all-you-can-eat dinners. On weekends hundreds of people flock here for the fish fries; on other nights, barbecued ribs, chicken, and shrimp are served. Its owner is the friendly Linda Wells, whose father built the restaurant in 1971.

Bluff Lake Catfish Farm is open Fri through Sun for dinner, and prices are moderate. Call (563) 652-3272 or see blufflakecatfishfarm.com for more information.

Ten miles west of Maquoketa on IA 64 lies the town of **Baldwin**. From Baldwin, follow the signs 1 mile north and 1 mile west to the **Tabor Home Vineyards and Winery**. Its owner, Paul Tabor, caught the wine-making bug early. Growing up on a farm that has been in his family for more than a century, he enjoyed wine-making as a hobby. Later Tabor earned a doctorate in microbiology and worked as a professor at Indiana State University, but his interest in wine-making continued. He enjoyed experimenting with different varieties of vines on the home farm and eventually hatched the idea of establishing a commercial winery there. In 1996 Tabor Home Vineyards and Winery became the first Iowa winery with its own vineyard to be established since Prohibition.

Visitors to the winery can sample its award-winning vintages in a light-filled tasting room. The shop overlooks the winery's indoor production facilities and also includes a touch-screen kiosk with information about grape and wine production in Iowa. In the summer, free live entertainment is offered on many Sunday afternoons on the veranda of a century-old barn that overlooks the vineyard.

For more information on the Tabor Winery, call (563) 673-3131 or see taborhomewinery.com.

From the Tabor Winery travel west on IA 64 to the town of **Anamosa**, site of the **Grant Wood Art Gallery**. At the center you can see Grant Wood prints and view videos about Wood's life and art, as well as a display of American Gothic caricatures. The center also stocks tourism information and sells a selection of Grant Wood prints, books, note cards, T-shirts, and other memorabilia. The gallery (319-462-4267; grantwoodgallery.org) is at 124 E. Main St. It is open weekdays from 9 a.m. to 2 p.m.

Before leaving Anamosa take note of the impressive architecture of the **Anamosa State Penitentiary** located at the west end of downtown. Beginning in 1873 prisoners labored to construct the prison using stone quarried from the nearby Stone City area. Upon its completion, Iowans dubbed it the White Palace of the West, a tribute to its imposing architecture, beautiful stone walls, and immaculate landscaping. The prison today looks much the same as it did a hundred years ago, down to the regal stone lions guarding its entrance. During the summer months a formal garden in front of the prison is filled with blooming flowers.

West of Anamosa lies lovely *Stone City*, once a thriving quarry area and later the site of two summer art colonies run by Grant Wood during the early 1930s. Visit the *General Store Pub*, housed in an 1897 building immortalized by Wood in his Stone City Iowa painting. In addition to serving food and drink, the pub frequently hosts live music. In the summer, you can enjoy a beer and burger on its deck overlooking the Wapsipinicon River. The pub (319-462-4399; generalstorepub.com) is at 12612 Stone City Rd.

Next head south to Iowa's second largest city, *Cedar Rapids*. The city made international headlines in June of 2008 when it suffered a devastating flood. More than 10 square miles (about 14 percent of the city) were inundated when the Cedar River overflowed its banks. Since then the people of Cedar Rapids have worked valiantly to rebuild and improve their city.

A center for revitalization efforts is the *NewBo District*. Artists and entrepreneurs have revitalized this neighborhood, which forms the heart of the historic Czech community of Cedar Rapids (about one-third of the population in Cedar Rapids is of Czech origin, making it the dominant ethnic group in the city). NewBo is short for New Bohemia, and you'll see many references to Czech and Slovak traditions and culture as you wander its streets.

The *National Czech and Slovak Museum* explores the history and culture of these eastern European ethnic groups. Particularly interesting are its exhibits on Cold War history, including information on the Prague Spring and ordinary life behind the Iron Curtain. The building also celebrates the artistic vibrancy of these cultures. Don't miss the displays of beautifully embroidered folk costumes. The museum (319-362-8500; ncsml.org) is at 1400 Inspiration Place SW.

Czech Village, an area within the NewBo District, has shops, restaurants, and bakeries that carry on the eastern European theme. Note the beautiful, two-story-high mural by artist Sirus Fountain that portrays the two patron saints of the Czech and Slovak people: St. Wenceslaus and St. Ludmilla.

Another premiere attraction in the neighborhood is the *NewBo Market*. Inside the all-weather structure are produce stands, artisan shops, food vendors, and a demonstration kitchen for cooking classes. It's also a center for live music, festivals, and even outdoor yoga. You'll find the NewBo Market (319-200-4050; newbocitymarket.com) at 1100 Third St. SE.

Art lovers will want to explore Cedar Rapids' many ties to Grant Wood, one of America's best-known and -loved artists. The *Cedar Rapids Museum of Art* has the world's largest collection of his art. Tour its exhibits and you'll

American Regionalist

If the farmland surrounding Cedar Rapids looks familiar, it's because you may have seen it in an art museum. Grant Wood often found inspiration for his paintings here, creating such masterpieces as *Young Corn*, *American Gothic*, and *Daughters of Revolution*.

Grant Wood was born on a farm near Anamosa in 1891 and moved to Cedar Rapids as a child. He spent much of his life here, working as a public-school teacher, carpenter, and woodworker as he pursued his passion for art. In 1930 he achieved national fame with his *American Gothic*, the often-parodied portrait of a stern-faced Iowa farmer and his daughter (in reality, its models were Wood's dentist and his sister, Nan). He became the most famous of the American Regionalists, a group of artists who in the 1930s and 40s painted scenes of rural and small-town life. During his lifetime, Wood received both praise and criticism for his sometimes positive and sometimes acerbic portrayals of his fellow Iowans.

While *American Gothic* resides at the Art Institute of Chicago, the Grant Wood Trail in eastern Iowa includes many sites connected to the famous artist.

be able to trace the development of his signature style. While he was initially much influenced by Impressionism, trips to Europe led him to find inspiration in the works of the Northern Renaissance artists. He blended their more realistic, hard-edged style with Midwestern themes to create such works as *Woman with Plants* and *Young Corn*, both of which are on display at the museum. The museum also has works by artists such as Marvin D. Cone, Mauricio Lasansky, and Malvina Hoffman, as well as a fine collection of Roman art. The museum (319-366-7503; crma.org) is at 410 Third Ave. SE. It is open Tues through Sun.

You can learn more about Iowa's most famous artist at the **Grant Wood Studio** at 5 Turner Alley, which is where he lived and worked during 1924–35. *American Gothic* was painted here in 1930. The studio is owned and operated by the museum and is open on weekends from Apr through Dec.

The **African American Museum of Iowa** (319-862-2101; blackiowa .org) tells the story of Black history and culture in the state. Located at 55 Twelfth Ave. SE near Czech Village, its exhibits include Endless Possibilities, which traces Iowa's African American history from its origins in West Africa through slavery, the Civil War, the Underground Railroad, and the Civil Rights Movement.

An environmental treasure in the area is the **Indian Creek Nature Center**, which has 210 acres of wetlands, riparian forest, maple sugarbush, tallgrass prairie, and oak savanna. Visitors can enjoy hiking, cross-country skiing, and fishing, as well as its Amazing Space building, which has a bird-viewing room

newdealmurals

During the Depression, the Works Progress Administration commissioned artists to paint murals across the state. You can see these WPA murals in towns that include:

Cedar Rapids: Harrison School

Monticello: Post Office

Marion: Post Office

Tipton: Post Office

DeWitt: Post Office

and nature displays. One of its most popular events is a Maple Syrup Festival held each March, which includes pancakes topped with real maple syrup handcrafted at the center.

Indian Creek Nature Center (319-362-0664; indiancreeknaturecenter.org) is open daily Mar through Oct, and Tues through Sun during the winter.

Before you leave the Cedar Rapids area, check out the **Cedar Valley Nature Trail**, a 67-mile route that follows a former railroad line between Cedar Rapids and Waterloo. One advantage of the trail is that its grade is never more than 3 percent, making it an easy place to hike, bike, or cross-country ski. The path winds through grasslands, woods, wetlands, and farms, with abundant wildlife along the way, from wild turkeys to white-tailed deer. To enter the trail from Cedar Rapids, drive north on I-380, take exit 25, and follow the signs to the trailhead. See cedarvalley naturetrail.com for more information.

Other sites of interest in Cedar Rapids include the historic Brucemore Mansion, and Duffy's Classic Cars, a car dealership with restored automobiles

Sledding Hills

One of the charms of an Iowa winter is sledding. Here are four places to head downhill when the snow conditions are right:

Eagle Point Park, Clinton: On the bank of the Mississippi, you can enjoy beautiful views as well as steep hills.

Wanatee Park, Marion: This 998-acre park (which is named for Meskwaki artist and advocate for Native American and women's rights Jean Adeline Morgan Wanatee) has a wide-open hill that's a magnet for sledders.

Pres Hill, Mount Vernon: Named after the First Presbyterian Church that stands at the top of the hill, this section of Third Avenue North is closed to traffic when snow conditions are right.

Morehead Pioneer Park, Ida Grove: On Sunday, a motorized tow rope makes it easy to get back uphill in this 258-acre park.

dating from decades past. For more visitor information on Cedar Rapids, call (319) 731-4560, or see tourismcedarrapids.com.

South of Cedar Rapids, visit *Cedar Ridge* (319-857-4300; crwine.com) at 1441 Marak Road in Swisher. This winery and micro-distillery makes award-winning bourbon whiskeys, vodkas, rums, brandies, and other spirits as well as wines. Take a tour to see the entire process of how the drinks are made. The free tours are offered on Sunday at 1 and 3 p.m.

Just east of Cedar Rapids is *Mount Vernon*, home to *Cornell College*. Cornell boasts of the fact that it is the only college in the nation whose entire campus is on the National Register of Historic Places. A very pleasant afternoon may be spent wandering through this lovely old hilltop campus and the adjacent downtown area, where there are specialty stores and places to eat. In the winter make sure you bring your sled along because when there's snow, Third Avenue North's "Pres Hill" is blocked off and left unplowed for some winter fun.

Take US 30 West out of Mount Vernon to end your trip to this region with a visit to the *Palisades-Kepler State Park*, located 10 miles east of Cedar Rapids. During the autumn months especially, this beautiful park skirting the banks of the Cedar River makes an ideal picnicking spot and a wonderful place to while away a Sunday afternoon. For more information call (319) 895-6039 or see iowadnr.gov.

Places to Stay in Cultural Crossroads

DAVENPORT

The Current
215 N. Main St.
(563) 231-9555
thecurrentiowa.com
expensive

CEDAR RAPIDS

The Hotel at Kirkwood Center
7725 Kirkwood Blvd. SW
(319) 848-8700
thehotelatkirkwood.com
moderate to expensive

IOWA CITY

hotelVetro
201 S. Linn St.
(319) 259-7111
hilton.com
expensive

A Bella Vista Bed and Breakfast
2 Bella Vista Place
(319) 338-4129
abellavistabandb.com
moderate

LECLAIRE

Wide River Winery Inn
106 N. Cody Rd.
(954) 242-6878
moderate

Grasshopper's Guesthouse
228 N. Second St.
(563) 289-4652
shopthehop.com
moderate

MAQUOKETA

Decker Hotel & Restaurant
128 N. Main St.
(563) 652-1875
moderate

MUSCATINE

Strawberry Farm Bed & Breakfast
3402 Tipton Rd.
(563) 262-8688
strawberryfarmbandb.com.
moderate

Places to Eat in Cultural Crossroads

ANAMOSA

Tyler & Downings Eatery
122 E. Main St.
(319) 462-5533
tyleranddowningseatery
.com
moderate

AMANA

Ox Yoke Inn
4420 220th Trail
(319) 622-3441
oxyokeinn.com
moderate

CEDAR RAPIDS

Black Sheep Social Club
600 First St. SE
(319) 200-7070
moderate

Lost Cuban
219 Second Ave. SE
(319) 362-2627
inexpensive

CLINTON

Rastrelli's Restaurant
238 Main Ave.
(563) 242-7441
rastrellis.com
moderate

CORALVILLE

Backpocket Brewing
903 Quarry Rd.
(319) 449-3700
backpocketbrewing.com
inexpensive

DAVENPORT

Front Street Brewery
208 E. River Dr.
(563) 322-1569
frontstreetbrew.com
moderate

IOWA CITY

Orchard Green
521 S. Gilbert St.
(319) 354-1642
orchardgreenrestaurant
.com
moderate to expensive

Pullman Bar & Diner
17 S. Dubuque St.
(319) 338-1808
pullmandiner.com
moderate

LECLAIRE

Crane & Pelican Café
127 S. Second St.
(563) 289-8774
craneandpelican.com
moderate

SOLON

Big Grove Brewery
101 W. Main St.
(319) 624-2337
biggrove.com
moderate

Rural Charms

Southeast Iowa is rich in rural pleasures. In the Kalona area you'll find one of the largest **Amish-Mennonite Community** settlements west of the Mississippi, while a few miles south lies Mount Pleasant, home of the Midwest Old Threshers Reunion that celebrates the state's agricultural heritage. The southern part of this region has been shaped in countless ways by two great rivers: the mighty Mississippi and the scenic Des Moines. In this part of southern Iowa, you'll find that many legacies from the nineteenth century still remain in the villages of Van Buren County and in the Mississippi River ports of Fort Madison and Keokuk.

Amish Country

Begin your tour of Amish country in **Kalona**, a place where buggies travel the highways next to cars, Amish farmers work the land with horse-drawn equipment, and on the downtown sidewalks women in black dresses and bonnets mingle with those in blue jeans and T-shirts. About 1,200 Amish people live in the area, as well as many Mennonites.

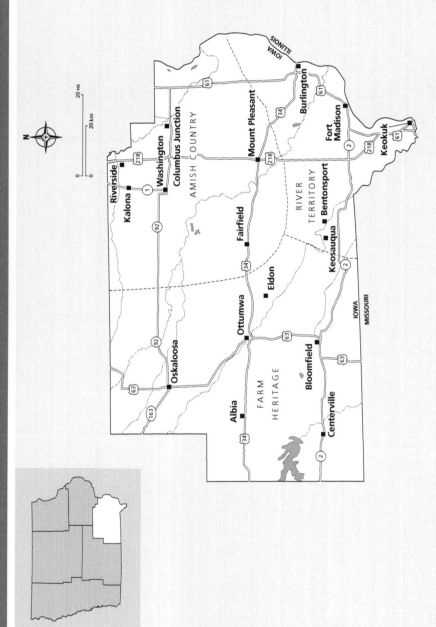

RURAL CHARMS

Although the Amish live in the countryside and limit their contact with the outside world, Kalona itself welcomes visitors to its tidy and prosperous downtown. Here you'll find a wide selection of antiques, bakery goods, and locally made gifts and craft items, including the hand-stitched quilts for which the area is famous. In late April the town hosts the **Kalona Quilt Show and Sale**, which is one of the Midwest's largest quilt shows. Each year several thousand people attend this nationally advertised event featuring hundreds of new and antique quilts made by the local Amish and Mennonite women. The show is held at the Kalona YMCA located at 511 C Ave. A small admission fee is charged. Call (319) 656-2240 or see woodinwheel.com for information.

The **Kalona Historical Village** (319-656-3232; kalonaiowa.org) is a great place to learn about the history and culture of the area. The village, which is at 715 D Ave., contains a dozen restored nineteenth-century buildings that include a one-room schoolhouse, general store, log house, buggy shop, and an old railroad depot. Also on the grounds is the **Iowa Mennonite Museum and Archives**, a repository for the documents and history of the Mennonite community in the area, and the **Quilt & Textile Library**. The village is open Mon to Sat, 10 am to 5 pm (shorter hours in winter). Admission is $12; $3 for children.

Each September the village hosts the **Kalona Fall Festival**, a down-home celebration with plenty of delicious food, homemade crafts, and demonstrations of old-time skills like spinning, weaving, cornmeal grinding, and wood sawing. For me the smells alone are worth the trip: Big pots of bubbling apple butter send a heavenly aroma through the crisp air, a smell rivaled only by that of bread baking in the village's outdoor oven.

The Kalona Fall Festival is held the last Fri and Sat in Sept.

Stop by the **Kalona Brewing Company** (319-656-3335; kalonabrewing .com) at 405 B Ave. for lunch or dinner washed down with a craft beer. Its owners use locally sourced and organic products as much as possible, including grass-fed beef and produce from eastern Iowa farms.

The countryside around Kalona has many small shops and businesses. The **Stringtown Grocery** is among the most popular. Run by the Amish, it has a large variety of bulk items, fresh produce, and garden supplies. You'll find it at 2208 540th St. **Golden Delight Bakery** at 2289 Johnson-Washington Rd. will tempt you with a heavenly array of baked goods, while **JK Creative Wood** at 2410 105th St. sells finely crafted, handmade items. And if you're in need of a new leather belt—or a new harness for your buggy—stop by the **Stringtown Buggy Shop** at 2484 540th St. SW.

Another fascinating introduction to the area can be had on a **Kalona Byways Tour**. Sponsored by the Kalona Area Chamber of Commerce, the narrated tours wind through back roads and include stops at local stores. A variety of tours are offered, some of which include meals. Call (319) 656-2660 for information.

Downtown Kalona is also home to the **Max-Cast Foundry**, where Stephen Maxon and Doris Park have been creating metal works of art since 1988. Inside the industrial-looking building is a warren of rooms overflowing with metal scraps, tools, molds, half-finished projects, and vats of peculiar smelling chemicals—a laboratory where humble materials are transformed into objects of beauty.

Visitors can shop in a gallery located at the front of the foundry. If Maxon and Park have time, you can also take a guided tour of the operation. The two work primarily with cast iron, aluminum, and bronze. Park draws much of her inspiration from the natural world, creating sculptures of unusual or underappreciated animals like snapping turtles and toads. Maxon has a more eclectic style, often creating fantastical creations that blend diverse elements. Many pieces display a sly sense of humor—including toes that look like they're peeking out of the ground and bookends sculpted in the shape of brains—while others take ordinary objects like scissors and a well-polished apple as inspiration for works of art. You can also see the couple's work in downtown Iowa City at the corner of Iowa Avenue and Linn Street, where their statue of local historian Irving Weber waves jauntily at passersby.

Max-Cast Foundry is at 611 B Ave. It's typically open Mon through Fri, but it's best to call ahead before visiting its gallery. For more information call (319) 656-5365 or see max-cast.com.

A charming place to visit is **Sisters Garden**, at 4895 IA 1, Kalona. An old farmhouse has been converted into a shop that sells both the delightfully old and the delightfully new. During the spring and summer months, you can also buy potted herbs, annuals, and perennials. Among the things you can find here are handcrafted willow furniture pieces and many unique items with a garden theme. There are also a few picnic tables scattered about the yard so you can relax and enjoy yourself in this rural setting. Call (319) 683-2046 for their hours.

East of Kalona in the small town of **Riverside** lies an Iowa landmark of interest to all *Star Trek* fans: the **Future Birthplace of Captain James T. Kirk**. In 1985 the Riverside City Council voted unanimously to declare a spot behind what used to be the town's barbershop as the place where Captain Kirk of *Star Trek* fame would one day be born.

Riverside has some official proof to back up its claim. Gene Roddenberry's book, *The Making of Star Trek*, says that Kirk "was born in a small town in the State of Iowa." The town contacted Roddenberry and received a certificate confirming its birthplace status, and thus was born one of Iowa's most famous future historical sites.

On the last weekend in June, Riverside celebrates Kirk's future birth date in the year 2228 by holding its **Trek Fest**. This gathering includes a talent show, carnival rides, and costume contest, plus sports events, a beer garden, and a parade on Main Street. Captain Kirk will undoubtedly be proud (once

TOP ANNUAL EVENTS

JANUARY

Bald Eagle Appreciation Days
Keokuk, third weekend in Jan
(319) 524-5599
keokukiowatourism.org

APRIL

Kalona Quilt Show and Sale
Kalona, last weekend in Apr
(319) 656-2260
kalonachamber.com

JUNE

Trek Fest
Riverside, last weekend in June
(319) 648-3501
trekfest.org

SEPTEMBER

Midwest Old Threshers Reunion
Mount Pleasant, Labor Day weekend
(319) 385-8937
oldthreshers.com

Centerville Pancake Day
Centerville, last Sat in Sept
(641) 437-4102
pactiowa.org

OCTOBER

Scenic Drive Festival
Villages of Van Buren, mid-Oct
(319) 293-7111
villagesofvanburen.com

NOVEMBER

Parade of Lights
Fort Madison, Fri after Thanksgiving
(319) 372-5471
fortmadison.com

he's born). For more information about Trek Fest, call (319) 648-3501 or see trekfest.com.

South of Riverside in the town of Washington, you'll find one of Iowa's destination restaurants: *Cafe Dodici*. Located on the town's central square at 122 S. Iowa Ave., the restaurant has the ambience of an art gallery, with chandeliers handmade in Florence and artwork from around the world. Its menu includes many Italian pasta dishes, from tortellini bianco to shrimp asiago, as well as entrees such as pistachio-encrusted lamb and raspberry salmon. The restaurant uses locally grown produce and meats as much as possible, varying dishes with the seasons.

The cafe's European style reflects the backgrounds of its owners. Lorraine Williams grew up in Washington but later spent twenty-five years living in Italy, where she married her husband, Alessandro Scipioni. On a typical evening, Cafe Dodici hums with conversation and laughter, a welcoming atmosphere set by its extroverted owners. "A restaurant is about much more than just food," says Williams. "It's a place where you should be greeted like an old friend."

Entrees are moderate to expensive. For reservations or more information, call (319) 653-4012 or see cafedodici.com.

From Washington, head east to *Columbus Junction*, where you'll find the *Columbus Junction Swinging Bridge*. A 262-foot suspension bridge made of steel cable and wooden boards, it stretches across a deep, wooded ravine and provides a suitably scary feeling as you stand in its center and sway back and forth.

The bridge's nickname is the Lover's Leap Bridge, a reference to a local legend that says that an Indian maiden jumped to her death in the ravine after hearing that her warrior sweetheart had been killed in battle. The bridge itself was first erected in 1896 so that citizens could travel between Third and Fourth Streets in Columbus Junction without making a detour around the ravine. Since then, the bridge has been replaced several times, most recently in 1921 when a professor of engineering at Iowa

didyouknow?

The chicken roulade at Cafe Dodici was voted one of the *Des Moines Register*'s "100 Things You Have to Eat in Iowa Before You Die."

State University designed a new bridge for the town. To reach the bridge, follow the signs on IA 92 on the west end of Columbus Junction.

From Columbus Junction head east to the *Port Louisa National Wildlife Refuge*. Located adjacent to the Mississippi River, its 24,149 acres include pristine wetlands, grasslands, and bottomland forests. During the spring and fall migration season, more than 60,000 waterfowl can be found here, including

Water Wilderness

Exploring the mazelike backwaters of the Mississippi can be intimidating to anyone unfamiliar with the area, but thanks to the **Odessa Water Trail**, paddlers can enjoy easy access to this water wilderness. The marked trail winds through 6,400 acres of marshes, ponds, lakes, and timbered chutes, an area that is home to thousands of waterfowl, shorebirds, and other animals, from playful river otters to basking turtles. The route is the third water trail in Iowa, and it's the only one that takes paddlers through a variety of water habitats rather than just on a river or stream.

The Odessa Trail is an interconnected set of routes that wind through both the Port Louisa National Wildlife Refuge and the adjoining Odessa Management Area. In all, the various segments of the trail include almost 70 miles of marked routes.

Parts of the trail are closed during the winter months, and changing water levels can affect paddling conditions. For more information call (319) 523-8381 or see louisa countyconservation.org.

mallards, pintails, canvasback, Canada geese, and snow geese. At any time of year, the refuge provides a haven for hundreds of fish, reptile, and amphibian species, as well as deer, muskrat, river otters, bobcats, mink, coyotes, and beaver.

While wildlife refuges can be found throughout the length of the Mississippi River, the Port Louisa Refuge has unique topographical characteristics. More than most refuges along the Mississippi, it's able to closely mimic the ebb and flow of water that existed here for millennia before the lock and dam system was installed. That means that its diverse habitats are regularly replenished by the waters of the river. The health of the refuge also benefits the surrounding area, helping to make Louisa County one of the premier waterfowl hunting and bird-watching areas in the state. The refuge is home to a number of rare and endangered species, including piping plovers, least terns, and peregrine falcons. For information call (319) 523-6982 or see fws.gov/refuge/port-louisa.

Next head west to the small community of **Swedesburg**, home of the **Swedish American Museum**. Swedish settlers began draining the marshy soil of Swedesburg—located in northern Henry County—for farmland beginning around 1860. The museum tells their story and is the location of several Swedish festivals throughout the year, including St. Lucia Day and Midsommar. Admission to the museum is free. Make sure you see the Huckster wagon, from which merchants sold their wares to outlying farms, as well as the wicker "cooling basket" used by the undertaker to hold the deceased body while the casket was being built. The museum is located at 107 James Ave., Swedesburg.

For more information call (319) 254-2317. Its hours are noon to 4 p.m., Thurs to Sat.

South of Swedesburg is **Mount Pleasant**, home to the **Midwest Old Threshers Reunion**, a celebration of old-time agriculture that draws more than 100,000 visitors each Labor Day weekend. The event began in 1950, when a small group of enthusiasts got together at the Henry County Fairgrounds to exhibit steam-powered equipment. (Before the development of the gas-engine tractor in the 1920s, smoke-belching steam engines provided the power that ran America's farms.)

Today the reunion has grown into a five-day event that draws visitors from throughout the country. Many are drawn by the wonderful old behemoth machines on display here: antique tractors and trucks, electric trolleys, steam trains, and all kinds of engines. Other attractions include live entertainment by nationally known performers, a log village, craft demonstrations, and food tents staffed by local church and civic groups that serve platefuls of ham, fried chicken, mashed potatoes, and various fixings. Take a ride on a trolley, attend classes in a one-room school, learn how to make soap, and watch a horse-pull competition—activities all meant to recall a largely vanished way of life.

If you can't make it to the reunion, the Old Threshers 160-acre site is still worth a visit. The permanent **Heritage Museums** (405 E. Threshers Rd. in Mount Pleasant) house scores of steam engines, antique tractors, agricultural equipment, and tools. There are also a farmhouse, barn, and exhibits on farm women and the use of water and electricity.

All Aboard!

The **Midwest Central Railroad** proves the old adage that the only difference between men and boys is the size of their toys (though that's not quite accurate, because women are involved with the railroad, too). These toys are indeed big. The volunteer-run railroad's two vintage, steam-powered trains make the ground shake as they rumble by, filling the air with great clouds of vapor.

This narrow-gauge railroad preserves a slice of train history on the grounds of the Midwest Old Threshers. The trains operate during the reunion in September and also for special occasions, such as the Fourth of July.

My favorite time to step on board the train is before Halloween, when the Midwest Haunted Rails operate. Each year during October weekends, the railroad offers delightfully spooky rides through a haunted landscape of ghosts, ghouls, open coffins, and headless horsemen. The high and lonesome sound of a train whistle in the night adds the perfect atmospheric touch to the scene. For more information call (319) 385-2912 or log onto mcrr.org.

The Midwest Old Threshers Reunion is held each year during the five days ending on Labor Day. Camping and motel accommodations are available. Admission is $30 for a five-day pass and $15 for a one-day pass. The Heritage Museums are open daily, Memorial Day through Labor Day, from 8 a.m. to 4:30 p.m. (weekdays only during the rest of the year). Admission is $5 for adults; children under ten are admitted free. Call (319) 385-8937 for more information on the reunion or museums, or visit oldthreshers.org.

Also on the Old Thresher grounds is the *Theatre Museum of Repertoire Americana* (405 E. Threshers Rd.), one of my favorite museums in the state. The facility houses the country's largest collection of tent, folk, and repertory theater memorabilia—show business that's in the rural, rather than Hollywood, style. Before the days of radio, movies, and television, hundreds of traveling theater companies crisscrossed the nation, bringing live entertainment to even the smallest of towns. This museum provides a colorful introduction to that forgotten past.

The museum owes its existence to Neil and Caroline Schaffner, former owners of the Schaffner Players. The two are best known for their stage characters of Toby and Susie, the wise country bumpkin and his sharp-tongued girlfriend. For nearly forty years their company performed throughout the Midwest, and after they retired they dreamed of establishing a museum to save the memories of early popular theater.

Mount Pleasant and the Midwest Old Threshers Association came to their rescue, and in 1973 the new museum opened its doors. Inside is a fascinating collection of costumes, advertising sheets, scrapbooks, scenery, pictures, and newspapers relating not only to the Schaffners' careers, but to all forms of early American theater. (Don't miss the beautiful hand-painted opera house curtains that were used as scenery for plays.)

The Theatre Museum of Repertoire Americana is open Memorial Day through Labor Day, Thurs through Sat. Call (319) 385-9432 or visit thetheatre museum.com for information.

While visiting Mount Pleasant, include in your plans a lunch or dinner at the *Little Mexico Restaurant*. Hostess and owner Anna Pang has created a bright and festive environment in which to enjoy great Mexican food. The walls are just the color of the mango margaritas and are enlivened by murals in the Mexican folk tradition. Her shredded beef tacos have received several awards. Located at 107 S. Jefferson St., Mount Pleasant; call for more information at (319) 385-8424. Prices are inexpensive to moderate.

Just south of Mount Pleasant lies the small community of *Salem*, home of the *Lewelling Quaker Museum*, 401 S. Main St. Built in the 1840s, this stone house served as a stop on the Underground Railroad; two of the hiding places can still be viewed. In 1847 a band of mounted men from Missouri, seeking revenge against Salem's Quaker community for helping Ruel Dagg's slaves to escape, positioned a cannon in front of the house (a replica of this cannon now rests on the grounds). They threatened to fire upon the house, but word was dispatched to the Henry County sheriff, who managed to disperse the men without violence. The museum is open Sun from 1 to 4 p.m. May through Oct, or by appointment. Call (319) 258-2000 for more information.

From Salem drive west on US 34 to the town of *Fairfield*, home to the state's most unusual institution of higher learning, *Maharishi University of Management (MUM)*. Much of the university looks like any tranquil Midwestern college campus—until you drive past its two huge, golden domes rising out of the Iowa prairie. The contrast symbolizes the interesting mixture at MUM, which combines traditional academic disciplines with the practice of transcendental meditation. Twice each day, students and faculty gather in the domes to practice a meditation technique that they say reduces stress and increases their creativity and productivity.

When representatives of the Maharishi Mahesh Yogi bought the campus of bankrupt Parsons College in Fairfield in 1973, many locals worried that their peaceful community would become a haven for leather-fringed hippies. Instead, MUM has helped stimulate an economic and artistic flowering in Fairfield that has made it one of the most dynamic small towns in the state. Many new businesses have been started by people associated with MUM, from health-food stores and restaurants to financial consulting firms and art galleries.

Ayurvedic Luxury

One of Fairfield's most successful enterprises is *The Raj*, a luxury hotel and health center that offers the indulgent delights of a full spa experience. Housed in a French country-style manor house, The Raj is set on 100 acres of rolling meadows and woods. Its treatments are based on *ayurveda*, an ancient system of preventive health care originally reserved for the royal families of India. It emphasizes prevention as the key to health and explores the relationship between mind and body through diet, exercise, meditation, relaxation, and purification procedures. Western-trained physicians working in conjunction with Indian doctors (called *vaidyas*) devise individualized treatment routines for guests looking to lose weight, reduce stress, and improve their health.

If you don't want to sample the spa, you can still visit *The Raj Restaurant*, which is open for brunch on Sunday. The vegetarian buffet is moderately priced. The Raj is located at 1734 Jasmine Ave. Call (800) 864-8714 or see theraj.com.

The ***Fairfield Arts and Convention Center*** is the most visible symbol of the town's cultural vibrancy. In addition to the 552-seat ***Stephen Sondheim Center for the Performing Arts***, the complex also includes three art galleries presenting permanent and touring exhibitions. The center hosts nationally touring performers and shows at affordable prices. The center (641-472-2000; fairfieldacc.com) is at 200 N. Main St.

For art lovers, the best time to visit Fairfield is on the first Friday of each month, when the town holds its ***Art Walks***. More than 25 galleries and art venues collaborate on the festive evenings. Each month's Art Walk is geared toward a theme, and during the summer, food and art vendors sell their wares to the accompaniment of live music in the town square's gazebo.

One of Fairfield's favorite gathering places is ***Revelations*** at 112 N. Main St., just off the town square. The multiple rooms of this combination bookstore/coffeehouse/cafe are filled with used and new books and comfortable chairs, perfect for browsing the volumes you've pulled from the shelves (don't miss the section on "Afterlife, Tarot, Channeling, and Prophecy"). The cafe has a wood-fired pizza oven and also serves tasty homemade desserts. Call (641) 472-6733 for information.

Before leaving the area, take a short drive north of town to ***Maharishi Vedic City***, which in 2001 became Iowa's newest city. You'll quickly see that this isn't your typical Iowa small town, for all the homes in this community are built according to the principles of Vedic architecture. All face east and have a central open space as well as a golden roof ornament. The town also includes the Maharishi Vedic Observatory, a 1.5-acre, open-air site with sundial-like instruments said to illustrate the inner structure of the universe. This is also the first (and I would guess the last) town in Iowa where the street signs are in Sanskrit.

Farm Heritage

Begin your tour of this predominantly rural part of southeast Iowa with a visit to the small town of ***Eldon***. There you'll find the ***American Gothic House*** (300 American Gothic St.), a home whose image is one of the most reprinted in the country, thanks to Grant Wood's having used it as a backdrop for his painting American Gothic. The picture of the pitchfork-bearing farmer and his daughter is one of the most familiar (and parodied) images in American art, and it has brought fame to the modest house that inspired it.

The home's brush with fame was entirely coincidental. While on a motor trip through southeastern Iowa in 1930, Wood saw the house and made a rough sketch on the back of an envelope of its Gothic-arched window and added two long-faced people in front. Later he looked around his home of Cedar Rapids for a farmer who would fit his ideal, but none was quite right. Finally he persuaded his sister, Nan, and his dentist, Dr. B. H. McBeeby, to be his models. Nan must have had a sense of humor, however, because she collected parodies of this painting during her lifetime and donated them to the Davenport Museum of Art.

After many years as a private residence, the home is now owned by the State Historical Society of Iowa and has been restored to its 1930s appearance. The adjacent **American Gothic House Center** has information on Grant Wood, the Regionalist Art Movement, and the history of the house. Call (641) 652-3352 or see americangothichouse.org for more information.

From Eldon travel north on IA 16 for 6 miles and then west on US 34 for 10 miles to **Ottumwa**. Whereas Riverside is the future birthplace of Captain James T. Kirk, Ottumwa can claim a famous citizen of its own: Radar O'Reilly of M*A*S*H fame.

Ottumwa is home to an attraction certain to delight children: **The Beach Ottumwa**. Why go to Florida when you can enjoy southeast Iowa's own beach, without all those pesky alligators? This indoor/outdoor facility has a wave pool, thrilling waterslides, sand volleyball, and millions of gallons of water. The surf's always up at The Beach Ottumwa, 101 Church St. Call (641) 682-7873 for information.

The **Pioneer Ridge Nature Area and Nature Center**, located 6 miles south of Ottumwa on US 63, offers fun of a drier sort. The site includes a two-story nature center, three stocked ponds for public fishing, and 10 miles of hiking trails. The center is open from 8 a.m. to 4:30 p.m., Mon through Fri. Call (641) 682-3091 or see wapellocounty.org for more information.

Another attraction in the area is the **Air Power Museum**, at 22001 Blue-grass Rd. The museum is home to nearly fifty old-fashioned aircraft and is the site of an annual reunion of antique-airplane enthusiasts each Labor Day weekend. The museum was a labor of love for its founder Bob Taylor, an aviation buff who soloed just before Pearl Harbor, served in World War II and Korea as a crew chief, and then returned to his hometown of Ottumwa to open a flying service in 1953. That same year he founded the Antique Airplane Association, an organization that claims members from throughout the United States and twenty-two foreign countries.

amishcountry

Davis County is home to more than 1,000 Amish. Here, as elsewhere, please do not take pictures of these fine, hardworking people.

At the museum you can see airplanes from the 1920s through the 1940s, plus various flight memorabilia. Most of the planes are civilian craft, with a few homebuilt ones on display as well. There's also a library for people doing research and renovation of antique aircraft.

The Air Power Museum is located west of Ottumwa, 3.5 miles northeast of **Blakesburg**. It is open from 9 a.m. to 5 p.m. on weekdays, from 10 a.m. to 5 p.m. on Sat, and from 1 to 5 p.m. on Sun. Call (641) 938-2773 or see antique airfieldia27.com for more information. Admission is by donation.

Southeast of Ottumwa and north of Floris (off CR J15) and located on the Wapello-Davis County line is **Mars Hill**. Built in 1857, it was one of Iowa's earliest religious buildings. It is constructed of hewn oak and walnut logs, some of them as large as 16 feet high and 8 inches thick, others as long as 28 feet. Mars Hill was a stop on the Underground Railroad. The adjoining cemetery has many old tombstones, the oldest dated 1846. This building is really amazing; go out of your way to pay it a visit (but be careful, for the site is said to be haunted!).

Travel US 63 south to the town of **Bloomfield**, home of the **Davis County Historical Museum** at 205 S. Dodge St., which is open from 1 to 4 p.m. on Sat during the summer. The museum complex contains a hand-hewn log cabin built by Mormons traveling west in 1848, a one-room schoolhouse, and a livery barn built in 1920. Inside the barn is a great mural painted by a local high school art teacher, which depicts the Civil War Guerrilla Raid of 1864, during which twelve raiders marched across Davis County, stealing horses and guns and killing three men in the process. Call (641) 664-2684 for more information or to schedule a tour.

Six miles west of Bloomfield, visit the **Dutch Country General Store** (641-722-3678; dutchcountrygeneralstore.com). The shop sells bulk candy, old-fashioned toys, kitchen and home décor items, and Amish- and Mennonite-made quilts and furniture. Enjoy free ice cream, popcorn, and coffee as you shop. You'll find the store at 17192 Highway 2.

Nearby (about 13 miles northwest of Bloomfield off IA 273) is pretty **Lake Wapello State Park**. It has thirteen family cabins with bathroom and cooking facilities, which may be rented by making reservations with the park ranger. Call (641) 722-3371 or see iowadnr.gov for more information.

From Lake Wapello State Park, travel north to **Oskaloosa**, one of the prettiest-named towns in Iowa. It's named after the wife of Chief Osceola of the Seminole Tribe, and its meaning is as lovely as it sounds: "Last of the Beautiful." Legend has it that Oskaloosa's husband believed that her beauty could never be surpassed.

In Oskaloosa's downtown, stop by **Smokey Row Coffee** on the town square at 109 S. Market St. The old-fashioned soda fountain, coffee shop, and cafe occupies a vintage building with high ceilings, scuffed wooden floors, and cozy booths. On open-mic nights, musicians perform underneath an old theater marquee installed on one wall. Call (641) 676-1600 or see smokeyrow .com for more information.

Adjoining Smokey Row is *The Book Vault*, a well-stocked, independent bookstore housed in a former bank. The old security vaults are now lined with best sellers, and in the back you'll find cooking and baking items. Ask the helpful clerks for a book recommendation—they're very friendly. For more information call (641) 676-1777 or see bookvault.indielite.org.

A major attraction 2 miles off US 63 north of Oskaloosa is the *Nelson Pioneer Farm and Museum* (2211 Nelson Lane; 641-672-2989; nelsonpioneer .org), a complex of restored buildings developed around the original pioneer homestead of Daniel Nelson, who acquired the land from the US government in 1844. The land was farmed by the Nelson family until 1958, when it was given to the Mahaska County Historical Society. The Nelson home and barn are both designated as National Historic Sites, and there are also a number of other buildings open for tours, including a log cabin, summer kitchen, meat house, post office, voting house, school, and Friends meetinghouse.

A good time to visit the Nelson Pioneer Farm and Museum is during its annual Fall Festival held on the third Saturday in September. More than thirty pioneer skills are demonstrated each year, along with special exhibits and musical entertainment. The farm is open May through Sept, Tues through Sat. Admission is $7 for adults and $2 for children.

didyouknow?

The Nelson Pioneer Farm and Museum is the site of the only mule cemetery in Iowa, the final resting place of Becky and Jennie, two white mules owned by Daniel Nelson that served in the US Artillery during the Civil War. They lived out the rest of their days on the farm and now have a special plot near the museum.

In the rolling, wooded countryside south of Oskaloosa, you'll find one of Iowa's premiere outdoor attractions: *Honey Creek Resort State Park*, which is located on *Rathbun Lake*, one of the state's largest bodies of water. The 828-acre site includes a beautifully designed lodge and twenty-eight elegant cottages overlooking an 11,000-acre lake. The 105-room lodge—which is decorated in Arts and Crafts style and includes a massive stone fireplace in its main lobby—features an indoor water park, fine-dining restaurant, outdoor patio, and meeting facilities. Outside lie multipurpose trails, scenic overlooks, picnic areas, a sand beach, boat slips, an RV campground, and an eighteen-hole golf course. The property is owned by the Iowa Department of Natural Resources and offers interpretive programs such as hiking, fishing, biking, stargazing, outdoor cooking, geocaching, and bird-watching.

If you like your nature served with a little bit of luxury, this is the place for you. For more information about Honey Creek Resort, call (641) 724-1450 or see honeycreekresort.com.

Near the resort you'll find **Rathbun State Fish Hatchery**, Iowa's largest warm-water fish hatchery. Catfish, walleye, saugeye, and largemouth bass by the millions are raised here each year before being released into Iowa streams, ponds, rivers, and lakes.

You can view the facility's operations on an elevated walkway. The hatchery is at 15053 Hatchery Place; call (641) 647-2406 for information. It is open Mon through Fri.

South of Honey Creek Resort lies **Centerville**, the county seat of Appanoose County. For many years the area was the site of a thriving coal-mining industry. Commercial mining began in 1863 and peaked in 1917, when 400 mines were operating in the area.

Though the last coal mine closed in 1971, you can learn more about the industry's history at the **Appanoose County Historical and Coal Mining Museum** in Centerville. Located at 100 W. Maple St., the museum (641-856-

anunusual friendship

Near the town of Agency, you'll see a sign for Chief Wapello Memorial Park, a little rest area that marks an important spot in Iowa's history. The park was once the site of an Indian agency (hence the town's name) where the 1842 Sac and Fox Treaty was signed to complete their cession of Iowa lands to the US government. This set the stage for the homesteading of Iowa in 1843.

The site is also a reminder of the unique friendship that sprang up between Chief Wapello, a principal leader of the Sac and Fox Nation, and General Joseph Street, director of the agency. After being forced from his home along the Mississippi by the government, Wapello led his people to settle near the Indian agency, due to his friendship with Street. The general died in 1840, and before Wapello died two years later, he asked to be buried beside him. Their graves rest undisturbed in the park to this day.

8040; appanoosehistory.com) is located in the town's former post office, built in 1903. It houses a coal-mine replica on its lower level, with mining tools and equipment that show the difficult working conditions endured by the early miners. The museum also includes information on the Mormon exodus that passed through here in 1846, as well as other aspects of southern Iowa history. The museum is open mid-May through mid-Oct, Mon through Sat, and Wed through Fri during the rest of the year. A small admission fee is charged.

There may be no such thing as a free lunch, but if you go to Centerville on the last Saturday in September, you'll sure get your fill of free pancakes! Why? Because it's **Pancake Day!** This wonderful festival, still entirely free of charge,

began in 1949 when local merchants got together to say "thanks" to their customers. It started small, but now twenty-six griddles cook up more than 80,000
pancakes. If pancakes aren't enough for you, there is also a parade with floats
and bands, ongoing entertainment, and the crowning of Pancake Day royalty.
For more information call (641) 437-4102 or see pactiowa.org.

Overnight guests will enjoy staying at *The Continental Hotel* (641-437-
1025; thecontinental.info) at 217 N. Thirteenth St. on the town square. The
hotel was built in 1893 and has hosted guests who included Booker T. Washington and (reportedly) Jesse James and Al Capone. Now a boutique hotel, it
includes *Lucile's Steak & Spirits*, which serves upscale comfort food.

River Territory

Next travel to scenic Van Buren County. *Keosauqua*, its county seat, has a
grand total of 936 people, and the pace in the county's other towns is just as
slow. Visitors agree that the quiet is part of the area's allure—that and an old-
fashioned atmosphere that's authentic, not manufactured.

Back in the mid-nineteenth century, however, life was more hectic in *Van
Buren County*. The meandering Des Moines River that flows through the center of the county was a busy passageway for steamboats, and the villages on
its banks were bustling ports. Mills, stores, and hotels filled the towns, and an
active social life kept both locals and visitors entertained. Unfortunately, the
years of prosperity ended abruptly when the US Congress decided that the
locks and dams along the river would no longer be maintained, thus making
the river un-navigable by the larger boats. Soon the towns settled into faded
obscurity, as all but a few residents packed up their bags and moved away.

Within the past few decades, the area has experienced a renaissance that
has preserved its historical character and charm while still making it a favorite
destination for growing numbers of visitors. Keosauqua is a good place to
begin your tour. The name comes from an Indian word meaning "great bend,"
a reference to the loop the Des Moines River takes around the town. Keosauqua was once a stop on the Underground Railroad and was also a fording spot
for the Mormons on their westward trek in the late 1840s.

Today the best-known landmark in Keosauqua is the *Hotel Manning*, a
two-story brick structure with wide verandas for watching the Des Moines River
flow by. The hotel was built in 1899 and through the ensuing years has with-
stood no fewer than four floods. I enjoy staying at the Hotel Manning because
it's like slipping into an old, comfortable shoe. The floors creak, the doors don't
always match, and there's a delightful air of faded gentility about the place that
makes it easy to imagine how it must have been when river travelers stayed

here a hundred years ago. The hotel's nineteen rooms are furnished with antique furniture and brightly patterned quilts, braided rugs line the floor, and steam radiators keep the building toasty warm in winter. The Hotel Manning is located at 100 Van Buren St. Rates range from inexpensive to moderate; call (319) 293-3232 for reservations.

Also in the area is **Lacey-Keosauqua State Park**, which with 1,653 acres is one of the state's largest parks. The great horseshoe bend the Des Moines River makes here offers beautiful vistas for hikers and campers. The park is named for John F. Lacey, an Iowan who served in the US House of Representatives in the late 1800s. An avid conservationist, he helped lay the legislative groundwork for the US national park and forest systems. The grounds include nineteen Native American burial mounds and nearly fifty structures built by the Civilian Conservation Corps during the Great Depression.

distinguished hotelguest

The poet T. S. Eliot was one of the Hotel Manning's famous guests. He signed the hotel register on September 13, 1919.

Next travel east to **Bentonsport**, a tiny village with a number of restored buildings and stores on its main street, which has been designated a National Historic District. Take special note of the Greef General Store, a structure built in the Federal style in 1853 that now serves as a showcase for local antiques and crafts. The town is also home to a community of artists, including potter Betty Printy. She has established a regional reputation with her distinctive Queen Anne's lace pottery. Using hand-dug local clay, Printy molds the pottery and then presses the wildflower Queen Anne's lace into the clay while it's still wet. The result is a beautiful tracery of lines and flowers. You can find her work at Iron and Lace. For information call (319) 592-3222 or see ironandlace.com.

Down the river from Bentonsport is the village of **Bonaparte**, also the site of historic preservation efforts. In 1989 its downtown area was named a National Historic Riverfront District, a tribute to the hard work of the village's citizens.

The best-known restoration in Bonaparte is **Bonaparte Retreat** at 713 First St. It is a fine restaurant housed in a nineteenth-century gristmill. Owned by Ben and Rose Hendricks, the restaurant is known for both the quality of its food and its decor and a pleasing mixture of steamboat and gristmill relics. The restaurant's menu includes steak, pork, and seafood.

Bonaparte Retreat (319-592-3339) is open Mon through Sat for lunch and dinner, and on Sun for lunch. Prices are moderate to expensive.

Ghost Hunting 101

Iowa's most famous haunted house sits on the banks of the Des Moines River in the small village of Bentonsport. The **Mason House Inn** is said to be haunted by no fewer than twenty spirits, including a ghostly cat. After initially wanting to keep its spectral inhabitants secret, owners Joy and Chuck Hanson now welcome public-ity about the inn's haunted reputation. In 2006 the Mason House was featured on a **Today Show** segment on America's most haunted houses.

When the Hansons purchased the Federal-style brick structure in 2001, they were told by the previous owner that the inn had a ghost. "That didn't bother us, but we soon began to suspect there was more than one spirit because there was so much strange activity in the house," says Joy. "Doors locked themselves, we'd hear our names being called when no one was there, and alarm clocks kept going off when we hadn't set them. Also, guests would often come to breakfast with stories of odd things happening at night, like door handles jiggling and tapping on the walls."

Today the Inn offers several ghost-hunting courses throughout the year. A typical class includes a primer in investigation techniques, an overview of the house's his-tory, and a description of the spirits who have previously made appearances. In the evening, class members go from room to room seeking to make contact with the ghosts.

Why do so many spirits congregate at the Mason House? The Hansons speculate that part of the reason is that the house has been a gathering place for the local community since it was built in 1846 and that many happy times happened within its walls. They also believe that the spirits watch over the house and that they enjoy the parade of people who come to stay in it. Guests who are leery of supernatural encounters can stay in the nonhistorical part of the inn, which isn't believed to be haunted.

"We have great respect for the spirits who live here, and I think they like that," says Chuck. "We know that they're the longtime residents here, and we're just temporary."

The Mason House Inn is at 21982 Hawk Dr. For more information call (319) 592-3133 or see masonhouseinn.com.

For more information about other attractions in the area, call the Villages of Van Buren at (800) 868-7822 or see villagesofvanburen.com.

West of Bonaparte on IA 2 lies the small village of **Cantril**. There you'll find **Dutchman's Store** (319-397-2322; dutchmansstore.com), a bulk grocery, dry-goods, and fabric store operated by a local Mennonite family. The old-fashioned establishment is open Mon through Sat.

From Van Buren County travel to **Keokuk**, a city that lies at the southeast-ern tip of the state. Keokuk was once known as the Gate City because of its position at the foot of the Des Moines rapids on the Mississippi. In the early days of settlement, steamboats were unable to go beyond this point, and all passengers had to disembark here, either to continue their journey on land or board another boat upriver. The city played an important role in the Civil War, when seven hospitals were established here to care for the wounded transported up the Mississippi from southern battlefields.

The **Keokuk National Cemetery** was one of the first national cemeteries designated by the US Congress and is the resting place for both Union and Confederate soldiers. It was also the first national cemetery west of the Mississippi and is the only one in Iowa. It's located at 1701 J St. and is open from dawn to dusk daily.

The city's most famous citizen was Mark Twain, who worked here as a young man in the printing shop of his brother, Orion Clemens. Most of the type for the city's first directory was set by Twain, who listed himself in its pages as an "antiquarian." When asked the reason for this, he replied that he always thought that every town should have at least one antiquarian, and since none had appeared for the post, he decided to volunteer.

The **George M. Verity *Riverboat Museum*** will take you back to those days when Keokuk was a busy river port. Built in 1927, the *Verity* was the first of four steamboats built to revive river transportation on the Mississippi. In 1960 it was retired and given to the city of Keokuk for use as a river museum. Today it contains many old-time photographs of riverboats and the river era, as well as other artifacts and historical items.

The *Verity* is berthed in Victory Park at the foot of Main Street on the Mississippi River. It is open daily from 9 a.m. to 5 p.m., Memorial Day through Labor Day, and a small admission is charged. Call (319) 524-4765 or see geomverity .org for information.

newdealmurals

During the Depression, the Works Progress Administration commissioned artists to paint murals across the state. You can see these WPA murals in towns that include:

Columbus Junction: Post Office

Mount Pleasant: Post Office

Sigourney: Post Office

Bloomfield: Post Office

While you're in Keokuk, take a self-guided walking tour that includes thirty beautiful old houses built at the end of the nineteenth and beginning of the twentieth centuries. The houses are all located on Orleans and Grand Avenues along the river and were built for the elite of this once-booming town. Don't miss 925 Grand Ave. This house was built in 1880 by Howard Hughes Sr., father of the famous junior and the inventor of the oil well drill. Hughes built the house for his mother and constructed it entirely without closets because

City of Christmas

The North Pole isn't the only place where elves work year-round to prepare for the holidays. In Keokuk, Santa's helpers come in the form of volunteers who stage the *City of Christmas*, a spectacular light extravaganza featuring more than one hundred handcrafted displays in the town's Rand Park.

Begun in 1989 with just a few displays, Keokuk's City of Christmas has grown to become a beloved holiday tradition. Financed by donations and run by volunteers, the event is truly a celebration of holiday—and hometown—spirit.

The people who *ooh* and *aah* from inside the nearly 20,000 vehicles that pass through the park each year may not realize the large amount of work that makes the City of Christmas possible. Most of the displays are constructed in the basement of Keokuk's senior center, with a half-dozen volunteers working steadily throughout the year. Several new designs are added each Christmas, and existing ones are improved.

While many of the designs feature familiar holiday themes, a growing number reflect the town's unique identity. One of the newest displays, for example, features a hand reaching down toward six lighted globes. The design pays tribute to three Keokuk children who were killed in a house fire in 1999 and to the three firefighters who died trying to save them.

she feared they were breeding grounds for disease. The tour ends at the lovely Rand Park. To get a wonderfully detailed map and brochure of this informative tour, contact the Keokuk Area Convention and Tourism Bureau at (319) 524-5599 or keokukiowatourism.org.

Also of interest in Keokuk are the Miller House Museum (once home to US Supreme Court justice Samuel Miller) and the Keokuk Power Plant/US Lock and Dam No. 19. When the power plant was completed in 1913, it was the largest electric generating plant in the world. Later a 1,200-foot lock, the largest on the upper Mississippi, was constructed to accommodate modern river traffic.

Thanks to the lock and dam, Keokuk is one of the most important winter feeding areas for the American bald eagle. As the birds' primary feeding spots in Canada and Alaska begin to freeze, they fly south to find food. As many as 1,400 bald eagles winter along the Mississippi between Minneapolis and St. Louis. Keokuk enjoys one of the largest populations because the lock and dam keep the water from freezing, thus enabling the birds to hunt for fish.

Eagles can be seen in the area from October to early April, but the best time for viewing them is from mid-December to mid-February. Early morning is the ideal time, when they can be seen soaring and diving for fish. During *Bald*

Eagle Appreciation Days each January, the Keokuk Area Convention and Tourism Bureau sponsors shuttle-bus service to and from observation areas, as well as seminars, lectures, exhibits, Native American activities, and films on the magnificent birds. It also puts out a brochure listing prime viewing areas; call (319) 524-5599 or see keokuktourism.org. If you do go eagle viewing on your own, bring a pair of binoculars and stay either in or next to your car. It's important that resting eagles not be disturbed; when they fly off, they burn up energy badly needed during the cold weather.

From Keokuk travel north on US 61 to ***Fort Madison***, a river town first established in 1808 as a government trading post and one of three major forts guarding the Northwest frontier. Rozanna Stark, the first white child to be born in the state, was born here in 1810. In 1813 the fort was attacked by Ho-Chunk, Menominee, and Sac warriors. The fort's soldiers fled, burning the structure as they left so all that remained was a blackened chimney (the chimney is now a monument on Avenue H and US 61). On the riverfront in Riverview Park, you can tour the rebuilt stockade of ***Old Fort Madison***, which vividly evokes the town's origins as a remote frontier outpost. Constructed on the riverfront in 1983 (partly with labor provided by inmates at the Iowa State Penitentiary in Fort Madison), the rough-hewn fort brings to life the often-precarious existence of its original inhabitants. Costumed interpreters describe how the residents coped with frequent raids, diseases such as malaria and typhoid fever, and the constant threat of starvation.

The tyrannical nature of the fort's commander, Horatio Stark, proved to be another hardship (a popular T-shirt in the gift shop bears the slogan, "The floggings will continue until morale improves"). Even by the standards of the day, Stark was considered a harsh disciplinarian of his men.

Special events are held at the Old Fort throughout the year, including a ***Muster on the Mississippi*** on Memorial Day weekend. Old Fort Madison (319-372-7700; oldfortmadison.org) is open Wed through Sun from 9 a.m. to 5 p.m. from June through Aug and on weekends in May, Sept, and Oct. Admission is $9 for adults, $3 for children.

After leaving the fort, enjoy handcrafted beers and pub food at ***Lost Duck Brewing Company*** (319-372-8255; duckbrewing.com) at 725 Avenue H.

Overnight guests to Fort Madison will enjoy the elegantly restored ***Kingsley Inn***, an eighteen-room hotel overlooking the Mississippi (rates are moderate). The brick structure was built in the 1860s as a whiskey and vinegar distillery. Call (319) 372-2144 or see kinglseyinn.com for reservations.

Each year on the weekend after Labor Day, Fort Madison hosts the ***Tri-State Rodeo*** (tristaterodeo.org; 319-372-2550). Since 1948 it has been one of the region's top professional rodeos, performed in a 10,000-seat outdoor arena.

The Toolesboro Indian Mounds

Seven Indian mounds are situated on a bluff overlooking the Iowa River near its junction with the mighty Mississippi. The largest one measures 100 feet wide and 8 feet high. Two thousand years ago, between 100 BC and AD 200, Native Americans constructed these mounds as sacred burial sites for the highest-ranking members of their nation, probably the chiefs and priests. The names of the tribes are lost to us, for no written language survives. They—or rather, their system of burial practices—are known to the modern world as the "Hopewell tradition." No village site has ever been found, perhaps because of the shifting course of the Iowa River over the centuries. We only know that these cultures shared a widespread system of belief and worship. They probably lived along river floodplains and buried their dead on the high bluffs as they did here. They had an extensive trade network; artifacts including marine shells, Chesapeake Bay sharks' teeth, Rocky Mountain obsidian, Great Lakes copper, Appalachian mica, and Gulf of Mexico pearls have all been discovered.

After AD 500 the mound builders disappeared from the archaeological landscape. Many of these ancient peoples' mounds were damaged or ruined by European-American land clearing, plowing, and clumsy excavation techniques. Fortunately, current archaeological exploration prefers nonintrusive studies, using such methods as aerial photography, surface surveys, and remote sensing—techniques that can see underground without disturbing it.

Visitors are welcome to visit the mounds anytime. Admission is free. They are located on IA 99 between Wapello and Oakville. The fine Educational Center is open from 12:30 to 4:30 p.m. Wed through Sun, Memorial Day through Labor Day, and on Sat, Labor Day through Oct. Call (319) 766-4018 for more information.

Watch cowboys compete in bareback riding, steer wrestling, bull riding, and other events as well as enjoy concerts by nationally known performers.

For more information about Fort Madison, contact the Fort Madison Area Convention & Visitors Bureau at (319) 372-7700 or see fortmadison-ia.com.

From Fort Madison head north on US 61 to the Mississippi River port of **Burlington**. The Sac and Fox Tribes called the great bluffs bordering the river here *Shoquoquon*, a name meaning "flint hills." Many tribes gathered flint from area hillsides in the early nineteenth century for use in their weapons and hunting tools. Their days in the area were numbered, however, for in 1805 Zebulon Pike landed in what is now the city of Burlington, and within thirty years the territory was thrown open to white settlers. Burlington was the first capital of the Iowa territory from 1838 to 1840 and an important steamboat, lumber, and railroad center in the nineteenth century.

A good place to begin your tour of the city is the **Port of Burlington Welcome Center** at 400 N. Front St. Located on the bank of the river, the 1928 building once was a coal-loading site for barges. Now it houses an information center with historical displays and a video of local attractions. The center (319-752-8731) is open daily.

Next take a stroll along Burlington's most famous landmark, **Snake Alley**. Ripley's Believe It or Not has dubbed Snake Alley the "crookedest street in the world," and each year it continues to draw many visitors. The alley and the Victorian homes that surround it have been named to the National Register of Historic Places. You can approach the top of Snake Alley along North Sixth Street between Washington and Columbia Streets.

Visit **Mosquito Park**, named for its size, not its bite! You will find this little gem tucked away at Third and Franklin Streets. Set on bluffs just north of the downtown district, it offers a captivating view of the rolling Mississippi below.

Another jewel is located at St. Mary's Catholic Church in West Burlington at 520 W. Mount Pleasant St. **Our Lady of Grace Grotto**, completed in 1931, was constructed of thousands of imported and native stones and features split-rock sidewalks and crystal-rock walls. Forty different varieties of trees are found in its garden. For more information call (319) 752-6733.

The Crookedest Street in the World

Building a town along the steep hillsides surrounding the Mississippi River required considerable ingenuity. In 1894 Snake Alley was constructed as an experimental street connecting the downtown business district and the neighborhood shopping area on North Sixth Street in Burlington. This 275-foot-long, zigzagging street rises nearly 60 feet up the bluff and is constructed of tilted bricks designed to allow better footing for horses. The switchback design proved to be less successful than was hoped, however, as drivers often lost control of their horses on its steep curves. Plans to construct more streets on its model were abandoned.

Snake Alley nevertheless proved useful. Horses were "test-driven" up the winding curves at a gallop, and those that reached the top with the least difficulty were deemed fit enough to haul the city fire wagons. When cars were first offered for sale, they had to endure the same test, as auto dealers used Snake Alley to show off the vehicles' power, with prospective buyers clinging in terror to their seats. While Snake Alley is no longer open to cars, it continues to be the town's most distinctive landmark.

Each June, the ***Snake Alley Art Fair*** is held on Burlington's signature street and surrounding area. In addition to arts and crafts, the event includes live music, kids' activities, and plentiful food. See artcenterofburlington.com for information. And on Memorial Day weekend, the ***Snake Alley Criterium*** (snakealleycriterium.com) draws cyclists from around the nation to race up Burlington's most famous street.

For more information on Burlington, call (319) 752-6365 or see greater burlington.com.

Places to Stay in Rural Charms

BENTONSPORT

Alexander's Cottage
21930 Wall St.
(319) 592-3152
alexandersbentonsport
cottage.com
inexpensive

BURLINGTON

Candlelight Manor Bed & Breakfast
303 S. Sixth St.
(319) 758-0428
candlemanor.net
moderate

FAIRFIELD

Seven Roses Inn
1208 E. Burlington St.
(641) 209-7077
sevenrosesinn.com
moderate

KALONA

Carriage House Bed and Breakfast
1140 Larch Ave.
(319) 471-2832
carriagehousebb.net
moderate to expensive

KEOKUK

The Eagle's Nest
1229 Grand Ave.
(319) 524-8643
moderate

KEOSAUQUA

Sunrise Inn & Retreat
17248 Highway 1
(652) 334-4123
sunriseinnandretreat.com
moderate

OTTUMWA

Oak Meadow Delight
2814 Oak Meadow Dr.
(641) 682-0580
oakmeadowdelightbedand
breakfast.com
moderate

Places to Eat in Rural Charms

BURLINGTON

The Drake
106 Washington St.
(319) 754-1036
thedrakerestaurant.com
moderate to expensive

La Tavola
316 N. Fourth St.
(319) 768-5600
latavolaburlington.com
moderate

FAIRFIELD

India Cafe
50 W. Burlington Ave.
(641) 472-1792
indiacafeiowa.com
inexpensive

FORT MADISON

The Palms Supper Club
4920 Avenue O
(319) 246-1419
palmsia.ia
moderate to expensive

KEOKUK

Angelini's Ristorante Italiano
1006 Main St.
(319) 524-9009
angeliniskeokuk.com
moderate

MOUNT PLEASANT

The Grange Public House
129 S. Jefferson St.
(319) 385-3121
grangepublichouse.com
moderate

OTTUMWA

Canteen Lunch in the Alley
112 E. Second St.
(641) 682-5320
canteenottumwa.com
inexpensive

Bridge Country

South central Iowa can be thought of as "bridge country" in two different ways. In Madison County you can discover the sites made famous by the popular novel and film *The Bridges of Madison County*. In Des Moines and its neighboring cities—a region sometimes called the "golden circle"—you can explore the metropolitan area that serves as a bridge between Iowa's rural communities and its increasingly urban central core.

South central Iowa is also home to the ethnic enclave of Pella, where Dutch traditions remain strong, as well as other rural treasures along the southern border.

Golden Circle

Begin your tour in *Grinnell*. J. B. Grinnell, the founder of the town, was the recipient of Horace Greeley's famous dictum: "Go West, young man, and grow up with the country." Josiah Bushnell Grinnell made Grinnell a stop on the Underground Railroad; more than 1,000 freedom-seeking slaves passed through Grinnell in the pre–Civil War years. In 1859 he gave refuge to John Brown following his raids in Kansas and Missouri. Learn more about this influential man and this

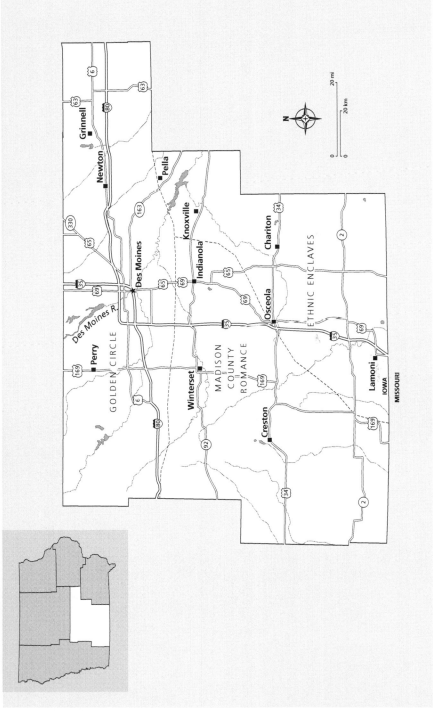

didyouknow?

The first intercollegiate football game played west of the Mississippi took place in 1889 when the University of Iowa and Grinnell College teams met on the gridiron.

community when you visit the *Grinnell Historical Museum*, which is housed in a ten-room late-Victorian residence at 1125 Broad St. Besides the furniture and artifacts of an earlier era, there is a barbed-wire collection and several carriages (including a surrey with fringe on top) made by the old Spaulding Carriage and Automotive Works of Grinnell. Call (641) 236-7827 or see grinnellhistorical museum.org for more information.

Grinnell College, one of the nation's top liberal arts colleges, attracts students from fifty states and more than fifty countries. They contribute to the town's vibrancy and work in some of the downtown businesses. Stop by the *Grinnell College Museum of Art* (641-269-4000; grinnell.edu) at the Bucksbaum Center for the Arts to see exhibitions of regional, national, and international art, and then stroll across the scenic campus.

Downtown, have a meal at *Prairie Canary Restaurant & Bar* (641-236-0205; prairiecanary.com), a moderately priced restaurant that makes creative use of locally sourced meats and produce. It's located in a historic building at 924 Main St.

For a treat (and maybe even a few tricks) visit *Uncle Bill's Farm* in October. You can pick a pumpkin, get lost in a corn maze, climb into a tree house, feed the pygmy goats, and ride on a kid-sized train. Uncle Bill's Farm is located at 244 400th Ave. in Grinnell. Open Fri through Sun and admission is $13. For more information call (641) 236-7043 or see unclebillsfarm.com.

Continue west to *Newton*. At the *Jasper County Historical Museum* (1700 S. Fifteenth Ave. W) you can view displays on local history. The museum's largest exhibit tells the story of the Maytag Company, which manufactured washers here from 1907 to 2007. The museum (641-792-9118) is open Tues

AUTHOR'S FAVORITES

Neal Smith National Wildlife Refuge	Carnegie Library Museum
Iowa State Fair	Cutler-Donahoe Covered Bridge
Iowa State Capitol	Des Moines Metro Opera
Living History Farms	John Wayne Birthplace and Museum

Twister Alert!

On June 17, 1882, the state of Iowa almost lost the town of **Grinnell**. Storms had been raging across the state all day and were to meet with a furious uproar in Grinnell. Ten miles away in Kellogg, two black clouds united and formed a tornado that swept northeast to Grinnell. In the west, in Carroll County, another tornado was moving swiftly to the southeast.

As if by appointment, the two twisters met in the very center of the town of Grinnell. It was a clash of titanic proportions that sent at least six smaller tornadoes spiraling outward. Thirty-nine people were killed, and the college was in ruins. The only property salvaged was the college bell.

Seven years later in 1889, the downtown district was again almost destroyed by a devastating fire. We are lucky to have this town still on the map. J. B. Grinnell, the founder, was instrumental in rebuilding the town twice. Earlier he had given lots to the college, stating that they would have to be given back to him or his estate if liquor was ever sold on them. Could it be that the tornadoes knew more about what was going on than he did?

through Sun from 1 to 4 p.m. from May 1 to Sept 30. A small admission is charged.

Near Prairie City, visit the **Neal Smith National Wildlife Refuge**. This is one of the few places in the nation where you can close your eyes and listen to an ancient sound: the restless, melodic swish of prairie grasses swaying in the wind. Founded in 1990, the 6,000-acre site is the largest reconstruction of a tallgrass prairie ecosystem in the nation. It is named after Neal Smith, a former congressman from Iowa with a long-standing interest in environmental preservation.

"We're just beginning a thousand-year project," says Pauline Drobney, research biologist at the refuge. "It took a long time for these landscapes to evolve, and bringing them back is also a long-term effort. This is the first time prairie restoration has been tried on this large a scale, and there's a lot that we have to learn as we go along."

In the middle of the refuge sits the **Prairie Learning Center**, an airy, light-filled building that shows why this landscape is worth saving and how it is being restored. In the Fire Theater visitors can learn more about the engine of destruction and rebirth that makes prairies possible. Fire is essential because it clears away

clothesline
capitalofiowa

Newton was once the home of nine washing-machine companies and was called "the Washing Machine Capital of the World."

Prairie Wonders

When pioneers first saw the endless grasslands that covered much of the heartland of the United States, they reasoned that the soil must be poor because there weren't many trees here. Some even called it a desert. Only later was it discovered that the prairie plants had in fact created the richest soil on earth, rich loam that extended to a depth of 4 feet in places.

Within a few short decades, settlers had plowed the prairie and sowed the land with crops like corn and wheat. Prairie plants remained in only a few scattered remnants. In Iowa alone the loss was catastrophic: When pioneers first came to the state, tallgrass prairie covered 85 percent of Iowa's 36 million acres. Today, less than 1 percent of that prairie remains.

A mature tallgrass prairie provides an abundance of life: hundreds of plant, insect, and bird species, plus scores of mammals, amphibians, reptiles, and even fish species. Each is precisely adapted to the extremes of temperature and precipitation found in the Midwest, from blazing summer heat and frigid winters to great floods and lingering droughts. Some prairie plants exhibit amazing ingenuity. Needlegrass, for example, has a seed with a sharp point and a tail that changes with the weather. When it's dry, it twists; when it's wet, it untwists. Thus the changing weather creates a seed that literally screws itself into the ground.

old thatch, releasing seeds and allowing new growth to flourish. It also keeps the prairie free of trees. Before the arrival of the pioneers, some fires were set by lightning, but the native peoples of the region also periodically burned the prairie, knowing that it kept the land attractive to grazing animals like buffalo and elk.

After touring the center, experience the prairie firsthand by either car or foot. An auto tour route and several hiking trails wind through the refuge, each providing lovely views of a rolling landscape of swaying grasses, blooming flowers, and expansive sky. You can also view the refuge's herds of buffalo and elk. Animals like these play a role in the ecosystem of the prairie, for their grazing, trampling, and manure stimulate plant growth. Visitors may also see another prized species at the refuge: regal fritillary butterflies, an endangered species that has been reintroduced in the past two years. Other rare and endangered animal species here include the Indiana bat, Henslow's sparrow, northern harrier hawk, short-eared owl, and upland sandpiper.

The Prairie Learning Center is at 9981 Pacific St., Prairie City. The entrance is at the southwest corner of Prairie City, at the IA 163–Prairie City interchange. The center is open Mon through Sat, 9 a.m. to 4 p.m., and on Sun from noon to 5 p.m. The refuge trails and auto tour route are open daily from sunrise to sunset. Admission is free. For more information call (515) 994-3400 or see tallgrass.org.

From the wildlife refuge head west to **Des Moines**. The past decades have brought a host of accolades for Iowa's capital, from #7 Hippest Mid-Sized City in America to #3 Top City for New College Grads.

The city's ongoing transformation is due in part to billions of dollars of private and public development money. During the past several decades a host of new attractions has kept construction crews busy, including the Iowa Events Center, with multiple venues for concerts, athletic events, and conventions; the dazzling Science Center of Iowa; a revitalized East Village neighborhood; and a continuing reclamation of the riverfront with pedestrian paths and parks.

The new developments—in combination with established city landmarks such as Living History Farms, the Des Moines Art Center, and Blank Park Zoo—are luring increasing numbers of visitors to a city whose staid image is getting an extreme makeover.

Wells Fargo Arena is one of the city's most prominent landmarks, a glass-sided structure that dominates the Des Moines riverfront just north of the downtown. The space plays host to some of the nation's hottest touring acts. The arena is connected to the city's enclosed 4-mile skywalk system, so that no matter what the weather is like outside, you can easily walk to all the

TOP ANNUAL EVENTS

FEBRUARY

BRR (Bike Ride to Rippey)
Perry, first weekend in Feb
(515) 465-4601
perryia.org

MAY

Tulip Time Festival
Pella, first weekend in May
(641) 628-4311
pellahistorical.org

JUNE

Des Moines Arts Festival
Third weekend in June
(515) 243-0388
artswork.art/desmoinesartsfestival

AUGUST

National Balloon Classic
Indianola, early Aug
(515) 961-8415
nationalballoonclassic.com

Sweet Corn Festival
Adel, second Sat in Aug
(515) 993-5472adelpartners.org

Iowa State Fair
Des Moines, third week in Aug
(800) 545-FAIR
iowastatefair.org

OCTOBER

Madison County Covered Bridge Festival
Winterset, second weekend in Oct
(515) 462-1185
madisoncounty.com

A Bell of Friendship

On the grounds of the Iowa State Capitol, you can see a bell house and large bronze bell that are a gift to Iowa from the people of Yamanashi, Japan. The landmark is a testimony to the generosity of Iowans and to the remarkable friendship that has blossomed between the two lands.

The friendship between Yamanashi and Iowa began in 1959 when Yamanashi suffered two devastating typhoons. Richard Thomas, an Iowan who had served in the US military in Japan after World War II, helped organize an Iowa Hog Lift that sent thirty-five pigs and 1,500 tons of corn to Yamanashi to help rebuild its shattered agricultural industry. That act of generosity laid the foundation for America's first sister-state relationship with Japan, a bond that continues to this day with frequent visits and exchanges.

The bell and bell house were sent to Iowa in 1962. The bell house was built in Japan and shipped to Iowa in boxes for assembly here. The bell, which weighs 2,000 pounds, is similar to those found in temples in Japan.

The story of the Iowa Hog Lift is told in the children's book **Sweet Corn and Sushi: The Story of Iowa and Yamanashi** by Lori Erickson.

attractions in the downtown. You can find the arena at 730 Third St. Call (515) 564-8000 or see iowaeventscenter.com for a listing of upcoming events.

Both kids and adults will love the **Science Center of Iowa**, a beautifully designed facility near the Des Moines riverfront on the south end of the downtown. Instead of exhibits, the center has six "experience platforms" that bring the wonders of science to vivid life, as well as an IMAX Dome Theater and a state-of-the-art "Cosmic Jukebox," which allows visitors to customize their own star shows. Throughout the facility, the focus is on self-guided exploration and the ties between science and our everyday lives.

Because science changes so rapidly, the center is not a static place. Its calendar includes more than sixty live programs ranging from "Kitchen Chemistry" to "Fire and Ice," an exploration of thermodynamics. In addition, its experience platforms will be changed on a rotating basis in the coming years, with the result that there will always be something new at the Science Center.

The Science Center of Iowa is open Thurs through Sun and is located at 401 W. Martin Luther King Jr. Pkwy. Admission is $15 for adults and children ages 2–12. For more information call (515) 274-6868 or see sciowa.org.

Des Moines is also drawing renewed energy from the revitalization of existing neighborhoods. A prime example is the **East Village**, a 6-block area that sits below the gold-domed Iowa Capitol, the center for state government. For decades the area had been in decline, until a flood of new investment flowed into the district to restore old buildings, build loft-style apartments, and install new street lighting. Its streets include an inviting array of stores, galleries, and restaurants.

Visitors to the East Village should begin with tours of its two best-known landmarks: the granite-and-glass **State Historical Museum** (515-281-5111; iowaculture.gov/history/museum) at 600 E. Locust St. is a treasure trove of exhibits that tell the story of the state, and the **Iowa State Capitol**, a showcase for nineteenth-century craftsmanship that is considered one of the nation's most beautiful capitol buildings. Completed in 1886, the building has a 23-carat golden dome and is filled with ornate mosaics, intricate wood carvings, and hand-painted murals. Admission to both attractions is free.

Just across the Des Moines River lies another revitalized area, the **Court District**. Each Saturday during the growing season, the neighborhood hosts the city's large farmers market, but at any time of year visitors enjoy its eclectic array of restaurants, clubs, and stores. Popular spots include **Court Avenue Restaurant and Brewing Company** (courtavebrew.com; 515-282-BREW) a microbrewery and eatery at 309 Court Ave., and **Spaghetti Works** (spagworks .com; 515-243-2195), a casual dining spot at 310 Court Ave. known for its Italian specialties. Both offer moderately priced meals.

The neighborhood also provides easy access to another major city project, the **Principal Riverwalk**. The route connects the east and west sides of Des Moines with walking paths and bridges and links to the many bike trails that fan out from the city. Be sure to visit the **Robert D. Ray Asian Gardens** on the east bank of the river, across from the Iowa Events Center. Named in honor of a former governor, their exquisite landscaping will make you think you've been transported to China.

Terrace Hill is the official residence of the Iowa governor and one of the finest examples of Second Empire–style architecture in the country. The home was constructed at a cost of $250,000 in the 1860s and was home to a couple of the city's most prominent citizens for many years. It was built for the state's first millionaire, B. F. Allen, who sold it to the F. M. Hubbell family, who donated

Fresh from the Farm

The **Des Moines Farmers Market** is one of the largest in the country. Covering 9 city blocks, it includes more than 300 farmers, bakers, artisans, and entrepreneurs. Don't miss it if you're in Des Moines on a Saturday morning from May through Oct.

it to the state in 1971. Since then more than $3 million has been spent on its renovation. Much of the effort has gone into refurbishing the home's main-floor rooms in their original Victorian splendor. The lower two floors are included in the tour open to the public, with the exception of one room on the second floor used as quarters for visiting families and dignitaries. The third floor houses the offices and family quarters of the governor. Terrace Hill is located at 2300 Grand Ave. It is open Mon through Sat, except during Jan and Feb. Call (515) 281-7205 or see terracehill.org for tour times.

Salisbury House is another Des Moines mansion that will bring you back in time—to Tudor England. The home at 4025 Tonawanda Dr. is modeled after a centuries-old Tudor dwelling in Salisbury, England, and features a great hall with beamed and raftered ceiling, rich tapestries, oriental rugs, stained-glass windows, and ornate wall paneling. It was built by a wealthy cosmetics manufacturer, Carl Weeks, who purchased many of the home's furnishings in England. He also amassed a 3,500-volume library that includes such treasures as a page from the Gutenberg Bible and a copy of the Kelmscot Chaucer produced by William Morris. For information call (515) 274-1777 or see salisbury house.org.

For a green retreat that's especially appreciated on a frosty winter day, stop by the **Greater Des Moines Botanical Garden** (909 Robert D. Ray Dr.). Its 80-foot geodesic dome is filled with lush tropical and semitropical plants as well as a variety of floral shows. Don't miss the bonsai collection, rated one of the ten best in the United States. Some of the plants have been in training for more than a hundred years! On pleasant days you can spend an enjoyable time wandering through its outdoor gardens as well. Its newest addition is the Ruan Reflection Garden, an ellipse-shaped installation that includes a reflection pool and fountain surrounded by thirty-four Japanese katsura trees and a hedge of American hornbeam. It's open Tues through Sun. Call (515) 323-6290 or see dmbotanicalgarden.com for information.

The **Blank Park Zoo** (blankparkzoo.com; 515-285-4722) has more than 800 animals from five continents in exhibits that simulate the animals' natural habitats. A highlight is the zoo's Discovery Center that features indoor habitats for bats, butterflies, snakes, and fish. Kids will especially enjoy the chance to feed parakeets and giraffes. The zoo is located at 7401 SW Ninth St. and is open daily, 10 a.m. to 4 p.m. Admission is $16 for adults; $10 for children.

The **Des Moines Art Center** (desmoinesartcenter.org; 515-277-4405) is a work of art in itself, with each of its three buildings designed by a world-renowned architect: Eliel Saarinen, I. M. Pei, and Richard Meier. Inside are works by luminaries who include Georgia O'Keeffe, Henri Matisse, and Edward

Hopper, as well as traveling exhibitions by contemporary artists. The center is at 4700 Grand Ave. and is open Tues through Sun.

Three miles east of the center, visit the **Pappajohn Sculpture Park**, a permanent installation of thirty-one works set on 4.4 acres of rolling green lawn in central Des Moines. The park is considered one of the top sculpture gardens in the nation, with works by more than two dozen internationally recognized artists. Favorites include Spanish artist Jaume Piensa's *Nomade*, a giant figure made of small steel letters painted white, and British sculptor Barry Flanagan's *Thinker on a Rock*, a large bronze rabbit immersed in contemplation. The park is open from sunrise to midnight and admission is free.

The best time to sample the artistic treasures of Iowa's capital city is during the **Des Moines Arts Festival** (desmoinesartsfestival.org; 515-286-4950). Each year more than 1,000 applicants from around the world compete for 180 spots, making this one of the most competitive art fairs in the nation. In addition to many forms of visual art, the three-day event includes live theater, dance, music performances, and interactive art activities. Booths line the streets surrounding the Pappajohn Sculpture Park along with two food courts. You can also enjoy screenings of dozens of films from around the world during the **Interrobang Film Festival**, which is held during the festival at the Des Moines Central Library.

Located in Union Park on the Des Moines River, the **Heritage Carousel** features thirty animals and two chariots that are accessible to wheelchairs. Note the handsome hand-painted local scenes as you ride. The fine wooden carousel runs on a variable schedule; call (515) 323-8200 or see heritagecarousel.org for more information.

For an afternoon of browsing, shopping, and munching, check out **Historic Valley Junction** in **West Des Moines**. The area was settled by coal miners and was once a bustling railroad center with a wild reputation, but as the importance of the railroad faded, so did the town's spirit. Then in the late

Art Route Des Moines

Think of this as a kind of yellow brick road of creativity that makes it easy to find art in Des Moines. The 6-mile route is marked by painted circles and chevrons on its sidewalks and intersections. Follow them to find nearly ninety pieces of public art, including the many colorful murals that line streets and alleyways in the city. Some highlight the history of a neighborhood, others make a political statement or amuse with their whimsy. All are a vibrant part of the Des Moines landscape. For information see dsmpublicartfoundation.org.

1960s, the area began to come to life again, as small-business owners (many of them antiques dealers) opened their doors in the area's historic old storefronts. Today Valley Junction is a popular shopping district filled with more than 150 businesses, which include upscale restaurants, fancy boutiques, antiques stores brimming with mismatched treasures, and specialty stores selling everything from lace to jewelry to kitchen tools. On Thurs evening mid-May through Sept, Valley Junction is also the site of a farmers market. For more information see valleyjunction.com or call (515) 222-3642.

The Valley Junction district is located on Fifth Street and the surrounding area in downtown West Des Moines. Take I-235 to the Sixty-third Street exit, and then go south and follow the Valley Junction signs.

One other stop, just west of Des Moines, is definitely worth a visit before you leave Polk County: *Living History Farms* in Urbandale. This is a 500-acre agricultural museum that tells the story of farming in the Midwest, from a 1700 Ioway Indian village to displays on twentieth-century farming. In between, several eras are highlighted, including an 1850 pioneer farm, an 1875 town, and a 1900 farm. The artifacts come to life through the efforts of interpreters dressed in historical clothing who re-create the daily routine of early Iowans. On each farm the buildings, planting methods, and livestock are authentic to the time periods represented, and visitors are invited to try their hand at old-time skills

Come to the Fair

As the inspiration for a novel (Iowan Phil Stong's **State Fair**), three motion pictures, and a Rodgers and Hammerstein Broadway musical, the **Iowa State Fair** is undoubtedly the nation's most celebrated fair. It is also the single largest event in the state, attracting more than 1 million people to Des Moines each August.

The eleven-day fair showcases Midwestern life at its most wholesome. Here you can see hundreds of buffed and groomed animals raised by 4-H kids, marvel at behemoth farm equipment, devour turkey legs big enough to feed a family of four, scream on a neck-snapping roller coaster, take in a superstar stage show, and try the latest gadgets hawked by fast-talking barkers.

The fair's most celebrated attraction is its butter cow created by sculptor-in-residence Sarah Pratt. Pratt uses about 550 pounds of butter to craft the animal, which is exhibited in a forty-degree cooler in the Agriculture Building. Each year she also creates an additional sculpture, which has ranged from Garth Brooks and Elvis to Grant Wood's **American Gothic** couple. Now that's fat put to a good use!

For more information on the annual extravaganza, call (800) 545-FAIR or visit iowastatefair.org.

like wool carding and apple-butter making. Tractor-drawn carts transport visitors between the five period sites on a regular schedule, and walking trails through native woodlands are also open between the sites.

Throughout the year special events and festivals are held at Living History Farms, from bobsled parties and hayrides to pioneer craft shows and early twentieth-century plowing exhibitions. On July 4 there's an old-fashioned Independence Day celebration, and during the fall there are several events centered on the harvest. Another popular attraction at Living History Farms is its historic dinner program, which runs during the winter months. Interpreters prepare and serve authentic meals based on recipes from each farm's era. Reservations are required.

To reach Living History Farms, take exit 125 (Hickman Road, US 6) off the combined I-35 and I-80. The farms are open Tues through Sat May through Oct from 9 a.m. to 4 p.m. Admission is $19 for adults and $12 for children. Call (515) 278-5286 for more information or visit lhf.org.

Every April, Des Moines hosts the **Drake Relays**, bringing together track competitors of all skill levels, from high school to professional, to compete with their peers. On a lighter note, Drake University, whose mascot happens to be a bulldog, hosts the **Beautiful Bulldog Contest** in which dozens of bulldogs compete for the title. But don't get your hopes up—it does not include a swimsuit competition. The contest serves as a kickoff to the relays and is held the third week in Apr; see godrakebulldogs.com for more information.

Finally, one more exciting Des Moines–based event needs to be mentioned: **RAGBRAI (Register's Annual Great Bicycle Ride Across Iowa)**. The seven-day bike ride is sponsored by the *Des Moines Register* newspaper and draws thousands of participants who toil up and down Iowa's hills at the end of each July. The event began in 1973 and was the first statewide bicycle ride in the country. A mixture of endurance test, parade, and party, RAGBRAI has become an Iowa tradition that's well-loved both by its participants and by the small towns that feed and shelter the riders as they pass through. For information visit ragbrai.com.

For more information about attractions in the Des Moines area, call the Greater Des Moines Convention and Visitors Bureau at (800) 451-2625 or visit catchdesmoines.com.

Northwest of Des Moines lies the small town of **Perry**. In its downtown, visit the **Carnegie Library Museum**, which serves as a hymn of praise to that most glorious of American institutions, the public library system. Located in the town's original Carnegie Library, a graceful stone building constructed in the Beaux Arts style in 1904, the museum celebrates libraries and their most

Iowa Bison

Bison once roamed across all of Iowa before becoming nearly extinct in the late-nineteenth century. Thankfully the species has staged a comeback thanks to the efforts of many individuals and public institutions. In Iowa you can see bison herds at the Broken Kettle Grassland Preserve north of Sioux City and the Neal Smith Wildlife Refuge near Des Moines, as well as on private farms.

Bison are the largest mammal in North America, with adult males tipping the scales at 2,000 pounds. Calves weigh 30 to 70 pounds at birth.

You can judge a bison's mood by its tail. When it hangs down, the bison is usually calm. But if it's standing straight up, watch out! It might be ready to charge. And no matter what position the tail is, exercise care around these animals, who can charge at any moment. Despite their size, they can run 35 mph and are extremely agile.

important American patron, Andrew Carnegie. Beginning in 1896, Carnegie (a Scottish immigrant who became the wealthiest industrialist in America) built nearly 1,700 libraries across the United States, ensuring that even the poorest citizens could be introduced to the world's literary riches.

Filled with light from large windows, the library museum is a cozy and inviting place, furnished as it was in its early years with a fireplace, oak desks, Windsor chairs, wooden book stacks, and cast-iron radiators. Its shelves include books and displays that tell the story of the important role libraries have played in the nation's history. Browsers can learn more about topics that include Midwestern authors, best sellers of the early nineteenth century, banned books, and the importance of libraries to immigrants. The displays show that throughout their history, public libraries have been both lending institutions and places that nurture community spirit—gathering spots where farm wives visited with town women, young men and women courted, and the issues of the day were debated.

You'll find the library museum at 1123 Willis Ave. It's open Tues through Sun, and admission is free. For more information call (515) 465-7713.

Just outside the library museum's doors lies the ***Hotel Pattee***, a jewel-like property luxuriously restored to its original Arts and Crafts style. The AAA Four Diamond Award property, which first opened in 1913, was completely restored in 1997.

Each of the hotel's forty guest rooms is meant to celebrate a different aspect of Iowa and the Midwest. Some are named after personages important to the town and state, while others, like the Dutch and Mexican rooms, pay tribute to Iowa's immigrant heritage. The hotel features more than 130 pieces of original art, most by Midwestern artists. Its restaurant, **Pattee Café**, features decor that re-creates a luxury train-dining experience from years past.

The Hotel Pattee is at 1112 Willis Ave. Rates are moderate to expensive. Call (515) 465-3511 or see hotelpattee.com for more information.

Perry visitors can relax in **Soumas Court**, an outdoor gathering place next to the Hotel Pattee. The shaded enclave is named after former mayor George Soumas, a son of Greek immigrants and World War II hero. A bronze statue of the well-loved town character sits at one of the tables, holding court over a coffee cup as he often did in life. The court is also the site of the "Wall of Witnesses," a tribute to Perry citizens such as Flora Bailey, the town's first librarian, and jazz musician Roy "Snake" Whyte.

Madison County Romance

Author Robert James Waller's decision to set his first novel in **Madison County**, Iowa, sparked a remarkable series of events that helped revitalize this primarily rural region. First the book landed on national best-seller lists, then Hollywood decided to turn the love story into a movie, and then, before the town quite knew what was happening, Clint Eastwood and Meryl Streep were exchanging passionate kisses on Roseman Bridge. Since then, **Winterset** has become a mecca for fans who travel from around the world to see the sites immortalized in the book and movie. This formerly sleepy town may never be the same, but few in Winterset are complaining.

The covered bridges of Madison County were a tourism attraction long before the book was written. Nineteen bridges were built in Madison County between 1855 and 1885, and they were covered to help preserve their large flooring timbers, which were more expensive to replace than the lumber used to cover the bridge sides and roof. Most were named after the resident who lived closest. Six of these covered bridges remain today, all of which are listed on the National Register of Historic Places. For many years the bridges have been the focus of the **Madison County Covered Bridge Festival**, held each year on the second full weekend in October, when bus tours to all the bridges are offered and the town square comes alive with food and craft booths, a car show, a parade, and other entertainment.

A visit to Winterset is enjoyable at any time of year, however—especially if you happen to be enamored of the story of Francesca and her photographer friend. Begin your tour with a visit to the **Madison County Welcome Center** (madisoncounty.com; 515-462-1185), which is located on the town square at 73 Jefferson St. There you can pick up brochures on the area's attractions as well as a map that lists the locations of all the bridges in the surrounding countryside.

The most famous of the bridges is perhaps the **Roseman Bridge**, where Francesca left a note inviting Robert to dinner. The bridge is located about 10 miles southwest of Winterset and spans a picturesque bend in the Middle River. Another lovely spot is the **Cedar Bridge**, which is located a few miles northwest of Winterset. In the novel, Cedar Bridge is where Francesca goes to observe Robert taking photographs.

A good place for a picnic is the **Cutler-Donahoe Covered Bridge** located in the Winterset City Park. This little park is also the site of Clark's Tower, a three-story limestone structure that serves as a pioneer memorial and offers outstanding views of the surrounding countryside.

Winterset has other attractions in addition to sites relating to the book and movie. Before Robert James Waller ever came to town, the **John Wayne Birthplace** put the town on the map. The famous actor was born here in a modest frame house on May 26, 1907. Back then he was called Marion Robert Morrison, son of a pharmacist who worked in a local drugstore. The Morrison family lived in the home until Marion (or John or the Duke) was three, when they moved to nearby Earlham in northern Madison County.

The **John Wayne Birthplace and Museum** celebrates both the Hollywood legend and the small-town boy. The $2.5 million building, which in 2015 replaced a much smaller facility, is a testimony to the enduring appeal of Wayne, who appeared in more than 175 movies in a career that spanned five decades. Two-thirds of its funding came in the form of small donations from fans around the world.

A visit to the museum begins, appropriately, with a movie, an eight-minute documentary with scenes from many of his movies, from *The Searchers* and *Stagecoach* to *Sands of Iwo Jima*. Exhibits describe his personal life and professional career and include an artifact that fills an entire corner of the room: a 1972 Pontiac station wagon, one of the last cars that Wayne owned. Because he was so tall, he had the roof raised so he could fit more comfortably in its driver's seat. Posters of his films line the walls and display cases showcase photographs, film scripts, props, and artifacts that include the eye patch he wore in *True Grit* and his hat from *Rio Bravo*.

After touring the museum, take a short walk to the four-room cottage where Wayne was born. Standing in the little house gives one an appreciation for the extraordinary life of the actor. From his small-town beginning, Wayne went on to become one of the most famous men in the world. The John Wayne Birthplace and Museum is at 205 S. Second St. It is open daily from 10 a.m. to 5 p.m. Admission is $20; $10 for children. Call (515) 462-1044 or see johnwayne birthplace.org for more information.

The *Iowa Quilt Museum* is located in a historic building on the town square in Winterset. It presents three or four exhibits a year of vintage, art and modern quilts. It is open 10 a.m. to 5 p.m., Mon through Sat, and noon to 4 p.m. on Sun (from Nov through Mar it closes at 4 p.m. Mon through Sat). Call (515) 462-5988 or see iowaquiltmuseum.org for more information.

At the *Madison County Historical Complex*, you can learn more about the local history of the area. This impressive 25-acre historical site contains a museum, an 1856 restored mansion, a log schoolhouse, a post office, a general store, an 1870 train depot, a blacksmith shop, a stone barn, and what is probably the only outhouse in the state of Iowa to be listed on the National Register of Historic Places (made of stone, the privy was at one time wallpapered and heated for the comfort of its users). Also on the property is the Zion Federated Church, an 1881 structure that was moved to the complex in 1988 through the support of local residents.

In the complex's museum you can view exhibits on local history that include vintage clothing, quilts, farm equipment, and Indian artifacts. In the basement is another treasure, a huge collection of fossils and minerals that the Smithsonian Institution offered to buy before it was donated to the museum.

The Madison County Historical Complex is located at 815 S. Second Ave. It is open May through Oct. Its hours are Mon through Sat from 11 a.m. to 4 p.m. and Sun from 1 to 5 p.m. A small admission is charged. Call (515) 462-2134 or see historyonthehill.org for more information.

West of Winterset in the small town of *Greenfield*, the *Hotel Greenfield* makes a good base for explorations in this part of Iowa. The hotel first opened its doors in 1920 but had declined into shabbiness before a multimillion-dollar restoration in 2011. Each of its twenty guest rooms is unique, with antique furnishings and modern amenities. The hotel (641-221-0034; visithotelgreenfield .com) is at 110 E. Iowa St. and prices are moderate.

Adjoining the hotel is another historic gem: the *Warren Cultural Center* (warrenculturalcenter.com), a turreted, three-story brick building dating from

1896. It now houses a restored opera house as well as an art gallery and *Ed & Eva's* (641-743-2566), a shop featuring Iowa-made arts and crafts.

From Greenfield, head southwest to *Corning*. History buffs will want to explore the *French Icarian Village* that sits on a windswept patch of prairie 3 miles east of town. The Icarian Community was the longest-lived, non-religious communal society in the United States. The sect—which was particularly known for its commitment to education and the arts—lived in the area from 1852 to 1898. The site's white clapboard schoolhouse and refectory host interpretive programs and historical reenactments. For information call (515) 321-9743 or see icaria.net.

The Icarian commitment to the arts is carried on today in the *Corning Center for the Fine Arts*. Located in a former hardware store in downtown Corning, it showcases the work of emerging and established artists. One of its most innovative programs is an artist residency. The current artist-in-residence can often be found concentrating on his or her work in a studio in the back of the store. The center (641-322-4549; corningfinearts.com) is at 706 Davis Ave. and is open Mon through Sat.

Corning is also home to the *Johnny Carson Birthplace*. The famed comedian was born in this modest home on a quiet Corning street in 1925. A video of his life includes a charming clip from a *Tonight Show* episode during

Freedom Rocks

In 1999 the seed of an idea for *Freedom Rocks* was developed by Bubba Sorensen, an art and design major at Iowa State University, after watching the movie *Saving Private Ryan*. The World War II tale of heroism and tragedy inspired Sorensen to honor veterans in a unique way. Near his home in southwest Iowa there was a large boulder covered with graffiti. Sorensen decided he would paint the uneven stone with a patriotic mural to honor veterans.

The community was moved by this gesture and named the decorated boulder The Freedom Rock. This single boulder drew so much attention that Sorensen was asked to create more murals in other locations.

Sorensen does a variety of projects in honor of veterans, but his murals on rocks have become his signature throughout Iowa. He has painted a Freedom Rock in all of Iowa's ninety-nine counties. Sorensen paints scenes from the nation's wars, from historic to current conflicts, featuring veterans who were killed in combat from the local area.

If you want to see the original Freedom Rock go to IA 25 near Menlo, 1 mile south of exit 86 on I-80. For a complete list of locations, see thefreedomrock.com.

which Carson called the 83-year-old woman who had been his babysitter in Corning. The birthplace (641-322-3212; johnnycarsonbirthplace.org) is at 500 Thirteenth St. and is open by appointment.

Another Iowa treasure can be found near **Orient** (just south of Greenfield). The **Henry A. Wallace Country Life Center** celebrates the philosophies and achievements of Wallace, who served as US Secretary of Agriculture and Vice President in the FDR administration. Visitors can tour the house where he was born in 1888 and then explore the ways the 40-acre property implements his ideals. The **Gathering Table Restaurant** (reservations required) builds its menus around the organic produce raised on the center's 4-acre garden and orchard, and people can also walk through its restored prairie. The center hosts programs on civility and sustainable agriculture, holds culinary and gardening classes, and maintains a Community Supported Agriculture (CSA) garden. The center (641-337-5019; wallace.org) is at 2773 290th St.

From Winterset travel east on IA 92 to **Indianola**, home of Simpson College and the site each summer of the **National Balloon Classic**. The event is one of the most visually spectacular festivals in the country. Each August more than one hundred pilots from around the country bring their magnificent balloons to Indianola to compete for cash and prizes. Throughout the festival the skies of Indianola are filled with brilliantly colored balloons, attracting thousands of visitors who crane their necks for hours on end to view the serene craft. Balloon flights are scheduled morning and evening (weather permitting), and during the day special demonstrations and competitions are held. After dark there's a Nite-Glo Extravaganza, when the bursts of flames that power the balloons light up the colored fabrics above them, creating vivid patterns against the night sky. During the Mass Ascension, nearly all the balloons rise at once, providing another picture-perfect opportunity. Paid balloon rides are offered each morning and evening, weather permitting.

Visitors bring their own lawn chairs to Memorial Balloon Field, where they can also enjoy live music, food vendors, and three nights of fireworks. Other events include a National Balloon Classic Sky Parade, when balloons fly over the Indianola city square, and a Summer Arts Festival at Simpson College. For information call (515) 961-8415 or see nationalballoon classic.com.

If you can't make it to Indianola for the balloon classic, you can still visit its **National Balloon Museum**. The architecture of the structure is a reason to visit in itself. The motif suggests two inverted balloons, which are approached through entrance arches that accentuate the feeling of entering a balloon. The exterior is trimmed with blue and yellow ceramic tiles that recall the color, serenity, and gracefulness of balloons.

Inside you'll be able to view exhibits that chronicle more than 200 years of ballooning history. On display are balloon envelopes, inflators, gondolas, and other equipment used in both hot-air ballooning and gas ballooning. Other items include memorabilia associated with scientific, competitive, and record-setting flights, including trophies, photos, and an extensive pin collection. The gift shop is fun to browse through as well, with its displays of posters, calendars, mobiles, and mementos relating to ballooning.

The National Balloon Museum is on the north side of town at 1601 N. Jefferson Way. It is open Wed through Sun except during January and February. A small admission is charged. Call (515) 961-3714 for more information or see nationalballoonmuseum.com.

Balloons aren't the only reason to travel to Indianola during the summer. Another attraction is the **Des Moines Metro Opera**, one of the top twenty summer opera companies in the world. Each season it presents three operas at the Blank Performing Arts Center on the Simpson College campus in Indianola. The singers are drawn from the ranks of the country's top young performers and present both classic and contemporary operas. Since its founding in 1973, the Metro Opera has attracted national and international attention for the quality of its performances. Iowans are fortunate to have such a premier cultural resource in their midst. For more information call (515) 961-6221 or see desmoinesmetroopera.org.

Iowa's growing wine industry is on display at the **Summerset Winery** at 15101 Fairfax St. in Indianola. Owner Ron Mark discovered a love for wine-making while growing up on a farm near Rising Sun, Iowa. As a young adult, four years in Italy deepened his interest in the process. Though Mark later pursued a career as an electronics technician, his dream of becoming a vintner didn't fade. In 1989 he and his family moved to a hilltop near Indianola and Mark began planting grapevines. In 1997 the Marks opened their winery.

Today the Summerset Winery grows more than 12 acres of grapes. Additional grapes are purchased from more than a dozen other Iowa vineyards. Its winery building includes wine-processing equipment, an underground wine cellar, a tasting room, and two large rooms for meetings and banquets. Special events, including live music, are offered throughout the year.

For more information call (515) 961-3545 or see summersetwine.com.

Ethnic Enclaves

Begin your tour of this region of Iowa with a visit to **Pella**, a pristine small town that looks as if it could be the set for a Walt Disney movie. The name Pella means "city of refuge," for it was here that a small band of Hollanders came in 1847 to found a new city based on freedom. Today that Dutch heritage is visible throughout Pella, especially in the downtown, with its European-style architecture, a large windmill in the city square, lovely flower beds, and the Klokkenspel, a musical clock with figures that perform five times daily. The gift shops around the square stock imported Dutch treasures, and at Jaarsma's and Vander Ploeg Bakeries, you can buy ethnic specialties that include the ever-popular Dutch letters—puff pastry baked in the shape of an S with an almond-paste filling.

The Molengracht Plaza (molengracht.com), located a half block south-east of the city square at Main and Liberty Streets, re-creates the canals that are found throughout Holland. A canal appears to emerge from under the street and then winds through the length of Molengracht Plaza. Shops and restaurants (all with exteriors that resemble eighteenth-century Dutch storefronts) line the Molengracht's bricked pedestrian walkways, making this a lovely place to stroll.

The Molengracht is also home to *The Amsterdam Hotel* (royalamsterdam .com; 641-620-8400), a European-style boutique hotel with thirty-eight rooms and suites. Its *Liberty Street Kitchen* serves upscale comfort cuisine. You'll find the hotel at 701 E. First St.

The best time to sample Pella's Dutch heritage is during its annual *Tulip Time Festival* held on the first weekend in May. Each spring the town comes to life with hundreds of thousands of tulips, and local residents dress in color-ful ethnic costumes as they host thousands of visitors from across the state. Highlights of the festival include folk dancing and crafts, parades, ethnic foods, and the crowning of the Tulip Queen. Another good time to visit is during the Christmas season, when Sinterklaas comes to help the town celebrate the season with traditions stretching back a hundred years.

The *Pella Historical Village* (507 Franklin St.) will give you the chance to learn more about the history that has shaped this town. It contains twenty-one buildings, some more than a century old, and an authentic grain-grinding windmill. Here you can see items that the early settlers brought from Holland, an outstanding collection of delft pottery, folk costumes, Dutch dolls, Hindeloopen folk art painting, and a miniature Dutch village. The buildings include a log cabin, blacksmith shop, gristmill, potter shop, store, and church, as well as the boyhood home of gunslinger Wyatt Earp. Another historic site in town

didyouknow?

Wyatt Earp, the famous gun-slinging marshal, grew up as an ordinary Pella boy. He and his family came to the town in 1850 when Earp was two years old. At the age of fifteen, he ran away to join the army—and was promptly sent back home to Pella by his father, an army officer.

is the Scholte House on the north side of the town square, former home of Dominie H. P. Scholte, the leader of the group of immigrants who founded Pella.

The historical village includes a full-size, functioning 1850 Dutch grain windmill. The mill has been laboriously reconstructed and houses a welcome and interpretive center where visitors can ride an elevator up four stories to the windmill's outdoor stage.

The Pella Historical Village is located 1 block east of the town square. It is open Mon through Sat, Mar through Dec. Admission is $10 for adults and $2 for children. Call (641) 620-9463 for more information or visit pellahistorical.org.

Southeast of Pella near the town of Leighton is one of Iowa's largest wineries, **Tassel Ridge Winery and Vineyards** (1681 220th St.; tasselridge.com). Founded in 2006, it specializes in wines made from northern grapes that are adapted to Iowa's cold winters and short growing season. Visit its scenic vineyard for tastings, tours, and special events that include wood-fired-oven pizza nights.

West of Tassel Ridge lies the town of **Knoxville**, which calls itself the Sprint Car Racing Capital of the World. Drivers have been racing at Knoxville

The Magic Is in the Dirt

The secret to Knoxville's status as sprint-car heaven lies in the sticky, tacky clay that lines its raceway. Cars get great traction on it, which makes for faster and more exciting races.

Racing has been part of Knoxville life since the early twentieth century, but it wasn't until 1954 that the sport began to take off. In that year the Marion County Fair board began holding weekly races.

Within a few years sprint-car racing dominated the Knoxville scene. The lightweight, open-wheeled vehicles have a single seat directly behind the engine. In 1958 large "wings" began to be added to the tops of cars, an innovation that forces air pressure downward, creating better traction and improving safety if the car rolls.

As their name implies, sprint cars are designed for short bursts of speed. At just 1,200 pounds and packing more than 700 horsepower, the cars have one of the highest power-to-weight ratios of any motor sport. Each race is between twenty and thirty laps and is as short as seven minutes.

Knoxville vibrates with racing action for approximately thirty-five nights from mid-April to mid-September, with 5,000 spectators filling the stands each evening. While many are from the surrounding area, drivers and spectators also flock to Knoxville from around the nation and the world, particularly during the Knoxville Nationals held in early August.

for nearly a century on a dirt track that is rated as one of the fastest in the nation.

In honor of its racing status, Knoxville has built the **National Sprint Car Hall of Fame and Museum** at the Marion County Fairgrounds off IA 14 at 1 Sprint Capital Place. The facility includes tributes to famous drivers, restored sprint cars, a gift shop, and booths for race viewing. The museum (641-842-6176; sprintcarhof.com) is open daily; a small admission is charged.

Southwest of Knoxville at the junction of US 34 and US 65 lies the town of **Lucas**, home to the **John L. Lewis Mining and Labor Museum**. The museum pays tribute to one of the most famous union leaders in America. Lewis was born in Lucas in 1880 and worked in the local coal mines before eventually becoming president of the United Mine Workers for forty years. The museum houses exhibits about his life, mining, and labor history.

The Lewis Museum (641-766-6831; coalmininglabormuseum.com) is located 2 blocks north of US 34 at 102 Division St. It is open Mon through Sat 9 a.m. to 3 p.m., mid-Apr through mid-Oct. A small admission is charged.

Just south of Lucas lies the major portion of the **Stephens State Forest**, one of the largest tracts of forest land in the state. The forest provides visitors with miles of trails that wind through deeply wooded country, as well as four stocked ponds and numerous campgrounds, three of which are set aside for equestrians.

Two other local park areas deserve mentioning. One is the **Pin Oak Marsh** (located on IA 14 south of Chariton), a 160-acre wetland where nature lovers can spot a variety of wildlife, like muskrat, mink, river otter, beaver, songbirds, shorebirds, and—during spring and fall migrations—ducks and geese. Bring your binoculars! Another favorite is the **Red Haw State Park**, known for its abundance of redbud trees. Visit in April to see it at its most beautiful. This 649-acre park is located just 1 mile east of Chariton.

While you're in the area, visit **Chariton**. Take the time to observe the clock in the clock tower of the **Lucas County Court House** (916 Braden Ave.), a lovely sandstone-faced Romanesque-style building. It was purchased— the clock, that is—at the 1893 Chicago World's Fair. When the people of Lucas County go out to shop for souvenirs, they mean business! The sidewalk surrounding the courthouse reinforces the time theme. In other words, look down as well as up if you want to know the time of day.

While you're on the town square, be sure to pay a visit to **Piper's Candy**. Piper's has been a landmark in Chariton since 1903. For many years it operated as a grocery store, but beginning in 1947 it also began selling handmade candy. Today the store is famous for its fudge, caramels, and toffee, which it ships around the country. Piper's is located at 901 Braden Ave., on the northeast

warning: buggycrossing

Lucas County is the home of a growing Amish community. Watch for horse-drawn vehicles!

corner of the town square. For more information call (641) 774-2131 or see piperscandy.com.

Burn off those calories by taking a hike or a bike ride down the **Cinder Path**, the first Rails-to-Trails location in the state (the railroad bed was converted to a trail in 1974). The grade is even, and the smooth cinder surface makes it easy to enjoy the 14 miles winding from the west edge of Chariton southwest to Humeston.

Your next stop in south-central Iowa should be **Lamoni**, home of the **Liberty Hall Historic Site**, an eighteen-room Victorian house that was home to the Joseph Smith III family from 1881 to 1906. Joseph was the oldest son of the founder of the Mormon Church and the first president of the Reorganized Church of Jesus Christ of Latter Day Saints (now known as the Community of Christ). His father, Joseph Smith Jr., was assassinated in 1844, and in the years that followed, the church divided into two main groups. One group followed Brigham Young to Utah; the other formed the Reorganized Church and named Joseph Smith III its leader. In the 1880s Smith and his followers established Lamoni as their headquarters, and Smith's home became the busy center of the new church. Though the church later moved its headquarters to Indepen-

newdealmurals

During the Depression, the Works Progress Administration com-missioned artists to paint murals across the state. You can see these WPA murals in towns that include:

Des Moines: Callanan Junior High and the Public Library

Pella: Post Office

Knoxville: Post Office

Corydon: Post Office

Osceola: Post Office

Leon: Post Office

Mount Ayr: Post Office

dence, Missouri, Liberty Hall has been restored to its original decor and today tells the story of the Smith family and the Reorganized Church. Many of the items inside are the Smiths' original furnish-ings. Don't miss the fold-down bathtub! Also on the property is a schoolhouse built in 1875, plus a museum shop sell-ing Victorian gifts.

The Liberty Hall Historic Site is at 1138 W. Main St. Admission is free, and hours are Tues through Sat from 10 a.m. to 4 p.m. Call (674) 784-6133 for more information.

The last stop to make in this region is **Creston**, west of Afton on US 34. Creston was founded in 1868 as a rail-road town and is the county seat of

Union County. Don't miss the *C. B. & Q. Railroad Depot* located between Union and Adams Streets. Inside, you can almost hear old steam engines chugging into town and whistles screeching in the distance. It is open weekdays; call (641) 782-7021 for information.

Equally charming is the *Frank Phillips Visitors Center* at 636 New York Ave. Housed in a 1931 Phillips 66 gasoline station, it not only serves as a tourism center but also commemorates Frank Phillips, an erstwhile Creston resident and barber who, with his brother, founded the Phillips Petroleum Corporation in 1917. This is a great place to stop, gather your bearings, and plan your next stops. The visitor center (641) 782-7021 is open from late May through early Oct.

Places to Stay in Bridge Country

ALLERTON

Inn of the Six-toed Cat
200 N. Central Ave.
(641) 873-4900
6toedcat.com
inexpensive to moderate

DES MOINES

Butler House on Grand
4507 Grand Ave.
(515) 991-1780
butlerhouseongrand.com
moderate to expensive

EARLHAM

Shady Brook's Floating Bed Tents
36026 Jewel Court
(515) 238-1998
shadybrookcampinghunting
.com
inexpensive

GRINNELL

Marsh House Bed & Breakfast
833 East St.
(641) 236-0132
moderate

INDIANOLA

The Corn Crib B&B
1301 S. K St.
(515) 961-3152
stayatthecorncrib.com
moderate

PELLA

The Dwelling Place Bed & Breakfast

935 Main St.
(641) 660-4962
dwellingplacepella.com
Inexpensive to moderate

WINTERSET

Judge Lewis House
1145 W. Summit St.
(515) 344-8027
judgelewishouse.com
Inexpensive to moderate

Places to Eat in Bridge Country

CLIVE

Cosi Cucina Italian Grill
1975 NW Eighty-sixth St.
(515) 278-8148
cosicucina.com
moderate

DES MOINES

Centro
1003 Locust St.
(515) 248-1780
centrodesmoines.com
moderate

Iowa Tap Room
215 E. Third St.
(515) 243-0827
iowataproom.com
inexpensive

The Royal Mile
210 Fourth St.
(515) 282-2012
royalmilebar.com
inexpensive

Splash Seafood Bar & Grill
303 Locust St.
(515) 244-5686
splash-seafood.com
moderate to expensive

KNOXVILLE

Baggio's Italian Restaurant
124 S. Second St.
(641) 205-8265
Inexpensive to moderate

NEWTON

Uncle Nancy's Coffeehouse & Eatery
114 N. Second Ave. W
(641) 787-9709
inexpensive

PELLA

Windmill Cafe
709 Franklin St.
(641) 621-1800
windmillcafepella.business
.site
inexpensive

WINTERSET

Mi Pueblito
103 N. First St.
(515) 462-1640
inexpensive

Fertile Plains

The rich soil of north central Iowa produces some of the nation's most bountiful harvests, on land that was once tall-grass prairie. In this region you'll find the fascinating railroad history of Boone County, the beauty of Clear Lake, and a host of other treasures that celebrate Iowa's rich past and vibrant present. From the Meskwaki Pow Wow to the Surf Ballroom where the memory of Buddy Holly is celebrated, north central Iowa offers an eclectic range of attractions.

Diverse Diversions

Begin your tour of this region of Iowa with a visit to the only Native American settlement in the state. The word *settlement* (rather than *reservation*) is important, because the land here was purchased by the Meskwaki, not set aside for them by the federal government. Using money from the sale of furs and ponies, the Meskwaki (also known as the Sac and Fox Tribe) first bought 80 acres of land near what is now the town of Tama in 1857. In the following years more land was purchased with tribal funds, and today the Meskwaki own more than 8,000 acres in Tama County.

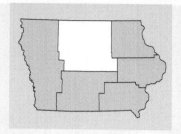

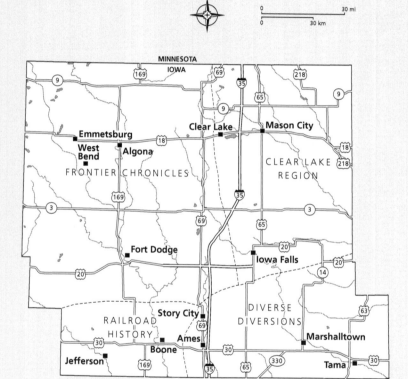

The best time to visit the settlement is during the ***Meskwaki Pow Wow***, which is held each year on the second weekend in August. This four-day celebration honors the traditional ways of the Meskwaki people, with various arts, crafts, and exhibits on display, plus old-time foods and costumed dancing. The Pow Wow has its origin in the Green Corn Dance, a religious and social event that was held each year at harvest time. The fresh corn was cooked for feasting, and the bounty of the land was celebrated with dancing, games, and socializing. Around the beginning of the twentieth century, more and more white visitors began attending the ceremonies, and in 1913 the festival gained its official name of the Meskwaki Pow Wow.

The traditions of the Pow Wow remain strong. The center of the festival is dancing, with members from the local tribe (and often guests from other parts of the country) performing dances that have been handed down for generations. The Buffalo Head Dance, for example, honors the magnificent beast that has played a central role in Native American culture and life, and the Swan Dance mimics the beautiful, rhythmical movements of a swan in the water. For the Traditional Women's Dance, the Meskwaki women don elaborately decorated dresses. The Pipe Dance is presented to honor distinguished visitors and warriors, and the Harvest Bean Dance is performed by young girls and boys to thank the Great Spirit for the abundance of food for the coming winter.

The Meskwaki Pow Wow is held each August at the settlement 4 miles west of the town of Tama. For more information call (641) 484-4678 or see meskwakipowwow.com.

At any time of the year you can visit the ***Meskwaki Cultural Center and Museum*** (meskwaki.org; 641-484-3185) at 303 Meskwaki Rd. Exhibits explore the rich culture and heritage of the tribe. In addition to displays of clothing, jewelry, pottery, photographs, and other items, the museum offers workshops, tours, and presentations. It's open weekdays from 8:30 a.m. to 4 p.m.

AUTHOR'S FAVORITES

Big Treehouse	Grotto of the Redemption
Reiman Gardens	Union Slough National Wildlife Refuge
Surf Ballroom	Historic Park Inn
Boone & Scenic Valley Railroad	All Iowa Lawn Tennis Club
Matchstick Marvels	

Traveling the Lincoln Highway

If you are traveling across the state, consider following the route of the first transcontinental highway, the **Lincoln Highway**. Funded by private industry and wealthy entrepreneurs, the Lincoln Highway spanned the country from Times Square to San Francisco, crossing twelve states and leading right through the heart of Iowa, from Clinton to Council Bluffs. The original idea for this Coast to Coast Rock Highway, as it was originally called, belonged to Carl Fisher, "an enthusiastic motorist," and the founder of the Indianapolis Speedway. Begun in 1913, the route has had many changes through the course of the years but what remains of it now roughly follows US 30. In this section of the state, you can drive from Tama in the east to Ogden in the west. Be on the lookout for old gas stations, cafes, bridges, and buildings. The Lincoln Highway originally passed through forty-nine towns; in forty-four of them, it went right down Main Street. For more information on the Iowa portion of the Lincoln Highway, visit iowalincolnhighway.com.

You can learn more about the Meskwaki and the history of the area at the *Tama County Historical Museum*, 200 N. Broadway, Toledo. The museum is open from 1 to 4:30 p.m. Tues through Sat. The building was built in 1869 and served as the county jail until 1970. Today it houses pioneer tools and utensils, antique toys, musical instruments, furniture, and clothing, plus a display of Meskwaki artifacts. Call (641) 484-6767 or see tamacountyhistory.org for more information.

And while you're in the area, drive to the neighboring town of Tama to see the *Lincoln Highway Bridge* on East Fifth Street near US 30. The bridge was built in 1915 to promote Tama as an oasis along the new transcontinental route of the Lincoln Highway (at that time, most of the highway was dirt). The bridge has a decorative railing that spells "Lincoln Highway" and is listed on the National Register of Historic Places. This is one of just a few remaining Lincoln Highway Bridges. The roadside park next to the bridge makes this a pleasant stop.

Next head west to *Marshalltown*, home to several attractions that will please active travelers. The *Marshalltown Aquatic Center* (641-754-5715; marshalltown-ia.gov) at 212 Washington St. features three waterslides, a lazy river, water basketball, and water toys, making this a perfect place to spend a hot summer day.

The *Grimes Farm and Conservation Center* owes its existence to Leonard and Mildred Grimes, who purchased the land in 1964. Over the years they have worked diligently to transform neglected acreage into a productive and beautiful farm that has woodlands, prairie, and wetlands as well as agricultural areas. The Grimeses have established waterways, constructed terraces, and significantly reduced soil erosion by planting grasses and using no-till agricultural practices. They have also donated a significant portion of their land to the Iowa Natural Heritage Foundation, ensuring that future generations will learn about responsible land stewardship.

During your visit to Grimes Farm, you can walk hiking trails and see educational displays in its conservation center. Guided interpretive programs are offered frequently. The conservation center is at 2359 233rd St. It is open Mon through Fri from 8:30 a.m. to 3 p.m. For more information call (641) 752-5490.

The **Big Treehouse** is guaranteed to captivate anyone who remembers the joy of perching in a tree as a child. Few of us had access to a tree house like this, however; this six-story structure has electricity, running water, piped-in music, and a spiral stairway from top to bottom. You'll find the Big Treehouse at 2370 Shady Oaks Rd. Call (641) 752-2946 or see bigtreehouse.net to schedule an appointment. A small donation is requested.

Marshalltown is also home to the **Iowa Funeral Museum**, which provides a fascinating window into death customs through the ages. Marty Mitchell, owner of the town's Mitchell Funeral Home, has been a collector of funeral artifacts for more than three decades. In 2017 he opened the Iowa Funeral Museum in a former convenience store adjacent to his funeral home. With more than 5,000 artifacts, it's one of only a handful of funeral museums in the United States. Tour its exhibits to learn about Victorian Era funerals, how embalming became popular during the Civil War so that bodies of soldiers could be returned home to their families, and the evolution of casket designs through the years. Other displays describe Egyptian burial practices and the 1963 funeral of John F. Kennedy. Despite its subject matter, the Iowa Funeral Home Museum isn't a depressing destination: Instead it's a powerful reminder that death touches all of our lives and that humans have dealt with this universal mystery in diverse ways. The Iowa Funeral Museum (641-844-1234; mitchellfh.com) is at 1209 Iowa Ave. W. Free tours are given by appointment.

Northeast of Marshalltown in the small town of **Gladbrook**, be sure to visit **Matchstick Marvels**. Here you can see how master craftsman Patrick Acton is able to turn ordinary kitchen matchsticks into incredible works of art. Ripley's Believe It Or Not! calls Patrick Acton "the best matchstick model maker in North America." Millions of matchsticks and gallons of glue have gone into the creation of the models on display, which include the battleship USS *Iowa*, the space shuttle *Challenger*, and the US Capitol. Don't miss Acton's model of the French cathedral of Chartres, which took two years and 174,000 matchsticks

TOP ANNUAL EVENTS

FEBRUARY

Winter Dance Party
Clear Lake, early Feb
(641) 357-6151
surfballroom.com

MARCH

St. Patrick's Day Celebration
Emmetsburg
(712) 852-4326
emmetsburgirishgifts.com

MAY

North Iowa Band Festival
Mason City, Memorial Day weekend
(641) 423-5724
masoncityia.com

JUNE

Scandinavian Days
Story City, early June
(515) 733-4214
storycitygcc.org

JULY

Floyd County Fair
Charles City, third week in July
(641) 228-1300
floydcountyfair.org

AUGUST

Pufferbilly Days
Boone, first weekend in Aug
(515) 432-3342
booneiowa.us

SEPTEMBER

Octagon Arts Festival
Ames, third weekend in Sept
(515) 232-5331
octagonarts.org

to construct. The model contains 136 hand-carved statues, ornate towers and spires measuring nearly 5 feet tall, and internal lighting.

Originally the collection was a traveling exhibit that appeared at art festivals, woodworking shows, and community festivals. It has now found a home in Gladbrook at 319 Second St. Matchstick Marvels (641-473-2410) is open daily from Apr through Nov, from 1 to 5 p.m. Admission is $5. See matchstickmarvels.com for more information.

South of Marshalltown in the small town of **Haverhill**, you'll find the **Edel Blacksmith Shop** (iowaculture.gov; 641-752-6664) at 214 First St. The shop was operated by German immigrant Matthew Edel between 1882 and 1940 and provides a vivid picture of the days before mechanized farming changed agriculture. Here Edel shoed horses, repaired tools and wagons, and manufactured implements like garden hoes and wedge makers. Edel was also an inventor who took out patents on such inventions as a perfection wedge cutter and cattle dehorner. Adjacent to the blacksmith shop is a two-story house constructed in the early 1880s, plus a summer kitchen where food was prepared during the warm months. Like the shop itself, they have been left largely unaltered and help complete the picture of what the life of a skilled craftsman was like some hundred years ago.

The Edel Blacksmith Shop (which is owned by the State Historical Society of Iowa) is open daily from noon to 4 p.m., Memorial Day through Labor Day.

Northwest of Haverhill lies the town of **State Center**, which prides itself on being the Rose Capital of Iowa. During the summer the town maintains a lovely rose garden at Third Avenue Southeast and Third Street Southeast, and each year on the third weekend in June, State Center hosts a **Rose Festival**.

Northwest of State Center, near I-35, lies the town of **Story City**, which is home to the only municipally owned carousel in the state. Built in 1913, the **Story City Carousel** first came to the town when its Iowa Falls owner agreed to let Story City use it for its Fourth of July celebrations. In 1938 the town purchased the merry-go-round, which was run each summer until 1979 when it became too dilapidated to use.

Instead of abandoning the carousel, however, the town decided to save it, raising the $140,000 needed to refurbish and repair it. A local antiques store and refinishing business took on the laborious task, and in 1982 the gleaming, revitalized machine was once again offering rides in its new home, a pavilion located in the town's North Park.

The merry-go-round is located in North Park at 700 Grove Ave. It is open Wed through Sun from Memorial Day through Aug and weekends in Sept. For more information call (515) 733-4214.

After you ride the carousel, stop by South Park for a pleasant walk across the swinging bridge. The bridge was constructed in the early 1930s under President Franklin Roosevelt's Works Progress Administration (WPA) program, and the park is a delightful place for a picnic lunch.

Also in Story City is the **Factory Stores of America Outlet Center**, where you can find discounts on brand-name merchandise. The mall is located off I-35 at exit 124.

From Story City travel south on US 69 until you reach **Ames**, home to **Iowa State University**. ISU is one of the oldest land-grant institutions in the country and is an international leader in agricultural studies. More than 30,000 students are enrolled here in a wide variety of undergraduate and graduate programs. The campus itself is lovely and full of green areas, with historical markers scattered throughout so that visitors can take their own self-guided tours (ask for a map at the Memorial Union, 2229 Lincoln Way, on the south side of the campus). On your tour, stop by the library to see its large Grant Wood murals, and notice the sculptures by artist Christian Petersen that are located throughout the campus.

A major attraction on the Iowa State campus are the **Reiman Gardens**, 1407 University Blvd. This horticulture display area covers 17 acres south of Cyclone Stadium on Elwood Drive and includes eleven distinct gardens, including an herb garden, rose garden, wetlands garden, and campanile garden.

didyouknow?

Iowa State University has one of the largest public art programs in the United States. More than 2,500 works of art can be seen in public spaces across campus.

The gardens are a beautiful place to stroll, and garden tours are also offered. Don't miss the Christina Reiman Butterfly Wing, a beautiful structure that is designed to look like a butterfly in flight. The 2,500-square-foot wing houses a year-round tropical garden filled with exotic and native butterflies from six continents. The gardens' newest addition is Sycamore Falls, a 3-acre area with a custom-built tower, bubbling stream, reflecting pool, and waterfalls that tumble over native limestone walls.

The Reiman Gardens and Butterfly Wing are open daily from 9 a.m. to 4:30 p.m. Admission is $12 for adults, $11 for seniors, and $6 for children. For more information on this beautiful site, call (515) 294-2710 or visit reimangardens.com.

Two other sites should be part of your ISU tour. The **Brunnier Art Museum** in the Scheman Building features a fine collection of decorative arts as well as traveling exhibitions. Also worth a visit is the **Farm House Museum**, the oldest building on campus and a fully restored National Historic Landmark that is furnished to reflect the 1860–1910 period. Located on Knoll Road, the museum is open noon to 4 p.m. Mon through Fri. For more information on Iowa State University and its attractions and events, call (515) 294-4111 or see iastate.edu.

Before you leave Ames, take some time to explore the rest of the city. Downtown Ames has a variety of specialty shops, including the **Octagon Center for the Arts** (octagonarts.org; 515-232-5331), which features rotating exhibits, art classes, and a retail outlet. It's located at 427 Douglas Ave. Campustown, an area within walking distance of the university, also has shops and restaurants.

No visit to Ames would be complete without a stop at **Hickory Park Restaurant**, which serves succulent and tender barbecued meats, the kind that fall off the bone with a nudge and melt with a tang in your mouth. Its specialty is huge slabs of pork ribs, but its smoked chicken and beef ribs also have devoted followings. For dessert try one of Hickory Park's sinfully rich ice-cream treats. Regulars agree that a chocolate mint marvel sundae is the perfect ending to a meal of barbecued ribs.

Farmers Market Bounty

Each spring, my husband and I have the same argument. As he's calculating how many seeds and sets he can squeeze into our garden plot, I'm urging him to plant more flowers—not because of my reluctance to deal with a bountiful harvest, but because I know that come summer, I'd rather be strolling through our local farmers market instead of picking our own vegetables.

It's not the work involved, mind you. It's just that we can eat only so many cucumbers, and how can I not buy from the kindly old farmer who always tells me about the latest doings of his grandchildren? And every ripe tomato we grow ourselves is one less I can purchase from the gentle Mennonite family with daughters so shy they never make eye contact. The market, with its overflowing bushels of brilliantly colored apples, peppers, and carrots, its shocks of Indian corn, bouquets of broccoli, gleaming jars of homemade jams, and succulent ears of sweet corn, is a sensory feast that lures me out of the house each Saturday morning from June through October.

A farmers market is a primer in human relations as well as a place to buy food. Amish women in bonnets sell produce next to Vietnamese immigrants who offer piping-hot egg rolls; overalled farmers in seed-corn caps set up their tables next to long-haired twenty-somethings selling organic garlic; and matronly farm women offer advice on life, in addition to delicious fruit pies.

The rich soil of Iowa nurtures more than a hundred farmers markets. You'll find major ones in Ames, Cedar Rapids, Des Moines, and Iowa City, but nearly every small town in the state has a farmers market during the growing season (typically they're held on Saturday mornings, but often at additional times as well). There's no better place to sample the tastes of Iowa.

Hickory Park Restaurant is located at 1404 South Duff Ave. Lunches are inexpensive; dinners are inexpensive to moderate. Hickory Park is open daily from 10:30 a.m. to 9 p.m. Call (515) 232-8940 or see hickoryparkames.com for more information.

For another memorable dining experience, try the *Cafe Beaudelaire*, 2504 Lincoln Way. Close to the campus, this fine cafe specializes in moderately priced South American cuisine (you'll find some American favorites on the menu as well). Try to nab a window seat for some great people-watching. Call (515) 292-7429 or see cafebeaudelaire.com for more information.

For an overnight stay in Ames, check out the *Iowa House*, 405 Hayward Ave. A former fraternity house near campus has been transformed into a boutique hotel. It's conveniently located, and a full breakfast is served each morning. For more information or to make reservations, call (515) 292-2474 or visit iowahouseames.com.

Railroad History

For more than a hundred years, scenic **Boone County** has been the railroad center of Iowa. At one time this was a bustling coal-mining region, with the railroads serving as a lifeline to the rest of the world. That heritage lives on today in the **Boone and Scenic Valley Railroad**, an excursion and dining train based in the town of **Boone** that travels through some of the state's most spectacular scenery. The railroad is operated by the Boone Railroad Historical Society and offers a 14-mile trip through the Des Moines River valley from Boone to Fraser, passing through densely forested bluffs and valleys.

Rides on the Boone Railroad last about two hours and are offered Memorial Day weekend through the end of October, as well as during December and around Valentine's Day. The train depot is located at 225 Tenth St. You can also visit the **James H. Andrew Railroad Museum**, which has information on train history in Iowa and the nation. For information, call (515) 432-4249 or visit bsvrr.com.

A good time to visit Boone is during its annual **Pufferbilly Days**. Held in August, Pufferbilly Days is a celebration of the town's railroading heritage and a community-wide festival featuring train rides, a parade, antique-car show, live entertainment, a carnival, sports events, an arts festival, and model-train displays. For more information call (515) 432-3342 or see visitboonecounty.com.

Another piece of Boone County railroad history is preserved at the **Kate Shelley High Bridge** northwest of Boone and the **Kate Shelley Memorial Park and Railroad Museum** 5 miles southwest of Boone at 1198 232nd St. in Moingona. The two sites are named in honor of a local girl who became a heroine at the tender age of fifteen. In a terrible storm the night of July 6, 1881, Kate crawled across a railroad bridge longer than the length of two football fields to warn an oncoming passenger train of a trestle washout near her home. Two crewmen had already died when a locomotive crashed at the site, and Kate is credited with saving the lives of everyone on the oncoming passenger train. Kate's bravery did not go unrewarded: As word of her adventure spread, the young woman became a national heroine. A Chicago newspaper raised funds to pay off the mortgage on her family home, and a well-known temperance leader of the day arranged to send the girl to college.

In 1901 the North Western Railroad completed the world's longest and highest double-track railroad bridge over the Des Moines River, a marvel of nineteenth-century engineering skill (the bridge is now listed on the National Register of Historic Places). The span was christened the Kate Shelley High Bridge in honor of the local heroine, and in 1903 Kate was named the North Western station agent in Moingona. She held the position until shortly before her death in 1912. Later the Boone County Historical Society bought the depot and opened it as a museum, re-creating a typical passenger station of the late nineteenth century, complete with a period waiting-room bench, a potbellied stove, a ticket window, a telegraph, and a wide variety of railroad memorabilia.

The Kate Shelley Museum is open by appointment. The Kate Shelley High Bridge is located 3 miles northwest of Boone. For information on either the museum or the bridge, call (515) 433-6900.

The town of Boone is also proud of its status as the birthplace of Mamie Eisenhower, wife of the thirty-fourth president of the United States. You can learn about her life and times at the *Mamie Doud Eisenhower Birthplace*, a modest frame house where she was born in 1896. The home had been privately owned for many years before a town committee was formed in the 1970s to buy and restore it. After five years of work, the birthplace was dedicated in 1980. Though Mamie was originally against the idea of saving the house (out of modesty, it was thought), she later donated a number of items to the site. Today it is one of only a few first ladies' birthplaces that have been preserved.

Though Mamie returned to Boone a number of times as an adult, her stay here as a child was brief. Her father, John Sheldon Doud, came to Boone in the early 1890s and established a meatpacking company with his father. In 1897, one year after Mamie's birth, the family moved to Cedar Rapids and a few years later to Colorado. Mamie met her future husband in 1915 on a vacation in San Antonio, Texas, and began living the traveling life of an army officer's wife. Later, after eight years in the White House, Ike and Mamie retired to the farm home they had purchased in Gettysburg, Pennsylvania—the first and only home they ever owned. After Ike's death in 1969, Mamie continued living on the farm until shortly before her death in 1979.

Visit the birthplace today, and you'll gain more insight into the life of the first lady and her husband. The home has been restored to the 1890s period and contains many furnishings that were donated by Mamie's family. The primary bedroom has its original furniture, including the bed in which Mamie was born, and there is also a library of Eisenhower-related materials.

The Mamie Eisenhower Birthplace is located at 709 Carroll St. It is open June through Oct. A small admission fee is charged. For more information call (515) 433-6900 or see mamiebirthplacebooneorg.wordpress.org.

For a peaceful place to recover from all your sightseeing, visit the *Iowa Arboretum*, southeast of Boone near the town of *Luther*. The arboretum is an educational facility unlike any other in Iowa. Located on 415 acres in rural Boone County, it contains hundreds of species of trees, shrubs, and flowers in a quiet, scenic setting. Its main goal is to help Iowans appreciate and better understand plant life. Here you can learn which plants are best adapted to the soils and climate of Iowa and how to use these plants properly for landscaping, gardening, conservation, and other purposes. The arboretum also serves as an outdoor laboratory for testing the hardiness and adaptability of newly introduced plants and as a center for the preservation of rare and endangered plant species.

A vital part of the arboretum is its 40-acre Library of Living Plants, where you can view varieties of cultivated trees, shrubs, and flowers. Plants with similar uses are grouped together—small shade trees are located in one area, for example, and trees useful as windbreaks in another. With this arrangement, you can quickly "look up" the best plant for your needs.

Labels identify the native trees, shrubs, and wildflowers, and illustrated brochures will help you plan your own self-guided tour. Along the way you're likely to see some of the deer, birds, and wild turkeys that make their home here. Guided tours and educational programs are also offered.

The Iowa Arboretum is open weekdays from 9 a.m. to 4 p.m. and on weekends for special events. To arrange a guided tour, call (515) 795-3216. The arboretum is located about 30 miles northwest of Des Moines, 2.5 miles west of the town of Luther on CR E57. See iowaarboretum.com for more information.

Next head southwest to visit **Picket Fence Creamery** (515-438-2697; picketfencecreamery.net) at 14583 S Ave. in Woodward. This 80-acre, family-owned farm raises Jersey cows in lush pastures and pasteurizes and bottles the milk on-site. Stop by their store to purchase milk, ice cream, cheese curds, and other dairy products. They also sell beef, pork, buffalo, elk, lamb, chicken, eggs, and other items produced by nearly one hundred other Iowa families. Farm tours are offered for groups. The farm store is open Mon through Sat, with a Sample Sunday once a month that serves a tempting array of food and drinks.

Northwest of Woodward lies the town of **Jefferson**, where you can pay a visit to the **Mahanay Bell Tower**, a 168-foot structure topped by 47 cast bells. Take the elevator to the observation platform and you can see a view of seven counties. The tower was built with funds from the estate of William and Dora Mahanay, both residents of Jefferson. William was a sales representative for a surgical-instrument company as well as the owner of a substantial amount of Green County farmland. When he died, he specified that his estate be used for the construction of a tower on the southwest corner of the courthouse square.

didyouknow?

George Gallup, founder of the Gallup Poll, was born and raised in Jefferson, Iowa. Maybe he got his penchant for counting things from counting the walls of his octagon-shaped house, located at 703 S. Chestnut St. Whatever you do, don't "gallup" past this one!

The bells on top of the tower were made and installed by a Chicago company. The largest one, middle C, weighs 4,700 pounds and is 5 feet in diameter. The smallest is G, which weighs only 198 pounds. A four-octave carillon is played at the top of each hour. In June, a Bell Tower Festival is held, with live entertainment, food vendors, and athletic competitions.

The Mahanay Tower is located on the downtown square in Jefferson (it's difficult to miss) and is open to the public from Memorial Day through September from 10 a.m. to 4 p.m. daily. In May and Oct, it is open on weekends. Admission is $3 for adults. Call (515) 386-2155 for more information.

Jefferson is also home to **RVP-1875**, a historical furniture shop and museum located in the century-old Milligan Lumber Grain & Coal Building. It's owned by Robby Pedersen, a master furniture maker who has built more than 1,300 pieces of historically accurate furniture using tools, techniques, and finishes used in 1875. Stop by to observe Robby work and hear his stories about the historical significance of the pieces he creates. He also offers tours and classes. RVP-1875 (515-975-3083; rvp1875.com) is at 115 S. Wilson Ave.

Before leaving the area, stop by **Deal's Orchard**, which has been growing tasty apples since 1941. In addition to apples and other fresh produce, the Deal family sells more than 30,000 gallons of fresh cider each year. In mid-October they hold a Fall Festival with horse-drawn hayrides, a corn maze, and live music. Deal's Orchard is at 1102 244th St. Call (515) 386-8279 or see dealsorchard.com for more information.

Frontier Chronicles

Begin your tour of this region of the state in **Fort Dodge**. The city is the county seat of **Webster County**—though if a certain wrestling match in 1856 had turned out differently, Fort Dodge's destiny may have followed another path.

The story begins when John F. Duncombe, described in a newspaper of the day as "an engine in pants," arrived in Fort Dodge in 1855. At that time Fort Dodge was only a tiny settlement in contrast to the nearby thriving town of Homer. Duncombe, however, spearheaded an effort to have Fort Dodge named as the county seat. The citizens of Homer naturally objected, and an election was held to determine which town would get the coveted distinction. When the votes were counted, it was discovered that both sides had stuffed the ballot box—but the citizens of Fort Dodge were more successful in their voting fraud, as their town came out the winner. John D. Maxwell, the leader of the Homer faction, was furious. Then someone made the suggestion that Maxwell and Duncombe settle the issue with a wrestling match. For an hour the two battled it out in Homer's public square in front of a large crowd. Duncombe was declared the winner, and Fort Dodge was named the county seat and as a result became the leading commercial center in the area. Fort Dodge has good reason to be grateful for the athletic prowess of John F. Duncombe.

Fort Dodge's history has many more colorful episodes, and the best place to learn about them is at the city's *Fort Museum and Frontier Village*. The site is a re-creation of Fort Williams, a garrison built in 1862. The fort includes a frontier village with stockade, blockhouse, soldiers' quarters, general store, blacksmith shop, one-room school, log chapel, and drugstore, all with period furnishings. Also on display are exhibits on military and pioneer history.

Various special events are held at the Fort Museum, including *Frontier Days*, which is on the first weekend in June. This citywide celebration of Fort Dodge's past features a parade, Buckskinner's Rendezvous, live entertainment, historic home tours, and much more.

The Fort Museum is at 1 Museum Rd. A small admission is charged. For hours and more information call (515) 573-4231 or see fortmuseumfv.com.

Fee, Fi, Fo, Fum!

Did you know you were in the land of giants? One of the great American hoaxes has its origin in a great lump of Fort Dodge gypsum. Listening to a sermon in church while visiting in Ackley, George Hull, a native New Yorker, came up with the idea of staging a little resurrection of his own. Somehow he managed to ship a chunk (7,000 pounds' worth!) of Fort Dodge gypsum to Chicago. There, while Hull posed, a sculptor carved the rock into the figure of a 10-foot-tall man. Hull, his cousin, and the sculptor worked with wooden mallets and steel needles to give the giant an ancient and weathered "faux-cade." Then, using a circuitous route, the giant was shipped on to New York and given a midnight burial in a field on the cousin's farm near Cardiff.

About a year later, when some men were digging a well on the farm—surprise!—a huge stone foot appeared, then a leg, then two legs, and soon they had unearthed an amazing stone-like giant! Hull and his cousin didn't let the grass grow under their feet: They put up a fence, erected a tent, charged a ten-cent admission, and went into business. Scientists, scholars, and an Indian medicine man visited the Cardiff giant; theories were advanced and some suspicions were raised. In the meantime, dimes kept rolling in. Soon they had made more than $20,000!

Unfortunately (at least for the cousins) one visitor happened to be Galusha Parsons, a lawyer from Fort Dodge. And he must have known his gypsum because he recognized in the form of the giant the huge rock that had been shipped out of his hometown a year earlier. The jig was up and Hull, at last, revealed the true origins of the colossal man. But you will have to go to New York to see this sleeping giant lie. He is at rest in the Farmers' Museum in Cooperstown. Or perhaps, the "real" giant is on display at the Fort Museum. Who knows?

Also in Fort Dodge is the **Blanden Memorial Art Museum**, the first permanent art facility in the state of Iowa. You're likely to be surprised by the diversity and quality of its collection, which includes such treasures as Chagall's *The Fantastic Horsecart* (one of the painter's personal favorites), Miró's *The Cry of the Gazelle at Dawn*, and Maurice Prendergast's *Central Park*, plus bronzes by Henry Moore, an Alexander Calder mobile, and a collection of non-Western art, including Asian works from the seventeenth through nineteenth centuries, pre-Columbian art, and tribal objects from North America and Africa. The museum also sponsors traveling exhibits and art classes for both adults and children.

The museum was founded in 1930, a gift to the community from former Fort Dodge mayor Charles Granger Blanden in memory of his wife. Since then other benefactors have donated money and works of art to the museum, including the Philadelphia art collector Albert Barnes.

The Blanden Memorial Art Museum is located at 920 Third Ave. S. It is open Tues through Sat from 11 a.m. to 5 p.m. Admission is free. For more information call (515) 573-2316 or see blanden.org.

Visit **Dolliver Memorial State Park**, south of Fort Dodge, for a picturesque view of this part of the state. The Des Moines River and Prairie Creek flow through the park, embellished by canyons, bluffs, and Indian mounds. Cabins, campsites, and picnic shelters are available.

In **Dows**, visit the **Dows Depot Welcome Center**, an 1896 Northern/Rock Island Railroad Depot. It is furnished with period railroad memorabilia and serves as a handy place to gather information on the area. You'll find the depot at 100 W. Train St. Call (515) 852-3533 for information.

Just across the street is the **Quasdorf Blacksmith Shop Museum**, housed in a building built in 1899. The museum has displays relating to the days when blacksmith, wagon, and machine shops were an indispensable part of small-town life. For hours, call (515) 852-3533 for more information.

A good time to visit Dows is during **Corn Days**, which is held on the first weekend in August. Enjoy a parade, rodeo, and other live entertainment.

From Dows head north to the town of **Clarion**, home to the **Heartland Museum**. The museum, located in the town's Gazebo Park at 119 SW Ninth St., is housed in the early twentieth-century schoolhouse where O. H. Benson, superintendent of schools, introduced the 4-H emblem. Inside the museum you'll see various displays on 4-H memorabilia and history, including 4-H uniform style changes through the years. Other displays explore area history, including the career of Alvina Sellers, the "Iowa Hat Lady." Watch the video from her David Letterman appearance and see hundreds of the hats she created in her millinery shop. The museum is open Mon through Sat, Memorial Day

An Apple a Day

If an apple a day keeps the doctor away, then one of the healthiest places in the state to visit is *The Community Orchard* at the northwest corner of the airport in Fort Dodge. Owned by Denny and Emily Stucky, the orchard is a great place to visit between August 1 and Christmas. There is a cafe serving delicious desserts and lunches, a well-stocked gift shop, an AppleFest in early October, and much more. And you can't leave without taking home one of their frozen apple pies as a souvenir. I can't think of anything better than a perfect fall afternoon spent at Community Orchard. I'd start with apple pie, move on to lunch, maybe an apple dumpling next, some more apple pie . . . you get the idea! Call (515) 573-8212 or see community orchard.com for more information.

through Labor Day and Sat in Sept. Admission is $12 for adults; $6 for children. Call (515) 532-3453 or see heartlandmuseum.org for more information.

North of Clarion lies the town of **Britt**, which each August plays host to one of the state's most unusual events, the **Britt Hobo Days**. Hoboes have been traveling to the convention since 1900, though their numbers have dwindled, and by now most of them are well past middle age. Each year they return to Britt to swap stories, meet old friends, and enjoy the hospitality of the town.

Britt hosted its first hobo convention in 1900, eager to gain some publicity for the town and show the rest of the world that "Britt was a lively little town capable of doing anything larger cities could do." The national media did indeed report on the convention, not realizing that the town was serious in its intentions until hundreds of hoboes began arriving for the event. The travelers were treated to games and sports competitions, musical performances, and a clean place to stay, and the newspapers around the state gave Britt the publicity it had hoped for.

Though the 1900 convention was declared a rousing success, it wasn't until 1933 that Britt once again hosted the convention. Some townspeople were reluctant to sponsor the event again, but they were won over by those who pointed out that the convention was for hoboes, not tramps or bums. A hobo is defined as a migratory worker who is willing to work to pay his way; a tramp is a traveler who begs for food rather than works for it; and a bum is too lazy either to work or to roam around. At a time when many people were out of work and homeless, a hobo was seen as an honorable—even romantic—character.

The town agreed to host the convention again and renewed a tradition that continues to this day. Through the years the event has grown to include more activities, from the crowning of a hobo king and queen to the serving of free mulligan stew. Hoboes including Mountain Dew, Hardrock Kid, and Fry Pan Jack have become legendary in Britt, though today fewer and fewer of their brethren come to the event each year. A new breed is taking their place, however: "weekend hoboes," who love the open road but still have stable jobs. Both groups gather in Britt once a year to renew their ties to each other and the traveling life.

You don't have to be a hobo to attend the convention, however. Visitors are welcomed, and the town offers a full slate of activities for their amusement: a flea market, parade, antique- and classic-car show, musical entertainment, art show, carnival, and fireworks display. Visitors are invited to stop by the "hobo jungle" (the area where the hoboes camp) to listen to storytelling and singing and learn more about life on the road. For more information call (641) 843-3734 or see britthobodays.com.

If you can't make it to Britt for the convention, you can still learn more about the hobo life at the town's **National Hobo Museum**, 51 Main Ave. Located in the former Chief Theatre in downtown Britt, the museum celebrates hobo history through photographs, printed materials, musical instruments, and documentaries. It is open Memorial Day through Hobo Days weekend. For information call (641) 843-9104 or see britthobodays.com.

newdealmurals

During the Depression, the Works Progress Administration commissioned artists to paint murals across the state. You can see these WPA murals in towns that include:

Ames: Post Office and the Iowa State University Library

Forest City: Post Office

Algona: Post Office

Clarion: Post Office

Jefferson: Post Office

Plan a visit—especially during spring and fall migration seasons—to the **Union Slough National Wildlife Refuge**. Take CR B35 north from Britt to CR A42 and head east to **Bancroft**. This area was established in 1938 by the US Department of the Interior to help maintain the waterfowl population of the Midwest Flyway, including ducks, geese, trumpeter swans, and a wide variety of shorebirds. The slough is all that remains of a pre-glacial riverbed. Now 3,300 acres, it once covered more than 8,000. It marks the confluence, or union, of two watersheds: the Blue Earth River and the East Fork of the Des Moines. There is a picnic area and nature trail at the southern end of the refuge. For more information see fws.gov/refuge/union-slough.

Drive west to the town of **West Bend**, the site of the **Grotto of the Redemption**. The grotto was the lifetime work of Father Paul Dobberstein, who started its construction in 1912. As a young seminary student, he suffered a

The Remarkable Gift of the Prison on the Prairie

During World War II a German prisoner-of-war camp was established just outside the town of Algona. One of the 3,200 prisoners, an architect and noncommissioned officer named Eduard Kaib, enlisted the help of some of his fellow prisoners, and together they went to work to fashion a nativity scene. It was a way, Kaib thought, for them to fight their loneliness and their longing for their families and the festivities of Christmas in their native land. They pooled their money in order to purchase the materials they needed and built the figures to a one-half life-size scale, using concrete over wire frames. They finished the detailing with hand carving in plaster. The project took more than a year to complete, and it was displayed at the edge of the camp for the first time in December 1945.

When the camp was being dismantled after the war, the citizens of Algona asked that the nativity scene be left behind for the community to enjoy. Kaib and his helpers agreed, with the stipulation that no admission fee ever be charged. They helped the townspeople assemble the display in a newly repaired building. It remains open to the public during the Christmas season, and several of the prisoners have returned here to visit. One of them, freelance photographer Werner Meinel, stopped in Algona in 1963 while returning to his home in Massachusetts from a shoot in Alaska. Surprised that the nativity scene was still being displayed and touched by the friendliness of the Algona residents, he sent one of his prize-winning photographs—a pair of white swans flying side by side, titled *Correlation*—to be hung in the nativity building as a symbol of peace.

You can see the nativity at the *Camp Algona POW Museum* at 114 S. Thorington St. The museum, which gives information on the history of the POW camp, is open April through Dec. For information and hours call (515) 395-2267 or see pwcamp algona.org.

serious illness and vowed that if he recovered, he would erect a shrine to Mary. For forty-two years he labored to build the grotto in West Bend, setting into concrete ornamental rocks and gems from around the world. After his death in 1954, his work was continued by Father Louis Greving.

Today the Grotto of the Redemption covers an area the size of a city block. Contained within its twisting walls and encrusted caverns are nine separate grottoes, each portraying a scene from the life of Christ. Highlights include a replica of Michelangelo's *Pietà* and a life-size statue made of Carrara marble portraying Joseph of Arimathea and Nicodemus laying Jesus into the tomb. Adjacent to the grotto is St. Peter and Paul's Church, which includes a Christmas Chapel that is considered to be Father Dobberstein's finest work. It contains a Brazilian amethyst that weighs more than 300 pounds. The church's main altar (a first-place winner at the Chicago World's Fair in 1893) is of hand-carved bird's-eye maple.

The grotto, which is open year-round, is financed by the freewill donations of visitors. The grotto is located 2 blocks off IA 15 at the north end of town at 300 N. Broadway Ave. For more information call (515) 887-2371 or see westbendgrotto.com.

Also of interest in West Bend is the **Sod House** (201 First Ave. SE; 515-200-9234), a home built of earth and managed by the West Bend Historical Society to help preserve part of the pioneer heritage of the area. At one time sod houses could be found throughout the prairie states, for in a land of few trees they were a quick and inexpensive answer to the housing needs of new settlers. A sod home cost between $15 and $30 to construct, and its thick walls and roof were good insulation against the heat of summer and cold of winter.

don'trun hogwild

The first Kossuth County law (1856) was known as the hog law because it prohibited hogs and cattle from running around at large. Watch out for escapees!

The sod-house era in Iowa lasted only thirty years, from the 1850s to the 1880s. It ended when the expansion of the railroad made lumber cheap enough to be used as a common building material. The historical society also operates a country schoolhouse and a historical museum. All are open Sat during the summer and by appointment.

The town of **Emmetsburg**, which lies northwest of West Bend, is also worth a visit, particularly if you have a bit of Irish in your background. The town was settled by Irish immigrants and named in honor of Robert Emmet, the Irish patriot who was executed by the English in 1803. The customs and heritage of the old country remain strong here, especially during its **Emmetsburg St. Patrick's Day Celebration**. This three-day festival includes a Miss Shamrock Pageant, parade, musical performances, and various Irish-themed entertainments. For more information call (712) 852-4326 or see emmetsburg irishgifts.com.

Clear Lake Region

The region that surrounds beautiful Clear Lake is dominated by two towns, Mason City and Clear Lake. **Mason City** is gaining international attention for its architectural heritage. In fact, Condé Nast *Traveler* magazine has named it one of the world's fourteen best cities for architecture lovers.

The city's premiere architectural treasure is the **Historic Park Inn Hotel**, the last remaining hotel designed by Frank Lloyd Wright. Don't miss its beautiful Skylight Room, which has many elements designed by Wright, including its columns, mezzanine, and skylight. Take a docent-led tour and then enjoy a meal at **Markley & Blythe**, the inn's fine dining restaurant that's named after the two attorneys who introduced Wright to Mason City. The inn is at 7 W. State St.; for reservations call (641) 422-0015 or see historicparkinn.com For information on tours, see wrightonthepark.org.

Next visit the **Architectural Interpretive Center**, 520 First St. NE, which is adjacent to the **Rock Glenn–Rock Crest National Historic District**. The beautiful neighborhood includes eight houses designed by Walter Burley Griffin and Barry Byrne of the Chicago office of Frank Lloyd Wright, all built between 1912 and 1917. They comprise the largest collection of Prairie School homes to share a natural setting in the United States. The center describes how Mason City came to have such a concentration of Wright's designs and describes the distinctive features of his style, which is characterized by open, flowing designs, low roofs, and skillful use of natural materials.

Complete your Mason City architectural tour with a visit to the **Stockman House**, a Prairie School house designed by the famous architect. Constructed in 1908, the home was one of very few houses built by Wright in this period to address middle-class housing needs. It features such details as an open floor plan, ribbon windows, overhanging eaves, and exterior wood banding that emphasizes its horizontal lines. The Stockman House (530 First St. NE; 641-423-1923; stockmanhouse.org) is open for tours Mon and Wed through Sun from May through Oct (Sat only from Nov through April). Admission is $10 for adults and $5 for children.

Mason City is also the birthplace of Meredith Willson, who wrote the book, lyrics, and music for the award-winning musical *The Music Man*. Begin your 76-Trombones-Tour at the **Meredith Willson Boyhood Home**, 308 S. Pennsylvania Ave. Willson grew up right here in Mason City and based the show on his boyhood experiences. The house is chock-full of Willson family memorabilia and musical treasures.

Anyone who enjoys Willson's best-loved musical will feel right at home in **Music Man Square** at 308 S. Pennsylvania Ave. The square features storefronts based on the sets used in the Warner Brothers 1962 film version of the musical, from Mrs. Paroo's front porch (a gift shop) to the Pleez-All pool hall.

While you're on the square, be sure to visit the **Meredith Willson Museum**, where you can hear your favorite Willson songs and learn more about his life in music. The museum also includes exhibits about the importance of music in American culture, with displays on topics ranging from Civil

War bands and Victorian parlor music to swing bands. There's even an interactive radio sing-along booth where "adoring fans" will applaud your warbling.

The Meredith Willson sites are open Tues through Sun from 1 to 5 p.m. A small admission is charged for the museum. For more information call (641) 424-2852 or see themusicman square.org.

On your tour of the city, visit the **MacNider Art Museum**. Housed in a handsome Tudor-style building, the museum has a permanent collection focusing on American art and boasts

didyouknow?

Meredith Willson also wrote the popular holiday song "It's Beginning to Look a Lot Like Christmas."

works by such well-known artists as Thomas Hart Benton, Grant Wood, Alexander Calder, Moses Soyer, and Adolph Gottlieb. Another highlight of the museum is its collection of Bil Baird puppets and memorabilia. Baird, a native of Mason City, was a famous puppeteer whose creations appeared in the theater, in films, and on television for more than fifty years. His puppets starred in the *Ziegfeld Follies*, appeared in the movie *The Sound of Music*, and performed on television for Ed Sullivan, Jack Paar, and Sid Caesar. In 1980 Baird donated a major collection of his work to the MacNider Museum, including some 400 puppets and marionettes.

The Charles H. MacNider Art Museum is located at 303 Second St. SE. It is open Tues through Sat, and admission is free. For more information call (641) 421-3666 or see macniderart.org.

76 Trombones and More

Meredith Willson was born in Mason City on May 18, 1902. He loved music from an early age, and when he was seventeen he left Mason City for New York, soon earning a place in the legendary John Philip Sousa Band and then the New York Philharmonic. At age twenty-seven he launched his career as a composer and lyricist. Hundreds of songs later, Willson began writing a musical comedy about his state and hometown. The effort took more than five years.

The Music Man opened on Broadway in 1957 and became a smash hit. A few years later a movie version was filmed, with its premiere taking place at the Palace Theater in Mason City.

Willson's seventy-five-year musical career won him many awards. The most prestigious came in 1988, four years after his death, when he was awarded the Presidential Medal of Freedom, the highest honor bestowed on an American citizen.

More insights into the region's past can be found at another Mason City attraction. The **Kinney Pioneer Museum** off US 18 West, located on the airport grounds, includes a pioneer village with a one-room schoolhouse, log cabin, railroad caboose, jailhouse, and blacksmith shop. The museum is open May through Sept, Tues through Sun 1 to 5 p.m. and a small admission fee is charged. For information call (641) 423-1258 or see kinneypioneermuseum.org.

Lovers of the outdoors will enjoy the **Lime Creek Nature Center**, which sits atop the limestone bluffs of the Winnebago River. The center includes both live and static displays of a variety of animals, plus an outdoor amphitheater and more than 9 miles of trails through prairie, forest, and wetlands. The center is at 3501 Lime Creek Rd.; it is open daily. For more information call (641) 423-5309 or see cgcounty.org.

Another Mason City attraction is the **Northwestern Steakhouse**, purveyor of tender steaks and several Greek specialties. Its founder, Tony Papouchis, the son of a Greek Orthodox priest, came to the United States in 1912 and opened the restaurant in 1920.

Today, Tony's son Bill and his wife, Ann, run the business. Northwestern Steakhouse is located at 304 Sixteenth St. NW. Hours are 4:30 to 9:30 p.m. Mon through Sat, and prices are moderate. Call (641) 423-5075 or see northwestern steakhouse.com for more information.

Just west of Mason City on US 18 is **Clear Lake**, one of the state's most popular recreation areas. The lake itself is one of the few spring-fed lakes in Iowa, a lovely 3,600-acre expanse of water that draws boating and fishing enthusiasts, water-skiers, swimmers, and confirmed beach bums all summer. Even in winter the area is a popular tourist spot, with cross-country skiing, snowmobiling, and ice fishing for those who don't mind the cold.

The water is not the only attraction in Clear Lake. In the downtown area you'll find a number of antiques stores and specialty shops, and during the summer months many special events are scheduled, from fishing tournaments to band concerts in the park.

One way to see the area is on board the **Lady of the Lake**, a paddle wheeler that takes passengers on a 90-minute scenic cruise around Clear Lake. Cruises are offered May through Sept. Tickets are $16 for adults and $7 for children. Call (641) 357-2243 or see cruiseclearlake.com for information.

Don't miss the **Surf Ballroom** on your tour of Clear Lake. The ballroom is best known as the site of the last performances given by rock 'n' roll legends Buddy Holly, Ritchie Valens, and J. P. "The Big Bopper" Richardson. Following their concert, the three were killed nearby in the crash of their small plane in the early morning hours of February 3, 1959—an event that became the basis for Don McLean's hit song "American Pie." For devoted rock 'n' roll fans, the

Surf has become a landmark on the same order as The Cavern in Liverpool, where the Beatles got their start. People from around the country make pilgrimages here to relive the memories.

Even without the Buddy Holly connection, the Surf is worth a visit on its own. At a time when most ballrooms have gone the way of the horse and buggy, the Surf is a living reminder of the big-band era, when swing was king. Today it books a variety of music and dance bands, from country to big band to fifties and sixties classics. The most popular time to visit the Surf is during its annual **Winter Dance Party**, which is held on the weekend closest to the date of the fateful plane crash. In addition to concerts, the event typically includes a record show, family sock hop, dance lessons, and dance and costume contests.

The **Surf Ballroom and Museum** are at 460 N. Shore Dr. and are open for self-guided tours daily during the summer months and Mon through Fri during the rest of the year, with occasional closures for special events. A $5 donation is suggested. For information see surfballroom.com or call (641) 357-6151. The website also has directions to the memorial site where Buddy Holly, Ritchie Valens, and J. P. "The Big Bopper" Richardson died. While it's located on private land, visitors are welcomed.

Clear Lake is also home to the **Clear Lake Fire Museum**. The facility opened in 1986 and depicts a fire station from the early twentieth century.

Where the Music Lives

The original Surf Ballroom opened in Clear Lake in 1934. After being destroyed by fire, it was rebuilt across the street in 1948, decorated in a tropical theme with murals of surf and palm trees, and faux clouds projected on its midnight blue ceiling. Holding up to 2,100 people, the Surf has hosted many of the entertainment world's top names, from Roy Orbison and the Everly Brothers to Martina McBride and B. B. King.

Today its 1950s interior, restored to pristine condition, is like a time machine. Its hallways are lined with publicity photos of guest artists from past decades. Musicians have also left their mark on the walls of the Surf's dressing room, which is covered with hundreds of signatures (including a handwritten stanza of "American Pie" signed by Don McLean).

The Surf's museum, located in a lounge adjacent to the main ballroom, features additional information on the three musicians who lost their lives after playing here in 1959. Through the years the families of the men have contributed memorabilia, including a briefcase used by J. P. Richardson and handwritten lyrics of Ritchie's "La Bamba." Most poignant of all is the phone booth where Buddy Holly and Richie Valens made their final phone calls after finishing their concert.

Inside you can see some of Clear Lake's earliest firefighting equipment, along with other antique firefighting memorabilia. Highlights of the museum include the town's 1924 Ahrens-Fox fire truck, an 1883 hand-pulled hose cart, a fire bell, antique fire extinguishers, photographs, and brass poles.

The Clear Lake Fire Museum is located at 112 N. Sixth St. It is open Memorial Day through Labor Day on Sat and Sun from 1 to 4 p.m. Admission is free. Donations are welcomed. For more information call (641) 357-2613.

For a fun place to stay in the Clear Lake area, book a stay in the **McIntosh Woods State Park Yurts**. Inspired by the circular dwellings used by the nomadic peoples of central Asia, these camping yurts have conical roofs and canvas walls. McIntosh Woods State Park (641-829-3847; iowadnr.gov) has two yurts on the shore of Clear Lake, each accommodating four guests in bunk beds. The park is at 1200 E. Lake St., Ventura.

Before you leave the Clear Lake area, plan a visit to the viewing area of the **Cerro Gordo Wind Farm**, 6 miles south of Ventura on CR S14. The wind farm produces free, renewable, and clean energy and covers more than 10 square miles—the giant windmills are really quite impressive. Even though the wind farm covers a significant amount of land, only 18 acres of it are actually used by the wind farm because the rotors are more than 100 feet off the ground; therefore, the land beneath them can be used for grazing or crop production. The wind farm is open daily from daylight to dusk. Admission is free.

Continue your tour of north central Iowa with a visit to **Charles City**, which lies east of Mason City. The town boasts one of the largest county museums in Iowa, the **Floyd County Historical Museum**. The museum is housed

didyouknow?

Iowa is one of the top-ten states in the country as far as wind resources go—or blow. Iowa gets nearly 40 percent of its electricity from wind.

Cerro Gordo County, averaging winds of 17 mph, is one of the windiest spots in the state.

in the former Salsbury Laboratory Building, constructed in 1933, and contains more than forty rooms of exhibits. Its best-known display is a complete original drugstore that operated on Charles City's main street from 1873 to 1961. The store was founded by German immigrant Edward Berg and was later owned by John Legel Jr., who donated it to the historical society in 1961. Tour the store today and it's like stepping back a generation or more. The shelves are filled with patent medicines designed to cure every ailment known, plus items like cigar molds, chimneys for kerosene lamps, and ink bottles and cosmetics such as 7 Sutherland Sisters Hair & Scalp Cleaner.

Women's Rights Crusader

Born in 1859 in Wisconsin, Carrie Lane moved with her family to Charles City, Iowa, in 1866 and graduated from Iowa State University in 1880 as valedictorian and the only woman in her graduating class. Because her father opposed her ambition to receive a higher education, she worked for a year at a country school and then as a dishwasher and library aide for nine cents an hour to pay her way through college. During her college years, she fought for the right of women to participate on the university debating team and in military exercises. Nationally, she led the women's suffrage movement until the ratification of the Nineteenth Amendment in 1920. (When she married her second husband, George Catt, in 1890, they both signed a contract allowing her to work on suffrage issues for four months a year.) She founded the League of Women Voters, worked ardently for international peace, and remained a powerful and well-respected advocate for women's rights issues until her death at the age of eighty-eight in 1947.

When visiting the Charles City area, plan a visit to the **Carrie Lane Chapman Catt Girlhood Home** to learn more about this remarkable woman. The site is at 2379 Timber Ave. Call (641) 228-3336 or consult catt.org to see tour times.

Elsewhere in the museum you can see a restored 1853 log cabin, displays of old-time vehicles and tools, and materials relating to the history of the county. The museum also contains the nation's most complete collection of information relating to the founders of the gasoline-tractor industry, the Hart-Parr Company. The business was founded in Charles City and produced the first successful gasoline tractor in 1901. Another display contains information about Carrie Chapman Catt, a Charles City native and early leader in the women's suffrage movement.

The Floyd County Historical Museum is located at 500 Gilbert St. It is open Wed through Sat from 9 a.m. to 4:00 p.m. Admission is $5 for adults and $3 for children twelve to eighteen. For more information call (641) 228-1099 or see floydcountymuseum.org.

At the Charles City Public Library, tour the **Mooney Art Collection**, which features prints, engravings, and etchings by artists who include Rembrandt, Picasso, Cezanne, and Manet. The works were donated in 1941 by an Eastman Kodak Company executive who grew up in Charles City. They are an extraordinary treasure for a public library to have, particularly one in a small town. The library is at 106 Milwaukee Mall and is open during library hours. Call (641) 257-6319 or see charlescitypl.com for information.

If you have a yen for adventure, before leaving town experience the fun at the **Charles City Whitewater Park**. This quarter-mile section of the Cedar River has been reshaped into three types of whitewater appropriate to varying

Tennis amid the Cornfields

At the *All Iowa Lawn Tennis Club* near Charles City you may have the urge to speak with a British accent. That's because the grass lawn court is a replica of those at Wimbledon in England, complete with white picket fence and tall umpire's chair. Mark and Denise Kuhn created it from a former cattle feedlot on their farm in 2003 (Mark has been a Wimbledon fan ever since he listened to its matches on his grandfather's shortwave radio as a child). After the court was featured in a national magazine, it began to draw tennis enthusiasts from around the world. Tennis fans can play for free, but reservations must be made in advance. The Kuhns even have a strawberry patch so they can serve strawberries and cream after the matches. See alliowalawntennisclub.com for more information.

levels of paddler skill. Kayakers, stand-up paddleboarders, tubers, and river enthusiasts of all kinds are welcome. See ccwhitewater.com for information.

Amateur geologists will love paying a visit to the *Fossil & Prairie Park Preserve*, a 400-acre nature area along the Winnebago River, 1 mile west of Rockford on CR B47. It is one of only a handful of public fossil-collecting sites in the nation, with Devonian-era fossils in its quarry that can be easily collected by visitors of any age. The site also has historic beehive kilns, more than 60 acres of native prairie, a re-created sod house, hiking trails, and a visitor center.

The park at 1227 215th St., Rockford, is open year-round from sunrise to sunset. Its visitor center is open from 1 to 4 p.m. daily, weekends only during winter. For more information call (641) 756-3490 or see fossilcenter.com.

Places to Stay in Fertile Plains

AMES

Onion Creek Farm & Guest House
3700 Onion Creek Ln.
(515) 292-0117
onioncreekfarm.com
inexpensive

CHARLES CITY

Sherman House Bed & Breakfast
800 Gilbert St.
(641) 228-3826
shermanhousecc.com
moderate to expensive

CLARKSVILLE

New Day Dairy Guest Barn
31000 175th St
(319) 278-4455
newdaydairy.com
moderate to expensive

CLEAR LAKE

Larch Pine Inn Bed & Breakfast
401 N. Third St.
(641) 357-0345
larchpineinn.com
moderate

IOWA FALLS

River's Bend Bed & Breakfast
635 Park Ave.
(928) 951-1910
inexpensive to moderate

MARSHALLTOWN

Tremont Inn on Main
24 W. Main St.
(641) 752-1234
tremontonmain.com
moderate

NORA SPRINGS

Cupola Inn
20664 Claybanks Dr.
(641) 420-9227
cupolainn.com
moderate

Places to Eat in Fertile Plains

CLEAR LAKE

Lakeside Landing Kitchen + Bar
1603 S. Shore Dr.
(319) 569-3995
stayclearlake.com/lakeside-landing-restaurant
inexpensive to moderate

FORT DODGE

Tea Thyme
2021 Sixth Ave. S
(515) 576-2202
teathymeatsadies.com
inexpensive

IOWA FALLS

Coffee Attic & Book Cellar
604 Washington
(641) 648-6771
coffeeattic.net
Inexpensive

MARSHALLTOWN

Tremont Grille
22 W. Main St.
(641) 754-9082
tremontonmain.com
moderate

Smokin' G's BBQ
25 W. Main St.
(641) 753-4147
smokin-gs.com
inexpensive

MASON CITY

Birdsall's Ice Cream
518 N. Federal Ave.
(641) 423-5365
birdsallsicecreamco.com
inexpensive

MONTOUR

Rube's Steakhouse
118 Elm St.
(641) 492-6222
rubessteakhouse-montour.com
moderate to expensive

OGDEN

Lucky Pig Pub & Grill
113 W. Walnut St.
(515) 275-9946
inexpensive

Prairie Borderland

Western Iowa has a rich array of attractions to tempt travelers, including the Loess Hills, a rare and beautiful geologic formation that borders the Missouri River between Sioux City and St. Joseph, Missouri. Here you'll also find the scenic beauties of Iowa's Great Lakes region, plus the cultural treasures of the Council Bluffs area.

Spirit Lake Region

Tucked into the far northwestern corner of the state, the **Gitchie Manitou State Preserve** will interest travelers who love outdoor adventures. Located about 10 miles northwest of the town of **Larchwood** (follow CR A18), this beautifully preserved site contains the oldest rock bed (Precambrian) left exposed in Iowa. The outcroppings of Sioux quartzite that you see here, battered and polished by the winds for more than a billion years, are composed of sand compacted by silica. A century ago this lovely rock was quarried, and the resulting depression is called Jasper's Pool. The surrounding prairie and woodlands are also worthy of notice and have been attracting Iowa botanists for decades.

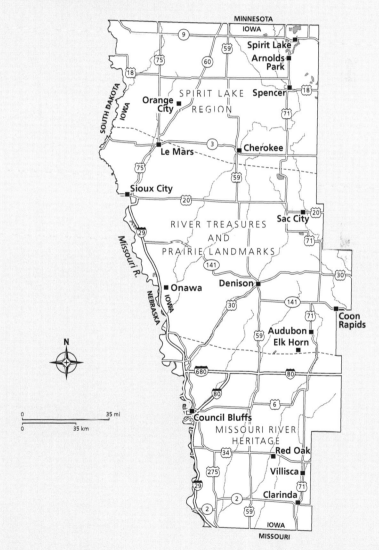

MINNESOTA
IOWA

Spirit Lake

Arnolds
Park

SPIRIT LAKE

Spencer

Orange
City

REGION

SOUTH DAKOTA

IOWA

Le Mars

Cherokee

Sioux City

RIVER TREASURES
AND
PRAIRIE LANDMARKS

Sac City

Missouri R.

NEBRASKA

IOWA

Onawa

Denison

Coon
Rapids

Audubon
Elk Horn

N

Council Bluffs

MISSOURI RIVER
HERITAGE

Red Oak

Villisca

Clarinda

IOWA
MISSOURI

0 ———— 35 mi
0 ———— 35 km

Continue your tour of western Iowa by exploring the **Iowa Great Lakes**. The region has been one of the state's most popular recreation areas ever since the railroad first came here in the early 1880s. Thirteen lakes are located here, the largest being **Big Spirit Lake** and **West Lake Okoboji** (at 136 feet deep, West Okoboji is the deepest lake in Iowa). Here you'll find some of the best swimming, boating, fishing, camping, and golfing in the state, in a beautiful setting surrounded by sparkling water. Once you visit you'll realize why Midwesterners have been flocking to the area for more than a hundred years.

Families will love **Arnolds Park Amusement Park**, Iowa's very own Coney Island. Built in 1889, the attraction is one of the nation's oldest amusement parks. Its park-like grounds on the shore of West Lake Okoboji are a scenic place to stroll and include a number of attractions.

The **Iowa Great Lakes Trail System** offers a great way to explore the area. The heart of the network is a hard-surface trail that connects the towns of Spirit Lake, Okoboji, Arnolds Park, and Milford. Spur trails provide additional biking opportunities on little-traveled country roads.

A highlight of any visit to Arnolds Park is a ride on one of the country's few remaining wooden roller coasters, the Legend. The ride made its debut in the park in 1929 and has thrilled thousands of children (and adults) with its clickety-clack ride and stomach-churning maneuvers. When Arnolds Park was being restored a number of years ago, a top priority was saving the local landmark. The Legend was completely dismantled, cleaned, repainted, and refurbished, and new side rails, bearings, cars, and brakes were installed. Today it is once again the park's featured attraction, drawing roller-coaster connoisseurs from across the country.

The Legend isn't the park's only asset. Nearly thirty rides and attractions, gift shops, restaurants, picnic areas, and sandy beaches will tempt you into relaxing. The park's Preservation Plaza upholds another lake tradition, that of dancing and musical performances by local and touring artists.

AUTHOR'S FAVORITES

Arnolds Park	Sergeant Floyd Monument
Hitchcock Nature Center	Prairie Pedlar
Whiterock Conservancy	DeSoto National Wildlife Refuge
Loess Hills Scenic Byway	Danish Immigrant Museum
Orange City Tulip Festival	

Iowa's Mythical University

No description of the Iowa Great Lakes region would be complete without mention of the **University of Okoboji**. Its campus is one of the largest in the world, stretching from the northern tip of Big Spirit Lake to south of Milford. As you walk through its campus, you'll see many signs of a strong school spirit: thousands of bumper stickers, sweatshirts, and pennants proudly bearing the university's name and hundreds of trash barrels that read "Help Keep your Campus Clean." Prospective students will be relieved to learn, however, that the administration of the University of Okoboji believes that standard academic pursuits like books and lectures are unnecessary to true learning. Instead, its students major in roller-coaster engineering at Arnolds Park, culinary arts at local restaurants, and human anatomy at local beaches.

The school was founded in the early 1970s, when Herman Richter (director of student affairs), his brother Emil (administrative dean), and Roger Stolley (director of admissions) ordered T-shirts emblazoned with the university's logo to wear at local sporting events. Before long, the joke had spawned a local—and then a national—phenomenon. Today there are U of O alumni chapters all over the country, made up of former visitors to the Great Lakes region. The school has its own radio station, KUOO, and even established an endowment fund that is used to support community projects. Each year many local events are sponsored by the school, including a homecoming weekend, winter games, and golf tournaments. Its football team, the Phantoms, is undefeated despite one of the most grueling schedules in college football.

It's not unusual for the Phantoms to play the University of Iowa at 1 p.m., Nebraska at 4 p.m., and Notre Dame at 8 p.m. At each game, all the tickets sold are for Row A, Seats 1 and 2 on the 50-yard line, with proceeds going for a dome over West Lake Okoboji. University officials concede that the school's amazing record is helped by the fact that no other teams ever show up to play, but they contend that their team's excellence is so intimidating that other schools know they could never win. Even if you can't get tickets for the U of O football games, you'll still enjoy your time as a student at the University of Okoboji. The tuition is low, the classes easy, and each year everyone graduates at the top of the class.

Arnolds Park is located on the south side of West Lake Okoboji off US 71. A day pass for the amusement rides is $38 for adults. The park is open daily (with some exceptions made for the local school year) from mid-May to mid-Sept. For more information call (712) 332-2183 or visit arnoldspark.com.

The *Iowa Rock 'N' Roll Music Association Museum* preserves the history of pop music in Iowa. It's filled with a potpourri of instruments, costumes, and memorabilia belonging to artists such as Buddy Holly, Richie Valens, Elvis, and J. P. "The Big Bopper" Richardson. Also on display are an old-time recording studio and radio booth, plus plaques displaying inductees into the Iowa

Rock 'N' Roll Hall of Fame, from Brenda Lee and the Everly Brothers to the Surf Ballroom in Clear Lake. The museum (712-330-0889; iowarocknroll.com) is at 243 Broadway in Arnolds Park. It's open daily from Memorial Day through Labor Day, and on weekdays during the rest of the year. A small admission is charged.

Arnolds Park is also home to the **Queen II**, a faithful reproduction of the 1884 *Queen* that plied the waters of the Iowa Great Lakes for eighty-nine years. Local volunteers are responsible for her existence, working both to help raise money for the boat and to help with her construction. More than half of the boat's $350,000 cost was raised through auctions, bake sales, and door-to-door solicitations. In 1986 the *Queen II* was officially launched, with Iowa governor Terry Branstad commissioning her as the Flagship of the Iowa Navy.

Today the *Queen II* offers multiple daily cruises throughout the summer on West Lake Okoboji. The cruises last for an hour, with the captain providing a narrative of the history and attractions of that region. The fare is $17. Call (712) 332-2183 or see arnoldspark.com for more information.

After your cruise, visit the nearby ***Iowa Great Lakes Maritime Museum***, a repository for antique wooden boats, memorabilia from the early days of the amusement park, a restored boathouse, and an exhibit of old-fashioned swim-suits that will make you grateful for the invention of Spandex. Don't miss its charming reproduction of a vintage Okoboji store, which will likely bring back a flood of memories for anyone who visited the area in decades past.

The Iowa Great Lakes Maritime Museum is located in the Okoboji Spirit Center at 243 W. Broadway St. in Arnolds Park. It is open year-round, with extended hours June through Aug. Call (712) 332-5264 or see okobojimuseum .org for information.

A more sobering Okoboji landmark was once the home of one of Iowa's most famous pioneers. The ***Abbie Gardner-Sharp Cabin*** dates back to the earliest years of white settlement. In 1857, forty-two pioneers were killed here on the shore of West Lake Okoboji by Wahpekuti Dakota warriors, violence that was part of a series of skirmishes between the two groups. The tragedy came to be known as the Spirit Lake Massacre.

The original cabin, which sits in a peaceful, tree-lined grove, is a monu-ment to courage and resilience as well as tragedy. Thirteen-year-old Abbie Gardner was taken captive after her family was killed but was eventually ran-somed in South Dakota. After years of depression and illness, she eventually recovered enough to write a book about the massacre. The success of the proj-ect earned her enough money to return to Arnolds Park and buy her family's cabin, the only building remaining from the tragedy. She converted the small building into a museum and welcomed visitors to the site for the next thirty

TOP ANNUAL EVENTS

JANUARY

University of Okoboji Winter Games
Okoboji, end of Jan
(712) 332-2107
uofowintergames.com

MAY

Tulip Festival
Orange City, third weekend in May
(712) 707-4510
octulipfestival.com

JUNE

Ice Cream Days
Le Mars, mid-June
(712) 546-8821
icecreamdays.com

Glenn Miller Festival
Clarinda, second weekend in June
(712) 542-2461
glennmiller.org

AUGUST

Sidney Iowa Rodeo
Sidney, first week in Aug
(712) 374-2695
sidneyiowarodeo.us

SEPTEMBER

ArtSplash
Sioux City, Labor Day weekend
(712) 279-6272
siouxcityartcenter.org

Apple Festival
Woodbine, late Sept
(970) 290-0071
woodbineia.com

NOVEMBER

Julefest
Elkhorn, last weekend in November
(712) 764-7001
danishmuseum.org

years. The cabin at 74 Monument Dr. in Arnolds Park is open Tues through Sun from Memorial Day through Labor Day. Admission is free. See abbiecabin .com for information.

Another Iowa Great Lakes attraction is *Cayler Prairie State Preserve*, a 1,200-acre tract that's one of the largest remaining areas of virgin prairie in the state. It is both a State Botanical Preserve and a National Historic Landmark, and it will give you a chance to see a little of Iowa's once-vast grasslands as they appeared more than a century ago. As you walk through its waist-high grasses, it's easy to imagine how it must have seemed to the early pioneers. Here you will find more than 250 types of grasses and wildflowers. Blooming begins in April with delicate pasqueflowers and ends in October with brilliant blue gentians. Other wildflowers can be found in bloom throughout the summer, with the height of color to be seen in early August. The prairie is also home to badgers, foxes, jackrabbits, meadowlarks, partridge, and the rare upland sandpiper.

Cayler Prairie is located three miles west of West Okoboji Lake. A parking lot is provided along the country road on the southwest side of the prairie.

Visitors are welcome during daylight hours but are urged to read the regulation signs before entering the prairie. The picking or digging of plants is forbidden because of the rarity of many of the prairie's species.

Southwest of Cayler Prairie is the town of **Orange City**, which takes great pride in its Dutch heritage. The town was founded in 1870 by settlers from Holland, who named their new home after Prince William of Orange, a prominent figure in Dutch history. Here you can tour a variety of Dutch-themed attractions and shop for traditional Dutch dolls, pottery, lace, baked goods, wooden shoes, and meats.

A good place to begin your tour is at the **Dutch Windmill Visitors Center**, 509 Eighth St. SE. The windmill stands more than 70 feet tall, with a dome that weighs five tons and vanes weighing more than seven tons. The center (712-707-4510; orangecityiowa.com) is open 9 a.m. to 4 p.m., Mon. through Fri.

On the third weekend in May each year, Orange City becomes even more of a Little Holland during its annual **Tulip Festival**. One of its most popular attractions is the Volksparade, when hundreds of people take to the streets with their buckets and scrub brushes to make the way clean for the festival's queen. Then board the Wilhelmina or the Juliana, the town's two horse-drawn streetcars, to see the rest of the sights in town. The Dutch street organ will likely catch your attention—one of only two in the United States, the organ was built in Holland and plays melodies for the enjoyment of passersby. The Dutch Dozen is a musical and dance group that will also entertain you, and in the evening you can kick up your own heels in a street dance or attend a theater performance.

At any time of year, you can tour the **Stadscentrum**, which is Dutch for "city center." The building contains wooden-shoe–making equipment, wooden shoes, and traditional costumes. You'll find it at 207 Central Ave. NE. It's open 9 a.m. to 5 p.m., Mon. through Fri. and by appointment. Call (712) 707-4510 for information.

At the **Old Mill** (102 Albany Place SE, at the entrance to the Diamond Vogel Paint Company), you can learn more about the Dutch heritage of Orange City. The mill is a replica of a nineteenth-century Dutch mill, with living quarters that show life as it was generations ago. Some of the furnishings were brought from Holland, and others came from local pioneers. The Old Mill is open Mon. through Fri. Call (712) 737-8880 for more information.

Next, take a walking tour of the downtown, which has many buildings with decorative features reminiscent of those in the Netherlands. Finish up at **Windmill Park**, which has six replica windmills, a small canal, and a replica of a traditional town water pump. During the spring, the park has the largest concentration of tulip beds in Orange City. And every Wednesday evening from Tulip Festival through the end of August, there's a free concert in the park.

Before leaving town, go across the street to the **Dutch Bakery** at 212 Central Ave. NE. There you can buy such treats as almond patties, St. Nick cookies, Dutch rusks, apple rolls, and Wilhelmina Peppermints imported from Holland.

For more information on attractions in the Orange City area, call the town's chamber of commerce at (712) 707-4885 or see orangecityiowa.com.

Southeast of Orange City lies the town of **Cherokee**. There you'll find the **Sanford Museum and Planetarium**. The facility was donated to the town by a local couple in memory of their son, Tiel Sanford, and opened in 1951.

didyouknow?

The Kneirim Bank in Kneirim (now a private residence) was robbed of $272 in 1934 by Clyde Barrow and Bonnie Parker.

Permanent exhibits at the Sanford deal with a variety of subjects relating to this region of the country and its past. Rocks, minerals, and fossil and animal specimens help explain the natural environment of the region. There are also displays about the Native American tribes who once lived in the area.

The Sanford Museum and Planetarium is located at 117 E. Willow St. It is open daily and admission is free. Planetarium shows are given each Wed and Sun at 4 p.m. For more information call (712) 225-3922 or see sanfordmuseum .org.

Before you leave the area, you might want to pay a visit to a natural landmark located about 2 miles south of Cherokee on US 59. Pilot Rock is an enormous boulder of red Sioux quartzite about 160 feet in circumference and 20 feet high. It was left behind when the last continental glacier receded and offers a panoramic view of the surrounding landscape. During pioneer days, Pilot Rock served as an important landmark for travelers.

Southeast of Cherokee lies **Storm Lake**, a lovely town of about 11,000 people on the shore of the 3,200-acre natural lake of the same name. Home to Buena Vista University, the town also boasts a beautiful network of parks that follows the shoreline, each park connected by a biking and walking trail that winds for about 5 miles.

In Sunset Park on West Lakeshore Drive, visit the **Living Heritage Tree Museum**, where you can see a unique collection of trees with illustrious histories. The Village Blacksmith Chestnut, for example, is a descendant of the tree that inspired the poet Longfellow to write "Under the Spreading Chestnut Tree." Another tree nearby was grown from a seed carried to the moon and back. Also in the museum is a tulip poplar descended from a tree planted by

newdealmurals

During the Depression, the Works Progress Administration commissioned artists to paint murals across the state. You can see these WPA murals in towns that include:

Emmetsburg: Post Office

Hawarden: Post Office

Storm Lake: Public Library

Sioux City: East Junior High and Castle on the Hill

Ida Grove: Post Office

Rockwell City: Post Office

Onawa: Post Office

Audubon: Post Office

Harlan: Post Office

Missouri Valley: Post Office

Corning: Post Office

George Washington at Mount Vernon, as well as an apple tree traced back to the famed Johnny Appleseed. Dozens of historically significant trees are interspersed amid serene landscaping near the lake. The park is open to the public at no charge, twenty-four hours a day.

The Victorian-era *Harker House* at 328 Lake Ave. N is also worth a visit. It was built in 1875 by a local banker in the French mansard-cottage style. The home, which contains many of the original furnishings, is open for afternoon tours on weekends. Call (712) 732-3267 or see harkerhouse.com for information. A small admission is charged.

Santa's Castle is a fun place to visit if you're in Storm Lake between Thanksgiving and Christmas (or any other time of the year if you make an appointment). Begun in 1962 with the purchase of four animated elves, the castle now houses what may be the largest collection of antique, animated Christmas figures in the world. These are real classics from old department store displays. They make their home in an original Carnegie Library building at 200 E. Fifth St. A small admission fee is charged. For more information or to arrange a tour, call (712) 749-9247 or see santascastle.org.

Northeast of Storm Lake lies the town of *Albert City* and a rather unusual historical museum. Don't miss the depot where a shoot-out following a bank robbery claimed the lives of three. You can still see the bullet holes in the walls and look at the gun used by one of the robbers. There are many vintage cars as well. Check out the funeral parlor where you can view old memorial wreaths and candlesticks, as well as a picture of the first motorized hearse. The *Albert City Historical Museum* is located at 212 N. Second St. It is open on Sun from 2 to 5 p.m., from Memorial Day to Labor Day. Call (712) 843-5684 for more information.

River Treasures and Prairie Landmarks

From Albert City head west to **Le Mars**, which is known for both its ice cream (see sidebar) and its street art. Ten of its downtown alleys are adorned with murals that range from the whimsical to the historical. **Le Mars Alley Art** (712-546-8821; lemarschamber.com) showcases the work of more than thirty area artists who use brick walls as their canvases. After your walking tour, you can see more artistic creations at the **Le Mars Arts Center** (712-546-7476; lemars arts.com), which is located in a 1903 Carnegie Library building at 200 Central Ave. SE.

Le Mars is also home to one of the nation's top steak houses (according to celebrity chef Rachael Ray). **Archie's Waeside** has been serving tender, aged steaks for more than sixty years. The third-generation restaurant was also given a James Beard American Classic award in 2015. Owner Bob Rand and his staff serve about 2,000 hand-cut steaks a week, feeding customers who come from three bordering states and beyond. You'll find the restaurant at 224 Fourth Ave. For information call (712) 546-7011 or see archieswaeside.com.

Next head to Iowa's western border. At the junction of Iowa, South Dakota, and Nebraska lies **Sioux City**. Ever since the Lewis and Clark expedition passed through here in 1804, Sioux City has been a focal point for travelers and settlers heading west. Located on the bank of the Missouri River, the city became a major nineteenth-century river port and the center of a booming stockyard and meatpacking industry. The Missouri River is still important to the city, though today it's prized primarily for its recreational attractions. Sioux City has developed its riverfront into an extensive park-and-trail system, with a number of historical points of interest along the way.

It's a Scoop!

It is a commonly known fact that we all scream for ice cream—and if there is one place where such screaming is more appropriate than others, that place is **Le Mars**, the Ice Cream Capital of the World! Here, in northwestern Iowa, more ice cream is made in one location than anywhere else in the world. That's because this is the home of Wells' Dairy Inc., makers of Blue Bunny ice cream and other popular frozen treats.

The **Wells Visitor Center & Ice Cream Parlor** at 115 Central Ave. NW sells all kinds of ice-cream delights at its antique marble bar. At the center you can also find out everything you want to know about the history of ice cream. Afterwards, walk around Le Mars to see its fifty-five ice cream sculptures, each more than 5 feet tall and painted by local artists.

Several of these attractions focus on Sergeant Charles Floyd, a member of the Lewis and Clark expedition who died here on August 20, 1804—the only casualty of the entire two-year expedition. His death is memorialized at the **Sergeant Floyd Monument**, a 100-foot-high white stone obelisk that is located on a high bluff overlooking the Missouri River. The monument became the country's first National Historic Landmark in 1960 and is located on US 75 near Glenn Avenue. It is 1/2 mile east and 1 mile north of exit 143 of I-29.

The **Lewis & Clark Interpretive Center** explores the dramatic story of the expedition in more detail. Interactive exhibits bring to life the hardships and challenges of this epic journey. At the entrance visitors sign on as members of the Corps of Discovery and then explore a day in the life of the expedition as it travels near Sioux City. You'll learn more about the military discipline that helped the team weather hardships, as well as the men's daily routines of cooking, standing guard, and setting up camp. The exhibits include animatronic mannequins, mapmaking tools, computers, hand-painted murals, brass-rubbing stations, and replicas of military equipment and Indian artifacts. A video presentation, produced exclusively for the interpretive center, is shown every fifteen minutes in the Keelboat Theatre. And don't miss the sculpture of Lewis, Clark, and their fearless Newfoundland dog, Seaman.

The Lewis & Clark Interpretive Center is at exit 149 off I-29. It is open Tues through Sun. Admission is free. For more information call (712) 224-5242 or see siouxcitylcic.com.

The young soldier who died near this spot is also remembered at the **Sergeant Floyd River Museum and Welcome Center**. The center is housed aboard an original 1932 Army Corps of Engineers vessel, named in honor of

With All the Honors of War

Regarding the death of Sergeant Floyd, the journals of Lewis and Clark read thus:

"20th August, 1804—I am Dull & heavy been up the greater Part of last night with Sgt. Floyd who is as bad as he can be to live. . . We set out under a jentle Breeze from the southeast. . . We came to make a bath for Sgt. Floyd hoping it would brace him a little, before we get him into his bath he expired with a great deal of composure . . . having Said to me before his death that he was going away and wished me to write a letter . . . . We buried him to the top of a high round hill overlooking the river & Country for a great distance situated just below a small river without a name to which we name & call Floyd's river, the Bluffs, Sergt. Floyd's Bluff. . . we buried him with all the honors of War, and fixed a Ceeder post at his head with his name title and day of the month & year . . . we returned to the Boat & proceeded to the Mouth of the little river 30 yd wide & camped a butiful evening. . . ."

Sergeant Floyd. From 1933 to 1975 the boat did towing, survey, and inspection work on the Missouri River, and in 1983 it was permanently dry-docked to serve as a combined welcome center and river museum. Tour exhibits on the Lewis and Clark Expedition and river transportation history and explore the third level of the boat, which has been restored to its original appearance.

The Sergeant Floyd Welcome Center and Museum is located off I-29 at exit 149. It is open daily from 9 a.m. to 4 p.m. and admission is free. Call (712) 279-0198 for information.

Another riverfront site recalls a more recent part of Sioux City history. The *Flight 232 Memorial* commemorates the heroic rescue efforts made by the Sioux City community after the crash of United Flight 232 in 1989. The monument includes a statue of Colonel Dennis Nielsen carrying a young child to safety. Nearby is the *Anderson Dance Pavilion*, a lovely public space that is used for festivals that include Labor Day weekend's ArtSplash. You'll find the memorial and pavilion on the riverfront in Gateway Park.

Sioux City is also proud of the renovation of its historic *Orpheum Theatre*. The Orpheum first opened in 1927 and was once one of the most magnificent movie palaces in America. During 2000–2001, hundreds of builders and artisans labored to restore the structure, using a mixture of antique and reproduction furnishings. Today the opulent 2,444-seat theater offers a full schedule of top-name performances, including touring Broadway shows. The Orpheum is at 528 Pierce St.; for a schedule of events, call (712) 258-9164 or see orpheumlive.com.

You can learn more about area history at the *Sioux City Public Museum*. After a twelve-minute orientation film, visitors can browse interactive science exhibits that include The Big Dig, which replicates a fossil dig site. Other exhibits give information on pioneer history and the Indian tribes that lived here before the arrival of white settlers.

The Sioux City Public Museum is located at 607 Fourth St. Its hours are Tues through Sat from 10 a.m. to 5 p.m. and Sun from 1 to 5 p.m. Admission is free. For more information call (712) 279-6174 or see siouxcitymuseum.org.

If you're a popcorn fan (and who isn't?), you won't want to miss the *Jolly Time Pop Corn Museum* at 1717 Terminal Dr. Jolly Time began as a basement business in Sioux City in 1914 and has grown into a nationwide company. Tour the museum's displays of vintage packaging, celebrity endorsements, and artifacts from the company's early years, then browse the Koated Kernels Retail Shoppe. The museum and shop are open Mon through Sat. For more information call (712) 560-6973 or see koatedkernels.com.

A fun place to visit while you're in Sioux City is the *Historic Fourth Street* area downtown. This area's early twentieth-century architecture now houses numerous pubs, restaurants, and antiques and specialty shops. The buildings along this street, noted for their Richardsonian Romanesque style, popular in the late 1800s, line a 2-block-long area from Virginia Street to Iowa Street. Two of the buildings, the Evan's Block and the Boston Block, are included on the National Register of Historic Places.

There are several places to eat on Historic Fourth Street. You can customize a pizza (with more than thirty different ingredients!) and sample a beer from more than 115 different varieties at **Buffalo Alice**. The restaurant is located at 1022 Fourth St. Call (712) 255-4822 or see buffaloalice.com for more information. For a sweet treat, stop by **Palmer's Olde Tyme Candy Shoppe**. Founded in 1878, the Palmer Candy Company has been run by the same family for five generations. Its signature candy is the Twin Bing, made of cherry nougat covered with roasted peanuts and chocolate. The Candy Shoppe sells a wide array of sweets and also has a small museum with antique candy-making equipment and vintage photos. You'll find it at 405 Wesley Pkwy. Call (712) 258-5543 or see palmercandy.com for more information.

After all that eating, it's time to venture out-of-doors. Take IA 12 north of town to CR K18, where you'll find **Five Ridge Prairie**. The ridges that give

The Loess Hills

Seen from a distance, Iowa's **Loess Hills** may appear little different from other rolling countryside in the state. But spend an hour, a day, or a week exploring them, and the region's unique character begins to unfold. These hills are a rare geological formation found only here and in northern China. Rich in natural beauty and ecological diversity, the Loess Hills are especially lovely in autumn, when brilliant colors light their woodlands and their prairies glow with gold and russet hues.

The Loess (pronounced "luss") Hills rise like a miniature mountain range on the western border of Iowa, stretching for 200 miles from Sioux City to the southern border of the state. The hills began forming at the end of the last ice age, when the wind picked up soils that had been finely ground by the glaciers and blew it into dunes alongside the ancient waterway that became today's Missouri River. Over thousands of years, the highly erodible soil was shaped by wind and rain into steep ridges, canyons, and valleys, each with their own microclimates that nurture a wide array of plants and animals. More than 300 species of native plants, 243 species of birds, and some of the state's largest remnants of virgin prairie can be found here.

The **Loess Hills National Scenic Byway** makes it easy to explore the region. The route winds through the most scenic portions of hills, with numerous side loops that lead into more remote areas. While the majority of the Loess Hills are privately owned, public parks and state forest land are also plentiful.

the 964-acre park its name include 8 miles of trails that wind through tall grass prairie and woodlands. Call the Plymouth County Conservation Bureau at (712) 947-4270 or see plymouthcountyparks.com for more information.

The **Hitchcock Nature Center**, located 15 miles north of Council Bluffs, is a good place to get an orientation to the Loess Hills. Its well-designed nature center gives a thorough introduction to how the hills were formed and to the distinctive flora and fauna of the area, from yucca and prairie rattlesnakes to scarlet tanager songbirds. Then set out on its 10-mile trail system, a web of paths that will take you up, down and through the hills. Even a short walk gives a sense of the beauty and diversity of the landscape. Some slopes feel almost like Wyoming, with mixed-grass prairie and semi-arid plants, while others are lush with vegetation.

The unique topography of the Loess Hills makes them one of North America's best places to watch migrating hawks and other raptors in the fall. Winds sweep through the Missouri River valley and are pushed upwards by the hills, creating updrafts and thermals that make it easy for the birds to fly south. The Hitchcock Nature Center has a 45-foot observation tower with splendid views of the action. On an autumn day, 200 raptors may pass by overhead, with numbers occasionally reaching into the thousands. The spot has been named one of the top twenty-five hawk-watching sites in North America by the National Wildlife Federation and was designated as Iowa's first Important Bird Area. The center is at 27792 Ski Hill Loop near Honey Creek. For information call (712) 545-3283 or see pottconservation.com.

To the north, **Preparation Canyon State Park** (712-456-2924; iowadnr .gov) offers more secluded hiking. Its 344 acres once included the town of Preparation, founded by Mormons who broke off from a Mormon wagon train headed to Utah in 1853. Today it has a wild and untouched air, with trails that wind along high ridge tops and then plunge into deep canyons. For a true getaway, you can stay in its hike-in camp sites, the only accommodations offered at the park. The park is at 206 Polk St. near Pisgah.

At the southern end of the Loess Hills, you can explore the nearly 2,000 acres of gorges and high ridges at **Waubonsie State Park** (712-382-2786; iowadnr.gov) at 2585 Waubonsie Park Rd. near Hamburg. In addition to 7 miles of hiking trails, the park (which is named after a Pottawattamie chief) includes cabins, a campground, horseback riding, boating, and fishing.

One of the more unusual businesses in the region is the **Loess Hills Lavender Farm**, an aromatic oasis located on a hillside north of Missouri Valley. Walk through its 2 acres of blooming plants and then visit its gift shop to sample lavender-infused lotions, soaps, and other products. Lavender grows very well here because the soil of the Loess Hills quickly percolates water away from the roots, which helps the plants to flourish. The farm is at 2278 Loess Hills Trail. For information call (712) 642-9016 or see loesshillslavender.com.

For more information, see visitloesshills.org. Another good resource is Cornelia F. Mutel's book *Fragile Giants*, which explores the Loess Hills and their delicate ecology.

From Sioux City travel east on US 20 for 60 miles and then head south on CR M43 to the **Prairie Pedlar** at 1609 270th St. in **Odebolt**. Here you can stroll through 7 acres of perennial and annual theme gardens filled with hundreds of varieties of flowers and herbs. This family-owned business also includes a gift shop and a greenhouse with hundreds of hard-to-find perennials and annuals. Special events include a Mother's Day Tea Party and Moonlight Garden Party in midsummer.

Owner Jane Hogue began the business more than twenty years ago and since then has seen her hard work blossom into an enterprise that draws visitors from across the state. Assisted by family members, Jane raises the flowers in the gardens and harvests, dries, and arranges them in delightful combinations.

The Prairie Pedlar gardens and gift shop are open Apr through mid-Oct, Mon through Sat from 11 a.m. to 4 p.m. and on Sun from 1 to 4 p.m. Call (712) 668-4840 or see prairiepedlar.com for more information.

Next head south to **Denison**, birthplace of one of America's favorite moms, actress Donna Reed. Reed was raised on a farm near Denison and completed her schooling here. After graduation she left Iowa to become an actress, starring in *The Donna Reed Show* and more than thirty movies. Reed returned often to Denison, remaining in contact with her family and friends in the area until her death in 1986.

The **Donna Reed Center for the Performing Arts** celebrates Denison's most famous daughter. The center is located in the former German Opera House, which first opened its doors in 1914. The Opera House was later converted into the Ritz Movie Theater, where Donna Reed fell in love with motion pictures. In 1988 the Donna Reed Foundation, with financial support from the community, corporate grants, and thousands of volunteer hours, saved the building.

Today the center (located at Broadway and Main Streets) houses the Donna Reed Foundation headquarters and the 550-seat Donna Reed Theater. A miniature replica of Bedford Falls, the town from the movie *It's a Wonderful Life*, is on permanent display, as are photos, personal items, and movie mementos from Donna Reed's life.

Denison is also the site of the **W. A. McHenry House**. This beautiful Victorian home was built in 1885 by Denison pioneer William A. McHenry. With six fireplaces and fourteen rooms (including a ballroom), the home was for

Al Capone's Favorite Whiskey

If you were traveling through this part of Iowa during Prohibition Days—and you didn't mind breaking the law—you would have made a beeline to the little town of Templeton (population 350) just east of Manning. There, a number of the town's citizens performed a valuable public service by making Templeton Rye whiskey. The drink commanded top dollar—the equivalent of $70 a gallon in today's dollars—and so impressed Al Capone that he started bootlegging it across the country. After Prohibition ended, the whiskey continued to be made in small batches for select patrons, but was not commercially available.

In 2006 Templeton Rye was reborn as a legal brand that still uses the original Prohibition-era recipe. Since then it has quickly attained a national reputation (while its flavor is superb, its association with Al Capone doesn't hurt its marketing efforts). Its visitor center at 209 S. Rye Ave. offers tours on Thurs, Fri, and Sat. Call (712) 669-8793 or see templetonrye.com for information. Tell 'em Al sent you.

many years a showplace for the area. Today it has been restored and contains a variety of historical artifacts, including the Academy Award won by Donna Reed for her role in *From Here to Eternity*.

The W. A. McHenry House is located at 1428 First Ave. N. It is open June through Sept on the first and third weekends. For more information call (712) 269-7594.

Southwest of Denison lies **Dow City**, site of the **Simon E. Dow House**. The historic home sits high on a hill with a commanding view of the surrounding countryside. Its builder, Simon Dow, was traveling through Iowa on his way west in 1855 when he decided to cut his journey short and remain here because he liked the area so much. Later he became a prominent cattleman, and in 1872 he built a substantial redbrick house that became the nucleus of a settlement called Dow City. At a time when the average home cost $2,000, Dow spent a princely $11,000 for his home.

The Dow House is unusual in that its floor plan is the same on all three floors. All the walls are three bricks wide to keep the home warm in the winter and cool in the summer, and ornamented keystones and carved roses are centered over the first- and second-floor doors. Today the home has been restored to its original appearance and will give you an interesting introduction to the lifestyle of a prominent, upper-middle-class citizen of the nineteenth century.

The Simon E. Dow House (712-263-2748) is located south of US 30 at the end of Prince Street in Dow City. It is open Memorial Day to Labor Day from 1 to 4 p.m. on Sat and Sun.

Before you leave this neck of the woods, plan a visit to the community of **Manning** on IA 141. Here you'll find what is probably the oldest building in Iowa, the **Hausbarn**, a combination house and barn built in the middle of the seventeenth century in the German region of Schleswig-Holstein and dismantled and shipped over to Manning, where it was reconstructed piece by piece in 1996. The Hausbarn is part of the **Manning Hausbarn Heritage Park**, a complex of sites celebrating the town's history and German roots. It is located at 12196 311th St. and is open daily from May through Oct. For more information call (712) 655-3131 or visit germanhausbarn.com.

A quite lovely place to tour in this area of the state is the community of **Woodbine**. Once a stop on the old Lincoln Highway, the town has relaid all of its downtown sidewalks with brick to match the oldest remaining brick segment of the first highway to span the country. Several stately Victorian houses still overlook this section of the road. Don't miss the old Lincoln Highway marker near the Harrison County Genealogical Center at 212 Lincoln Way. Then take a stroll through the White Floral Gardens at Eleventh and Park Streets, a lovely park filled with peonies, shrubs, and trees.

Plan a visit to the community of **Gray** at the end of May or June. "Gray" may be its name but gray is not its nature, especially during the summer months, when the **Heritage Rose Garden**, located on the first block of Main Street, comes alive with the fragrance and color of roses. This garden has been planted with old garden roses known for their hardiness, durability, fragrance, and beauty. Here you'll find rugosas, climbers, gallicas, albas, and lovely big-headed cabbage roses. Don't miss the angel garden and the other old-fashioned flowers. Call (712) 563-2742 for more information.

Traveling south on US 71, you may think your eyes are deceiving you but look again—it's **Albert the Bull** of **Audubon**. The world's largest anatomically correct bull stands as a monument to the beef industry and weighs in at 45 tons. Erected in 1963 and made of concrete and steel, he is 30 feet tall and has a horn span of 15 feet.

While you're in Audubon don't miss the wonderful mural in the post office of John James Audubon, artist and naturalist, for whom both the town and the county were named. Commissioned by the Works Progress Administration (WPA) in the 1930s, it was painted by Virginia Snedecher of Brooklyn, New York. The town also celebrates the famous artist with a series of mosaics in the downtown's Bird Walk. Call (712) 563-3780 for information.

Farther south toward **Hamlin** and easily seen from US 71 are the eighteen antique windmills that were donated by local farmers and are now used to show the way to **Nathaniel Hamlin Park and Museums**. This unusual park, part of the old Audubon County Home, includes a bluebird house trail, a preserved prairie, and an elk couple—not to mention what may well be the world's largest nail collection! The park is open on Fri, 10 a.m. to 4 p.m., Memorial Day through Sept. Call (712) 563-2742 for more information.

Southeast of Dow City you'll find the charming villages of **Elk Horn** and **Kimballton**, which are home to the largest rural Danish settlement in the United States. Danish immigrants settled the area in the late nineteenth century, and their descendants have worked hard to preserve their unique heritage.

Your first stop should be the **Museum of Danish America**, which tells the story of the Danish settlement of North America and the Danish-American ethnic heritage that lives on today. Located in Elk Horn, the three-story structure has a pitched roof and a half-timber, half-stucco finish that suggests a Danish farmhouse. Inside are exhibits that describe the immigrant experience both in the Old Country and the New World. Elk Horn was chosen as the site of the museum after a nationwide search because of its strong town spirit and commitment to the project. The Museum of Danish America (712-764-7001; danishmuseum.org) is located at 2212 Washington St. It is open daily. Admission is $7 for adults and $3 for children.

Next pay a visit to Elk Horn's **Danish Windmill**. The landmark brings to mind the bumper sticker that says, "You can tell a Dane, but you can't tell him much." If that weren't the case, it's doubtful the historic mill would ever have left its home in Norre Snede, in the Danish province of Jutland. It was during the worst days of the farm crisis in the mid-1970s that local resident Harvey Sornson came up with the idea of finding a Danish windmill to bring to the area. Many people thought the idea was crazy, but their skepticism gradually gave way to Sornson's persistence. A mill was located in Denmark, and an emergency town meeting in Elk Horn resulted in $30,000 being pledged to the project in just a few days. The 1848 structure was then laboriously dismantled and brought over piece by piece to Iowa. When it arrived it still had ocean salt on its timbers, and eighty-seven-year-old Peder K. Pedersen, who had left Denmark at the age of twenty-one and never returned, tasted the salt of a distant sea and cried.

Many of Elk Horn's townspeople worked together to reassemble the jigsaw puzzle of the dismantled mill, which was rebuilt in 1976. The total cost of the project eventually came to $100,000, a hefty amount raised through fundraising projects and contributions from all over the country. Today the windmill stands some 60 feet high, with four 30-foot wings that catch the wind, turn the gears, and grind locally grown grain. The base of the mill houses a welcome center with extensive tourist information, and the adjacent Danish Mill Gift Shop offers stone-ground flour and a wide selection of Scandinavian gifts and foods.

The Danish Windmill is located at 4038 Main St. It is open daily. For more information call (712) 764-7472 or see danishwindmill.com.

Another Elk Horn attraction that owes its existence to the town's volunteer spirit is **Bedstemor's House**, meaning "grandmother's house." More than a hundred volunteers have donated time, materials, and furnishings to restore the 1908 home. Inside you'll find a glimpse of the life of a Danish immigrant family from the early twentieth century. (To furnish the home, volunteers used a 1908 Sears Roebuck catalog as their guide.)

Bedstemor's House is located 3 blocks north and 1 block west of the Danish Windmill at 2105 College St. It is open Wed, Thurs, and Fri from 1 to 4 pm. For more information call (712) 764-7001.

Two miles north of Elk Horn you'll find its sister village of Kimballton, also an enclave of Danish-American culture. The town's pride and joy is the *Little Mermaid*, a statue modeled after the famous landmark in Copenhagen's harbor (the Little Mermaid, of course, is the immortal character from the fairy tale by Hans Christian Andersen). Kimballton's little mermaid is the focal point of the town's Little Mermaid Park on Main Street. Nearby is the Mermaid Gift Shop, featuring many imported gift items.

Whiterock Conservancy

Perhaps you want to spend a weekend in the country canoeing, hiking, or trail riding. Maybe you just want to kick back and do some fishing during the day and some stargazing at night. Maybe you'd like to learn more about alternative agriculture methods or beekeeping or how to start a prairie. Whatever your interests, you are sure to find something you like at *Whiterock Conservancy*.

The resort is located on the farm once owned by Roswell Garst, hybrid corn promoter and diplomat, who bought it in 1916 and added to it over the years until his death in 1977. It was here that Garst entertained Nikita Khrushchev and his family in 1959 during the height of the Cold War. Garst's progressive and entrepreneurial spirit lives on today in this 5,500-acre nonprofit land trust. The Whiterock Conservancy is a national leader in sustainable agriculture, low-impact recreation, and ecological restoration.

The resort is still owned by the Garst family, whose home is now a five-bedroom bed-and-breakfast. Additional lodging is available at properties that include the Hollyhock Cottage, which began its life as a chicken coop and then became Mrs. Garst's garden shed, and in the Oak Ridge Farm House, which can accommodate up to thirteen people. There are also camping sites.

For more information, call (712) 790-8221 or see whiterockconservancy.org. The resort, ½ mile east of Coon Rapids, is located at 1436 Hwy. 141 in Coon Rapids.

A good time to visit this area is during its two annual Danish festivals. *Tivoli Fest* is held each year on Memorial Day weekend. *Julefest* (the town's Christmas festival) is held the weekend after Thanksgiving and celebrates the season in true Danish style. Whenever you visit, you're likely to leave these friendly communities with an appreciation for their Danish heritage and with plans to return. For more information on attractions in Elk Horn and Kimballton, see danishvillages.com.

From the Danish villages head south to the small town of *Walnut*, which is known as *Iowa's Antique City*. More than a dozen antiques stores make Walnut one of the best havens for nostalgia buffs in the state. From antique brass beds to ice-cream parlor stools and vintage dollhouses, you're likely to find an eclectic mixture of treasures on a visit to Walnut. For more information, see iowasantiquecity.com.

Missouri River Heritage

From Walnut head west to *Harrison County*, which borders the Missouri River and contains some of the most varied and beautiful scenery in the state of Iowa: lush farmland, gently rolling foothills, and the fragile loveliness of the Loess Hills. The county is also known as an apple-producing area. The fruit was first planted here before 1880, and today Harrison County has more acreage in apples than any other county in Iowa. These beautiful orchards, many of which line the county roads, are located near the towns of *Missouri Valley*, *Mondamin*, *Pisgah*, and *Woodbine*. Several orchards have facilities for picking your own apples, and orchard tours are also available. Apples are available for sale from mid-August to the end of the season.

Near the town of Missouri Valley in Harrison County, you'll find one of the state's major wildlife areas, the *DeSoto National Wildlife Refuge*, located 5 miles west of I-29. The refuge lies on the wide plain formed by prehistoric flooding and shifting of the Missouri River. Each spring and fall since the end of the last ice age, spectacular flights of ducks and geese have marked the changing seasons along this traditional waterfowl flyway. During a typical year some 200,000 snow and blue geese use the refuge as a resting and feeding area during their fall migration from their arctic nesting grounds to their Gulf Coast wintering areas. Peak populations of 125,000 or more ducks, mostly mallards, are common in the refuge during the fall migration. Other birds commonly seen in the area include bald eagles, warblers, gulls, pheasants, and various shorebirds.

Bird life is not the only attraction at the refuge. Deer, raccoon, coyote, opossum, beaver, muskrat, and mink make their homes here and can often be seen by patient observers. During the spring and summer, the refuge is open for fishing, picnicking, mushroom and berry picking, hiking, and boating. Twelve miles of all-weather roads meander through the refuge, and during the fall a special interpretive brochure is available to guide visitors and explain the annual migration.

The visitor center at the refuge should definitely be part of your visit to Harrison County. In addition to its natural-history displays, viewing galleries, wildlife films, and special programs, the refuge center is also the site of the ***Steamboat* Bertrand *Museum***, a facility housing some 200,000 artifacts recovered from the steamboat *Bertrand*, a vessel that sank with all its cargo in the treacherous Missouri River in 1865.

Visit the *Bertrand* Museum today and you can view many of those items, a collection that provides a fascinating look at a vanished time. More than the story of the *Bertrand* is revealed here: The saga of the western expansion unfolds through the boat's artifacts and other exhibits depicting the history and wildlife of the Missouri River basin.

The *Bertrand* Museum, located in the DeSoto National Wildlife Refuge Visitor Center, is open from 8:30 a.m. to 4:30 p.m. daily. Additional interpretive

A Time Capsule of Frontier Life

The wreck of the **Bertrand** mirrors that of many steamers, 400 of which sank in the Missouri during the nineteenth century. The boat was a mountain-packet stern-wheeler designed for the shallow, narrow rivers of the West. She was built to carry supplies that would eventually find their way to the gold miners of the Montana Territory and was said to be loaded with 35,000 pounds of mercury, $4,000 in gold, and 5,000 gallons of whiskey—a fortune worth $300,000 or more back then. Luck was not with the steamer, for on her first trip upriver in 1865 she hit a snag and sank in 12 feet of water. The passengers and crew escaped unharmed, but the bulk of the cargo had to be abandoned. By the time a full-scale salvage operation could be mounted, the boat was irretrievable.

Over the years many treasure hunters searched unsuccessfully for the *Bertrand* and her costly cargo. With time, the Missouri changed its course, leaving the boat in a low-lying field under 25 to 30 feet of silt and clay. It wasn't until 1967 that the wreck was located after an extensive search by treasure hunters Sam Corbino and Jesse Pursell. Unfortunately for them, the cargo didn't contain the rumored riches, though it did contain bounty of another sort: some 10,000 cubic feet of hand tools, clothes, foodstuffs, furnishings, munitions, and personal effects, a virtual time capsule of nineteenth-century life. What was even more remarkable was that most of the cargo was in an excellent state of preservation, though the boat itself had to be returned to its resting spot once the artifacts were removed.

displays can be seen at the *Bertrand* excavation site 3 miles south of the visitor center. For more information call (712) 388-4800.

To learn more about the history of the region, visit the **Harrison County Historical Village and Welcome Center**. The site is arranged like a small pioneer village, with a one-room schoolhouse, general store, blacksmith shop, and frontier home. The adjacent **Iowa Welcome Center** (which is open daily) gives additional information on the area, including background on the ecology of the Loess Hills. The museum at 2931 Monroe Ave. in Missouri Valley is open daily Apr through Nov. For information call (712) 642-2114 or see harrison countyparks.org.

Next head south to the **Council Bluffs** area. The city is named for the council meeting that took place near here in 1804 between the explorers Lewis and Clark and the chiefs of the Otoe and Missouri Tribes. Council Bluffs later became a major stopover point on the Mormon Trail, and it was here that Brigham Young was elected president of the Mormon Church in 1847. By the mid-nineteenth century Council Bluffs had become a wild and lawless town, a place where "gambling and sin of almost every description flourished," to quote one observer of the day. The Ocean Wave Saloon was one of the most notorious sporting houses in the entire West until it burned to the ground during a violent thunderstorm (some held that it had been struck by lightning, while others believed it was the wrathful hand of God). Henry DeLong, a former regular customer of the establishment who had mended his ways, bought the property and gave it to the Methodist Church with the provision that it be used forever after as a church site. The Broadway Methodist Church now stands on the property, and it's most likely the only church in the country with a plaque on the front commemorating a saloon.

You can learn more about the history of the area at the **Western Historic Trails Center** at exit 1B off I-80/29. The site tells the stories behind the four trails that once passed through Council Bluffs: the route followed by Lewis and Clark, the journey of the Mormons west to Utah, and the California and Oregon Trails taken by the pioneers. The challenges and hardships of the trails are explored through exhibits and a film by award-winning filmmaker John Allen.

The site also includes 400 acres of hiking and biking trails that wind amid wildflowers and prairie grasses along the Missouri River. Admission to the center (712-366-4900) is free. It is open daily from 9 a.m. to 5 p.m. (closed Mon during the winter months).

Council Bluffs' most famous and influential citizen was Gen. Grenville M. Dodge, a man who has been called the greatest railroad builder of all time. Born in the East, Dodge first saw Council Bluffs while making a railroad survey and was so captivated that he made the city his home in 1853. In 1859 he

Iowa Bike Trails

Iowa has one of the best networks of off-road bicycling in the nation, with hundreds of miles of paved trails that wind through scenic landscapes. In addition to the bike ride known as RAGBRAI (a July event that takes a varied route each year from the western to eastern border), permanent trails will take you through river valleys, along the shores of lakes, past fields of corn and soybeans, and through deep woods. Here are some of the state's most beautiful trails:

- Wabash Trace Nature Trail: 63 miles running south from Council Bluffs to Blanchard

- High Trestle Trail: between Ankeny and Woodward, a 25-mile trail that crosses a 130-foot-high bridge

- Trout Run Trail: an 11-mile route encircling Decorah

- Raccoon River Valley Trail: a 72-mile loop connecting 14 towns in central Iowa

- Neal Smith Trail: 26 miles from Saylorville Lake to the north side of Des Moines

met Abraham Lincoln, and the two developed a strong friendship. After Lincoln became president, he appointed Dodge as the chief engineer of the first transcontinental railroad. During the Civil War, Dodge served with distinction in a number of positions and was responsible for creating the first military spy system. After the war he was elected to Congress without campaigning and later became an adviser to Presidents Grant, McKinley, Roosevelt, and Taft, as well as a business leader in Council Bluffs and the East.

Today you can visit the ***Historic General Dodge House*** to learn more about the life and times of this remarkable man. The home was built in 1869 and was designed by the architect responsible for Terrace Hill in Des Moines. The Second Empire–style mansion stands on a high hillside overlooking the Missouri valley and contains lavish furnishings; parquet floors; cherry, walnut, and butternut woodwork; and a number of "modern" conveniences quite unusual for the period. Today it has been restored to the opulence of the general's day and is open for tours.

The General Dodge House is located at 605 Third St. It is open from 10 a.m. to 5 p.m. Tues through Sat. It is closed during the month of Jan, and the last tour begins each day at 4 p.m. Admission is $10 for adults; $5 for children. For more information call (712) 322-2406 or visit dodgehouse.org.

General Dodge's wife, Ruth Anne, is commemorated by the ***Ruth Anne Dodge Memorial***. On the three nights preceding her death in 1916, Mrs. Dodge had a dream of being on a rocky shore and, through a mist, seeing a boat approach. In the prow was a beautiful young woman who Mrs. Dodge thought to be an angel. The woman carried a small bowl under one arm and extended the other arm to Mrs. Dodge in an invitation to drink of the water flowing from the vessel. Twice Mrs. Dodge refused the angel, but on the third night she accepted the invitation to drink—and died the next day.

Dodge's two daughters later commissioned Daniel Chester French, who also sculpted the Lincoln Memorial in Washington, to construct a statue of the angel in memory of their mother. Though the daughters were reportedly disappointed with the finished work, the monument is now considered to be one of French's finest works. Today you can see the graceful angel, cast in solid bronze, in Fairview Cemetery. As in Mrs. Dodge's dream, the heroic-size statue holds a vessel of water and beckons with her hand.

The Ruth Anne Dodge Memorial, locally known as the **Black Angel**, is located in Fairview Cemetery at Lafayette Avenue and North Second Street. (Also buried in the cemetery is Amelia Bloomer, the inventor of bloomers, the first trousers for women.)

Another historic monument in Council Bluffs is the **Squirrel Cage Jail**, once considered the ultimate in prison facilities. The unique design was patented in 1881 by two Indiana men with the idea of providing "maximum security with minimum jailer attention." Also called a "lazy-Susan" jail, the cell block consists of a three-story drum surrounded by a metal cage. Each of the three

A Mormon Refuge

The original name of Council Bluffs was Kanesville, a tribute to a man who was sympathetic to the plight of the more than 30,000 Mormon refugees who flooded into the area beginning in 1846. The pioneers were escaping religious persecution in Nauvoo, Illinois, where their leader Joseph Smith had been killed. By the time the Mormons left the area for Utah in 1854, they had established more than eighty communities in southwest Iowa, organizing churches, schools, local governments, and four newspapers.

Kanesville was renamed Council Bluffs in 1853, but the Mormon history of the area lives on in a number of sites. Fairview Cemetery holds Mormon pioneer graves, and the **Kanesville Tabernacle and Visitor Center** is a reconstructed log church similar to the one in which Brigham Young was upheld in 1847 as president of the Church of Jesus Christ of Latter-day Saints. The event is one of the most significant days in the history of the church.

The Kanesville Tabernacle includes a visitor center where you can learn more about Mormon history in the area. It is located at 222 E. Broadway and is open daily. Admission is free. Call (712) 322-0500 for information.

decks contains ten pie-shaped cells, with only one opening on each level of the drum. To enter a cell, the jailer would turn the central drum so that a cell doorway was lined up with the cage opening—like a squirrel cage. It may seem dehumanizing today, but in 1885, when it was opened, the jail was considered an improvement over the damp, unsanitary quarters prisoners had been kept in previously.

Though it remained in use up until the 1960s, the jail was declared a fire trap in 1969 because only three prisoners could be released at one time during an emergency. It was later in danger of being destroyed, until the Pottawattamie County Historical Society launched a heroic effort to save it. The jail was named to the National Register of Historic Places in 1972 and is now owned and operated as a museum by the historical society.

On a tour of the Squirrel Cage Jail, you'll also see the jailer's quarters and an office and a room filled with prison memorabilia. Today the site is one of only three lazy-Susan jails still standing in this country and is unique in being the only three-story one (it also may be haunted—be sure to ask your tour guide for the stories!).

The Squirrel Cage Jail is located at 226 Pearl St. It is open Thurs through Sat from 11 a.m. to 4 p.m. and on Sun from 1 to 4 p.m. (weekends only Nov through Mar). Admission is $7 for adults; $5 for children. For more information call (712) 323-2509.

Railroad buffs won't want to miss two sites in Council Bluffs that celebrate the rich train history of the area. The first is the **Union Pacific Railroad Museum**, located in the city's historic Carnegie Library building at 200 Pearl St. The museum takes visitors on a journey through 150 years of American history, with artifacts, photographs, and documents that trace the development of the railroad and the American West. Among its treasures are the promotional materials that helped attract immigrants to make the hazardous journey west, along with a sampling of the precious possessions they brought with them. You can trace the settlement of the West on an interactive map table that highlights the towns that grew up along the railroad's route. The museum also features displays about the heyday of passenger travel and the rail industry's efforts to promote the nation's first national parks. The museum (712-329-8307; uprr museum.org) is open Thurs through Sat from 10 a.m. to 6 p.m.

Council Bluffs is also home to the **RailsWest Railroad Museum**, which is housed in the former Rock Island Depot that once served the city. Inside the 1898 structure are railroad memorabilia as well as a model railroad that depicts the railroad operations of the surrounding region. The museum is located at 1512 S. Main St. and is open from 11 a.m. to 4 p.m. Thurs through Sat and Sun from 1 to 4 p.m. For more information call (712) 323-2509.

A fine place to eat is **Pizza King**, a combination steak and pizza restaurant at 1101 N. Broadway. Although the restaurant offers a full menu ranging from sandwiches to fine steaks, it is most famous for its thin-crust pizza, which is known far and wide as the best in the area. Visitors include regulars within a 50-mile radius as well as frequent interstate travelers who jump off at the US 6 exit. Pizza King is open seven days a week from 4 p.m. to 11 p.m.; prices are inexpensive to moderate. The phone number is (712) 323-4911.

For more information about these and other attractions in the city, call the Council Bluffs Convention and Visitors Bureau at (712) 256-2577 or see unleashcb.com.

From Council Bluffs you can also explore the **Wabash Trace Nature Trail**, which is one of southwest Iowa's premier attractions. The 63-mile trail stretches between Council Bluffs and the small town of **Blanchard** on the Iowa-Missouri border, following an old railroad bed through the Loess Hills and rolling farm country. The trail's gentle inclines are perfect for walking and biking, winding through many small towns where travelers can quench their thirst and grab a bite to eat. The Council Bluffs trailhead is located on US 275, near Lewis Central School. The trail's user fee is $2 per day, $20 per year. For information see wabashtrace.org.

didyouknow?

The town of Tabor (30 miles southeast of Council Bluffs) was once the headquarters of abolitionist John Brown.

Twenty-five miles east of Council Bluffs on US 6 you'll find the **Nishna Heritage Museum** in the town of **Oakland**. Housed originally in a 1905 dry-goods and grocery store, the museum now comprises four lots. Don't miss the bathtub in the barbershop, the scooter-bike, the collection of bride's dresses and children's clothes, and the Buster Brown display. The museum is located at 117 N. Main St. It is open from 9 a.m. to 3 p.m. Mon through Thurs. Call (712) 482-6802 for more information.

About 25 miles east of Oakland is the small town of **Lewis**, home of the **Hitchcock House** (63788 567th Ln.), one of the few remaining stations left in Iowa that were once stops on the Underground Railroad. Located on the route designated by the famous abolitionist John Brown, this brownstone house built in 1856 and inhabited by a sympathetic circuit preacher, his wife, and their eight children served as a shelter for escaping slaves en route to Canada before the onset of the Civil War. The house is open from May to Sept, from 1 to 5 p.m. Tues through Sun. A small donation is charged. Call (712) 769-2323 or see hitchcockhouse.org for more information or to schedule a guided tour.

From the town of Lewis, travel south to the town of *Villisca* on US 71. The town was the site of one of the state's most notorious crimes. In 1912 an ax murderer killed eight people in a home at 508 E. Second St., a crime that remains unsolved to this day. The murders have been the subject of a play and a documentary and are still the subject of some speculation. Paranormal investigators continue to flock here. The *Villisca Ax Murder House*, where the killings took place, has been restored to its 1912 appearance and is open for daylight tours and (for the brave) overnight stays. For information see villiscaiowa.com.

For your final stop in western Iowa, visit *Clarinda*, about 20 miles south of Villisca on US 71. Glenn Miller, the famous big-band conductor, trombonist, and founder of the Glenn Miller Orchestra, was born here in 1904, and his birthplace, purchased by his daughter in 1989, has been restored by the *Glenn Miller Birthplace Society* and is open 1 to 3 p.m. Tues through Sun. A great time to visit Clarinda is during the *Glenn Miller Festival*, held the second weekend in June. Highlights of the festival are informational talks and panels, musical performances, and dances. It is capped off by the society's own big band, which uses Miller's original Café Rouge bandstands. The museum is at 122 W. Clark St. Call (712) 542-2461 for more information or see glennmiller .org.

The *Clarinda Carnegie Art Museum* is located in the town's historic Carnegie Library at 300 N. Sixteenth St. Built in 1908, it's filled with treasures collected by Robert and Karen Duncan, who grew up in Clarinda and wanted to do something to help their hometown. It's a gem of a museum, well worth a detour, full of stunning modern art in a variety of media. The museum is open Sun and Wed from 1 to 4 p.m. Admission is free. For information call (712) 850-1175 or see visitccam.com.

Places to Stay in Prairie Borderland

AKRON

Hole N' the Wall Lodge
14396 Diamond Ave.
(712) 568-1010
holenthewalllodge.com
moderate

ATLANTIC

**Chestnut Charm
Bed & Breakfast**
1409 Chestnut St.
(712) 243-5652
chestnutcharm.org
moderate to expensive

CLARINDA

Celebrity Inn
1323 S. Sixteenth St.
(712) 542-5178
thecelebrityinn.com
inexpensive

EVERLY

Scharnberg Park Cabins
3430 145th Ave.
(712) 262-2187
mycountyparks.com
inexpensive

SIOUX CITY

The Warrior Hotel
525 Sixth St.
(712) 317-1011
thewarriorhotel.com
expensive

SPIRIT LAKE

Red Brick Farm
1983 Hwy. 9
(916) 879-5936
okobojiredbrickfarm.com
moderate

WEST OKOBOJI

Okoboji Country Inn
1704 Terrace Park Blvd.
(712) 332-2358
okobojicountryinn.com
moderate

Places to Eat in Prairie Borderland

ARNOLDS PARK

Smokin' Jakes
117 W. Broadway
(712) 332-5152
smokinjakes.com
moderate

Yesterdays
131 W. Broadway
(712) 332-2353
yesterdaysokoboji.com
moderate

COUNCIL BLUFFS

Tish's Restaurant
1207 S. Thirty-fifth St.
I-29 exit 53A
(712) 323-5456
tishs.com
moderate

712 Eat + Drink
1851 Madison Ave.
(712) 256-5525
sevenonetwocb.com
moderate

GLENWOOD

Bodega Victoriana Winery
60397 Kidd Rd.
(610) 312-7724
inexpensive

PISGAH

Dave's Old Home Café
200 First St.
(712) 456-2127
inexpensive

SERGEANT BLUFF

Aggie's
107 Sergeant Square Dr.
(712) 943-8888
aggiesbbq.com
inexpensive

SIOUX CITY

Main + Abbey
111 Third St.
(712) 226-7610
hardrockcasinosiouxcity
.com
moderate

Index